CHANGING THE WORLD

Changing the WORLD

A Framework for the Study of Creativity

David Henry Feldman,
Mihaly Csikszentmihalyi,
and
Howard Gardner

PRAEGER

**Westport, Connecticut
London**

Library of Congress Cataloging-in-Publication Data

Feldman, David Henry.
    Changing the world : a framework for the study of creativity /
    David Henry Feldman, Mihaly Csikszentmihalyi, and Howard Gardner.
        p.   cm.
    Includes bibliographical references and index.
    ISBN 0–275–94769–6 (alk. paper).—ISBN 0–275–94775–0 (pbk. :
    alk. paper)
    1. Creative ability. I. Csikszentmihalyi, Mihaly. II. Gardner,
    Howard. III. Title.
    BF408.F38   1994
    153.3′5—dc20   93–11868

British Library Cataloguing in Publication Data is available.

Library of Congress Catalog Card Number: 93–11868
ISBN: 0–275–94769–6
      0–275–94775–0 (pbk.)

First published in 1994

Praeger Publishers, 88 Post Road West, Westport, CT 06881
An imprint of Greenwood Publishing Group, Inc.

Printed in the United States of America

∞™

The paper used in this book complies with the
Permanent Paper Standard issued by the National
Information Standards Organization (Z39.48–1984).

10 9 8 7 6 5 4 3 2 1

Contents

Acknowledgments

We are first and foremost indebted to our colleagues on the Social Science Research Council's Committee on Development, Giftedness, and the Learning Process. For ten years (1980–1990) we met as a group and discussed creativity and related matters. What appears here reflects those discussions and exchanges in ways that it would be almost impossible to sort out. Jeanne Bamberger and Howard Gruber were there from the beginning, while Yadin Dudai, Helen Haste, Robert Siegler, and Robert Sternberg joined the group at various points and had significant impact. Each of these people has also made significant independent contributions to our understanding of creativity (and/or human giftedness), and a full appreciation for the work that was done during our ten years together would necessitate reading works by these authors as well as our own.

A great debt is also owed to the Social Science Research Council itself, and particularly to Dr. Lonnie Sherrod and Dr. Peter B. Read, who served as staff to our committee. Lonnie and Peter became full participants in the work, and gave much more than just logistical and technical support. Their substantive contributions are also, we hope, reflected in the work you are about to read.

Thanks as well to John Harney, at Greenwood Publishing, for his long standing interest in this project. He stood by patiently while the project took form, then gently provided guidance and support as it went through its various phases. It is a rare and welcome experience to work with someone whose interests seem to transcend the business of publishing.

Finally, we are very pleased to acknowledge the support of the Andrew W. Mellon Foundation for supporting our efforts through a grant to the Council. Jack Sawyer, then president of the Foundation, went out on a limb to push for our project because he thought that something worthwhile might come from it. If so, it is because of his faith in the work and the support that he and his colleagues gave. We are very grateful and hope that this book in some small way justifies the investment made in our project.

We dedicate this book to Mr. Sawyer and to Mr. Scott McVay, president of the Geraldine R. Dodge Foundation, whose helpful hand made all the difference.

Preface

When J. P. Guilford stood before the American Psychological Association in 1950, he was at the peak of his powers. On the strength of his role in helping the United States military carry out the most massive testing program in history, he had been elected president of the largest and most powerful professional association in the field. The topic of Guilford's address to the association? Creativity.

It was a daring talk. As Guilford pointed out, virtually no systematic research had been done on the topic of creativity. And none was reported in Guilford's presentation, either. Guilford's address was a call to arms, a rallying cry, a polemic aimed to convince his audience that research on creativity was essential to the future security of America. In measured tones, Guilford laid out a scenario that placed creative thinking as the most vital resource available to the country. Here is an example:

> We hear much these days about the remarkable new thinking machines. We are told that these machines can be made to take over much of men's thinking and that the routine thinking of many industries will eventually be done without the employment of human brains. We are told that this will entail an industrial revolution that will place into insignificance the first industrial revolution. . . . [E]ventually, about the only economic value of brains left

would be in the creative thinking of which they are capable. (Guilford 1950, p. 444–454)

Guilford went on to lay down a blueprint for the field he hoped to bring into existence. It was to be based on the idea of creativity as a trait or set of traits characteristic of creative individuals. As a leading proponent of psychometric testing, Guilford had a vision of a new set of tests for traits of creativity that would be far more accurate in finding talent than existing instruments (which were primarily IQ or IQ-derived tests).

His notion of creativity was to encompass the whole personality, including intellectual and nonintellectual traits. It also included recognition of the idea that creativity in one field is not necessarily the same as creativity in another:

> The hypotheses that follow concerning the nature of creative thinking have been derived with certain types of creative people in mind: the scientist and the technologist, including the inventor. The consensus of the philosophers seems to have been that creativity is the same wherever you find it. To this idea I do not subscribe. (Guilford 1950, pp. 444–454)

Given his experience and his purposes, it should be no surprise that Guilford would have chosen to focus his lens on particular kinds of creativity. After all, he and his colleagues had found that currently available IQ-derived tests were poor predictors of innovativeness, inventiveness, leadership, or flexibility within the military context. If the United States hoped to survive the Cold War (the McCarthy hearings were contemporaneous with Guilford's presentation), it would do so on the strength of its superior mental resources, and to tap these resources would require, Guilford believed, powerful new testing technologies.

The history of the field of creativity research for the next thirty years was guided by Guilford's vision of a new set of tests for creative traits. With substantial investment of funds from the military (particularly the Navy), Guilford and his coworkers staked out the intellectual traits and set about the construction of new tests based on factor analytic approaches and sophisticated psychometric techniques. Others, such as Frank Barron and Donald MacKinnon at Berkeley, began to try to isolate personality factors in various groups of relatively creative people, also with sizable grants from the military.

As we will show in the essay that follows this preface, Guilford's vision for the field was deeply flawed. Rather than usher in a new era of super sophisticated assessment, the quest for creativity tests turned out to be something of a fiasco. After twenty years of generous funding, military resources were abruptly withdrawn, the field went through a wrenching reexamination of its goals and purposes, and, partly as a result, all but ceased to exist as a vital force in research by the early 1970s (Wallach 1971). The 1960s themselves and their antiestablishment emphasis no doubt influenced how the field was perceived.

In the mid-1960s the current three authors entered the scene and began to try to study creativity. Although it was several years later that we actually worked together, we each struggled to understand what the field of creativity research was about, where it had gone wrong, and what, if anything, could be done to put it on a more productive track. What we had in common was that, each in our own way, we found the field of creativity research and scholarship to be seriously wanting.

By the mid-1970s the Social Science Research Council, an organization long known for its ability to jump-start a lagging field, was encouraged to see what it could do with the study of giftedness, of which creativity was by then a subcomponent. Two of us (Feldman and Gardner) were recruited to participate in early meetings of a group convened to give new direction to the broad field of research on the study of giftedness. As it turned out, the first three years of that committee's existence were a microcosm of the struggle going on in the broader field.

There were those of us who believed that the field had to make a radical shift in emphasis if it were to thrive, and there were others of us who believed just as firmly that the basic approach of the field (psychometric and IQ-based) was sound, but should be expanded into areas neglected in its first half-century. After three years of getting nowhere, despite the best efforts of a distinguished and able leader (Robert Sears), the committee was disbanded. It appeared that the field of research on giftedness (and creativity as well) was not ready for a new burst of energy.

At the urging of Howard Gardner, a subgroup of the original committee (Feldman, Gardner, and Howard Gruber) met independently and hatched a plan to start a new committee with a developmental emphasis and oriented toward the study of great giftedness and creativity. Guilford's approach was to assume that the same traits of creativity exist in all people in varying degrees, and that creativity could be as productively studied in an unselected sample as a sample of extremely accomplished individuals—a crucial mistake, we believed. Fortunately, Jack Sawyer, the head of the Andrew W. Mellon Foundation, saw some promise in our vision for the field and provided resources for our new venture.

After adding Jeanne Bamberger, a cognitively oriented student of musical development, to our core group, we set out to rechart the field. Our charge was broader than just to rejuvenate the field of creativity research, although we are reporting only on that aspect of the effort here. Attempts to impact the wider research community of the study of giftedness can be found in other publications that, directly or indirectly, were spawned by the committee and its funders (Feldman 1982; Horowitz and O'Brien 1985; Sternberg and Davidson 1986; Wallace and Gruber 1989). Mihaly Csikszentmihalyi joined the committee in 1983.

In addition, for briefer periods, Yadin Dudai, Helen Haste, Robert Siegler, and Robert Sternberg served as members. A number of other scholars consulted with the committee and a number of specialized small conferences were held. Each has had impact on the thinking that is represented in the present volume, and although not represented with chapters of their own, anyone who knows the work of the individuals who have served on the committee will recognize features of their work. Indeed, one of the remarkable things about working with the committee was how much it seemed to take on a life of its own, stimulating changes in viewpoint and making it often difficult to sort out where ideas originated or how they became transformed.

These qualities will be evident in the chapters to follow. Although six of the seven chapters list a single author, it will become clear to the reader that there is much overlap and mutual influence between and among them. This holds true as well for the impact of works of other committee members and people who have worked with the committee. The first chapter, jointly authored, is an effort to try to put into one essay a set of statements that all three of the present authors could live with. Its length is testimony to how difficult it is to capture the texture of our vision for the field of creativity research and scholarship.

In the simplest version of what each of us has tried to do in this field, it might be said that each of the three staked out a different area of the field. Gardner, with his long-standing interests in the brain and central nervous system, focused on the *person*. Feldman, having conceived of the idea of nonuniversal bodies of knowledge as a neglected arena of theory and research, began to conceptualize what the study of *domains* themselves might contribute to our understanding of creativity and how it develops. Csikszentmihalyi insisted that we heed the more contextual aspects of the process, ranging from the infrastructures that support preparation of recruits to the systems of selection of worthy new contributions; his focus has thus tended to be on the broader *field* within which creative work takes place.

This tripartite division of the field (with deference to former committee member Bob Sternberg, who has a penchant for dividing things into threes) arose from our discussions, and was first offered to the group in 1984 by

Csikszentmihalyi. It has proven useful and durable at least so far, and provides the main conceptual organization to this book. On the other hand, the reader will not see two chapters each by the authors on, respectively, *person, domain, and field.*

In our own individual work we have each ranged freely across the terrain of creativity. Gardner, the proponent of biological aspects, explores both domain and field as he examines Freud's Vienna and the features of medicine that both constrained and challenged his revolutionary idea. Csikszentmihalyi, with his exploration of genes and memes, shows that he is comfortable dealing with individual issues as well as broader, contextual ones. And Feldman, with the notions of coincidence and the transformational imperative, has clearly made forays across borders in both directions.

This is all perfectly in keeping with how the process has gone over the decade and more that we have collaborated. Although as concerned about marking individual contributions as most, there has been an easy give-and-take that has characterized our collaboration. It is less important to us at this point to be acknowledged individually for having thought of this or that idea than it is to see this field move with dispatch toward worthwhile new advances. Fortunately, we are assisted by a brace of able and committed scholars who have committed their careers to the effort. Many of these younger people knew little of the committee's work and pursued their research goals for their own purposes. Happily, they have contributed to the feeling of a rapidly arriving critical mass.

Unless we have badly misread the current scene, we are witnessing a robust rejuvenation of the field of creativity research. It has taken nearly two decades to restore momentum and redirect energy from the original plan laid down by the founder of the field, J. P. Guilford, whose brilliant conceptualization was powerful enough to lead (and in some ways constrain) the field for almost three decades.

It is hoped that works such as the present one will encourage the field of human creativity studies to grow and prosper. In the context of a world that might actually have a chance to live without an imminent nuclear threat, it is difficult to imagine a topic more vital to the well-being of our species and the species with whom we share the biosphere than the study of creativity.

CHANGING THE WORLD

1
A Framework for the Study of Creativity

David Henry Feldman
Mihaly Csikszentmihalyi
Howard Gardner

Creativity is one of those words that seems to be everywhere. It also seems to have many meanings, which often are not made explicit enough to avoid confusion and impede communication. For example, if someone says that she is leaving a job because it is not offering her enough opportunity to be creative, there are several possible meanings for what the word creative might refer to in this context.

Does she mean that there are few opportunities to choose her own objectives? Does she mean that she would like to be able to have more leeway in carrying out objectives set by someone else? Does she mean that there is little room for spontaneity and innovativeness in her place of work? Does she mean that the standards for excellence used to judge performance are such that there is little incentive to try to exceed them? It could be any of these, or any combination.

In this book we are primarily interested in one particular meaning for the term *creativity*, although we readily acknowledge that there are other meanings that could be our focus. The meaning that is of primary interest to us here is creativity as the achievement of something remarkable and new, something which transforms and changes a field of endeavor in a significant way. In other words, we are concerned with the kinds of things that people do that change the world.

We are thus concerned with what is sometimes called "big" creativity, in contrast, for example, to the more humble (but perhaps equally vital) tendency to bring a fresh and lively interpretation to any endeavor, whether humble or exalted. "Small" creativity can thus refer to a charming arrangement of fresh flowers to brighten up a room, or the use of a doorstop to weatherstrip an ill-fitting window, or a clever remark that lightens the tone of a conversation. In contrast, big creativity only occurs when something of enduring value is contributed to an existing body of knowledge, thereby transforming it.

Oddly, the field of creativity research has tended to shy away from investigating the sort of creativity that we find of greatest interest. Instead, other meanings have been explored. The most active among these have been: personality characteristics of individuals judged relatively more creative than their peers; relationships between intelligence test scores and scores on various instruments intended to measure creative abilities; effects of various intervention procedures on measures of divergent idea production and divergent idea quality (Amabile 1983).

Several works have explored the lives and experiences of remarkable individuals in the form of psychohistories or psychobiograpies; prominent examples include Erik Erikson's studies of Luther and of Gandhi (Erikson 1968, 1969) and Howard Gruber's study of Charles Darwin (Gruber 1981a). These works deal with unquestionably "big" creative achievement, and do add a great deal to our understanding of the processes through which specific individuals have achieved their greatest works. What has been true of this line of work is that it has failed to provide a coherent set of generalizations about the nature of great creativity and how it occurs. The field of creativity research is rich with examples from the lives of remarkable individuals, but lacks a framework for approaching the many issues that arise when trying to make more general sense of the data. To produce such a framework is the main purpose of this book.

ARE THERE NEW IDEAS?

Before turning to the matter of how to build a useful framework for investigating creativity, we should first recognize that there are voices within the scholarly community that have been arguing against the very idea of studying creativity as a separate psychological problem. For some of our colleagues, creativity, regardless of degree, is better thought of as a common sense word referring to certain unusual manifestations of perfectly ordinary processes. There tend to be two forms of such arguments.

One of these comes from those who see virtually all important contributions to knowledge as arising from preexisting physical structures present in the growing individual. Noam Chomsky, for example, has argued that the basic structures of human language are sufficient to account for both acquisition and all later forms of expression of linguistic competence (Chomsky 1968, 1980). Jerome Fodor has extended this argument to include all forms of human cognitive capacity, including mathematical, musical, and spatial intelligence (Fodor 1983). The argument rests on the belief that it is not possible to create something out of nothing, and if all that is necessary for even the most grand of achievements already exists in the person's capacities for growth, then it is in principle not possible for anything really new to be constructed.

This position has been quite influential both inside and outside academic circles, leading to increasingly strident arguments based on biological determination of human potential. The so-called "radical nativist" position has been one embraced by growing numbers of cognitive and developmental scientists. Robert Campbell and Mark Bickhard (1986) and David Henry Feldman (1989, also this volume) have argued that creativity should be studied as a distinctly human process, countering the biological argument by showing that much of what goes into the process of creativity actually comes from outside the individual, making it unnecessary to consider only what the individual's original capacities might be. Indeed, Feldman (1989, also this volume) has argued that the existence of human creativity actually proves that development occurs as well, countering another argument of the radical nativist group.

The second group that is skeptical of creativity as a distinct process comes from within the powerful new field of cognitive science. Its most prominent spokesman is Herbert Simon, who, along with several able collaborators, has tried to show that perfectly ordinary cognitive processes, combined and transformed in perfectly mundane ways, are capable of constructing some of the most profound scientific laws in the history of science, such as Kepler's third law. In fact, however, the premise of the work done in the AI computer laboratory isolates only one set among the larger number of creative processes that are involved in constructing a radically different point of view or new solution to a scientific puzzle (Csikszentmihalyi 1988a, also this volume; Simon 1988, 1990). Such processes as problem finding and problem formulation are as critical to creativity as problem solving, as are a number of other processes detailed in Csikszentmihalyi's writings (Csikszentmihalyi 1988a, b; 1990 Csikszentmihalyi and Robinson 1986).

For the purposes of the present volume, we acknowledge that important challenges have been mounted questioning the existence of creativity as a topic worthy of scientific study, but we believe these challenges do not offer sufficiently compelling arguments or evidence to lead us to abandon our efforts. Indeed, the contrary is true. The need for a framework that organizes and helps direct research and scholarship on the topic of creativity is one that is very real and that, in our view, merits the full attention of the scholarly community.

We must therefore reassert our assumption that new ideas actually do occur. Claiming that automobiles are nothing but recombinations of already existing technologies or arguing that evolutionary theory was anticipated by earlier theories and gathered all of its elements from them evades the obvious fact that these things represent qualitative changes in knowledge, technology, and culture which have had enormous impact. In any reasonable sense of the word, new things are brought into the world all the time. This is taken for granted at the biological level where the unique combination of genetic material makes every organism new in a not-trivial sense. And even if this were not true, the course of growth is unique for every organism. At the cultural level, the human environment is nothing if not a panoply of novelty and innovation, sometimes subtle, sometimes revolutionary, but always changing.

The question is not, then, if there is anything new under the sun, but how certain of the new things under the sun that we find valuable might have been constructed (Piaget 1971b, 1982).

HISTORY OF CREATIVITY RESEARCH

The beginning of the field of creativity research in the modern era is usually marked from J. P Guilford's presidential address before the American Psychological Association in 1950 (Guilford 1950). In this speech, Guilford laid out the conceptual basis for creativity research that would frame the vast majority of studies on the topic for more than twenty years (Guilford 1970). Only since the mid-1970s has there been a concerted effort within the research community to replace Guilford's conception with a different one. Perusal of current issues of research journals shows that there is still a steady stream of research activity using Guilford's framework; it is fair to say that as of this date, no rival paradigm has dislodged it despite widespread dissatisfaction and a growing sense of its limitations (Amabile 1983, 1985; Csikszentmihalyi 1988a, b, 1990; Csikszentmihalyi and Robinson 1986; Feldman 1974, 1980, 1982; Gruber 1981a, b; Simonton 1988; Wallach 1971, 1985).

The basic idea of Guilford's approach to creativity was to isolate various traits of intellect and personality that "creative" individuals might possess in greater quantity than others. By comparing more creative individuals with less creative ones, it could be shown on which creative traits the two groups differ. Guilford proposed a number of traits that he thought were promising candidates for differentiating more from less creative individuals, divided into traits of intellect and traits of personality. Among the intellectual traits, Guilford thought fluency of ideas, flexibility in thinking, and complexity of conceptual structure might be traits of creative people. As for personality, Guilford guessed, for example, that sensitivity to the environment might be a critical trait.

Guilford proposed that the best way to determine which traits are characteristic of creativity was to invent tests for the various qualities believed to be important, then to give these tests to individuals varying in their degree of creativity, as measured in some real-world way. If covariation occurs, it could be said that the traits tested were able to differentiate creative from less creative individuals.

Guilford also proposed the use of factor analytic methods for simplifying what could quickly become a cumbersome set of variables. Among many tests on a variety of specific topics, Guilford thought they might reduce to a smaller set of broad dispositional variables revealed through factor analytic techniques (see Gould 1981, for a readable discussion of how factor analysis works). Although not the only methodology that Guilford could have chosen for the purpose, factor analysis was central to how the field took shape. For Guilford, the most important reason for wanting creativity to be studied through factor analytic methods was that he wanted to be able to demonstrate that creativity is a separate dimension from IQ (Guilford 1950).

As a member of the team of psychometricians responsible for ability testing during World War II, Guilford had learned that IQ measures were unsuccessful in predicting leadership, innovation, or technological inventiveness. This inability of general intelligence measures to predict which individuals would excel in key areas important to the military was the primary motivation for studying "creativity" in the first place, as Guilford made clear in his 1950 address:

> When we look into the nature of intelligence tests, we encounter many doubts concerning their coverage of creative abilities. (Guilford 1950, p. 460)

And later:

> If the correlations between intelligence-test scores and many types of creative performance are only moderate or low, and I predict that such correlations

will be found, it is because the primary abilities represented in those tests are not all important for creative behavior. It is also because some of the primary abilities important for creative behavior are not represented in the test at all. (Guilford 1950, p. 461)

The task for research, then, was to construct the new tests that would be largely independent of IQ and would better predict creativity in the areas of technological and scientific inventiveness. This is essentially what was attempted during the twenty years following Guilford's 1950 address, largely supported by the Defense Department. It was not the only line of research pursued during that period, but it was by far the most prominent and influential, and the best-funded social science work ever undertaken in this country. The abilities research carried out by Guilford and his followers was complemented by a series of studies which attempted to isolate specific personality traits of creative individuals. This research, while quite different in technique from the abilities research, shared the basic trait framework Guilford laid down in his 1950 paper. Guilford's effort to define creativity as a total personality construct provided the rationale for abilities research as well as the more personality-oriented work which was influenced by psychoanalytic and ego psychology.

During the 1950s and 1960s an ambitious series of studies of creative personality was carried out under the leadership of Donald McKinnon, Frank Barron, and their associates at the University of California. With support from the Air Force and other agencies, the Berkeley group looked at individuals from several fields and compared those who were determined to be "more creative" from those who were rated "less creative." Although as we will see, many methodological issues confronted the abilities researchers and the personality researchers, such as validity and technical adequacy of measuring instruments, the Berkeley studies typically used a plausible criterion for determining actual creative accomplishment. Their technique involved seeking nominations from recognized experts in each field (e.g. architects, mathematicians) and then having other experts rate the nominated individuals with respect to demonstrated creative accomplishment (Barron 1955; Barron and Welsh 1952; Mackinnon, 1962). A study was done, for example, of Air Force officers to find which if any personality measures would differentiate the more from the less "creative" (Barron 1955; Barron and Welsh 1952). A set of personality indicators was found that occurred more frequently or with greater strength in the individuals rated as more innovative by their superiors. Preference for complexity among mosaic design patterns was one such finding, replicated many times with other samples.

Shift to Children

Over time, research on divergent thinking abilities shifted its epicenter from adults to children after the publication of the Torrance Tests of Creativity in the early 1960s (Torrance 1962). The Torrance tests were inspired by Guilford's divergent thinking model and included similar items to the Guilford-inspired tests of the 1950s, except that they were adapted for children. Instead of "How many uses can you think of for a brick?" there might appear an item like "Suppose the world were covered with fog. What would the consequences be?" Also included in the Torrance battery were nonverbal items such as completion of a drawing from a suggestive line or piece of colored construction paper. A number of researchers also made up their own tests, but virtually all were Guilford inspired (e.g., Getzels and Jackson 1962; Wallach and Kogan 1965).

The rationale for creativity research with children was that the earlier the "creative ability" could be identified, the greater the chance that something positive could be done to facilitate its being put to good use. Galvanized by the launching of Sputnik I in 1957 by the Soviets, a major national effort to increase scientific and technological achievement was undertaken, with creativity testing of children one component of that effort (Wallach 1970, 1971, 1985). Between 1960 and 1965, tests were developed for younger and younger children, so that by the mid-1960s there were even preschool "creativity" tests (Wallach, 1970, 1971, 1985).

Instead of trying to differentially predict creative manpower in adulthood, the research of the 1960s emphasized early identification of promising scientific and technological talent. Find the most promising children early, the argument went, and give them intense training in science and related subjects, provide incentives for choosing careers in the national interest, and the result would be a generation of superior talent. President John F. Kennedy capitalized on this trend when he set a goal for the country of putting a "man on the moon" by the end of the 1960s.

More important for the subsequent history of creativity research, investigators with vastly different reasons for doing work in creativity moved the field away from the pragmatic goals of scientific/technological talent identification, selection, and encouragement and toward the social reforms of the 1960s. As part of the emerging social agenda, creativity research was recast as a way of breaking out of the perceived stranglehold of conservative educational practices, and of showing how traditional practice was destroying creative expression. Rather than seeing their work as assisting in the Cold War effort, they saw it as a way to help bring about an easing of constraints on free expression, thus connecting creativity research with a long tradition of intellectualism in America (Clifford 1964; Getzels and Jackson 1962, 1963).

To oversimplify, creativity research moved in the 1960s from "conservative" to "radical," from serving national security interests to serving the cause of greater individual expression (Clifford 1964). As part of the social revolution of the 1960s, a revolution that placed the value of individual expression over that of social responsibility, creativity research contributed to the hoped-for demise of traditional lock step education.

The most influential work of this period was carried out by Getzels and Jackson (1962). The major purpose of their study was to differentiate between intelligence and creativity with the hope of expanding conceptions of intellectual giftedness to include more divergent expression. As they wrote in an article summarizing their work:

> It is, we believe, unfortunate that in American education at all levels we fail to distinguish between our convergent and divergent talents—or even worse, that we try to convert our divergent students into convergent students. Divergent fantasy is often called "rebellious" rather than "germinal"; unconventional career choice is often labeled "unrealistic" rather than "courageous"; it is hoped that the present work in cognition will help modify some of these stereotypic attitudes regarding children's thinking. (Getzels and Jackson 1963)

A decisive shift in the rationale for doing creativity research had thus taken place, a rationale associating creativity research with radical school and broader social reforms. Not surprisingly, given this shift, traditional sources of support for the work disappeared quickly. At the adult level as well, creativity research went applied and promised ways for people to become more effective and satisfied with work and life. Programs like "synectics" to "increase creativity" became popular (Gordon 1961), not for nationalistic reasons, but because being more creative was seen as a way to lead a fuller and more satisfying life. Not that practical purposes were ignored; many of the creativity improvement techniques were designed for business application, but the goal was not to work in the national but rather in the interest of personal, corporate, and competitive gain (Parnes 1967).

Michael Wallach, one of the leaders of creativity research during the 1960s, lamented the turn toward planned obsolescence and excessive faith in technology. In an influential review published in 1971, Wallach wrote:

> When technology changes its role, from an instrument for achieving a decent life for all members of society to a value in its own right, the only principle operating is one according to which the more fruits of technology, the better.

But one can question whether it is desirable to do whatever is necessary in order to have more cars, and then to have a new car every other year, and to have a telephone in each room of our house, and then to have a private helicopter instead of or besides a car, and a telephone that lets you see as well as hear the person at the other end, first in black and white, and a few years after that in color. . . . A society that values technology and its effects as goals in their own right must socialize its members into a willingness to fill the occupational roles spawned by a technological order. (Wallach 1971, pp. 2–3)

As creativity research moved away from technological, military, and scientific goals, its power base and sources of support virtually vanished. Creativity research became seen as part of the revolutionary social movement of the 1960s, part of the "problem" rather than a possible solution.

To an amazing degree, those who became involved in the field of creativity research seemed not to appreciate that a withdrawal of support had occurred and a change in assumptions had taken place. Guilford looked out at the field in 1970 and saw only positive things, predicting continued healthy growth for the research enterprise. Guilford could not have comprehended that the field as he knew it was doomed as a major national research effort. Guilford wrote in 1970, in the recently founded *Journal of Creative Behavior*:

Extrapolations from the present scene give us every reason to be optimistic about the future of things creative. But besides contemplating a rosy future, we should also consider whether we are missing any opportunities. (p. 157)

Validity

One of the most remarkable things about the creativity research enterprise was how far it got without producing data on the issue of validity. Guilford dealt with validity issues in 1950 in the following manner:

The question will inevitably arise, "how do you know your tests are valid?" There are two answers to this question. The first is that the factorial study of the tests is in itself one kind of validation. It will determine which tests measure each factor and to what extent. That is a matter of internal validity or factorial validity. It answers the question, "What does the test measure?" The second answer will be in terms of which factors are related to the creative productivity of people in everyday life. That calls for the correlation of factor measures with practical criteria. I feel very strongly that only after we have determined the promising facts and how to measure them are we justified in taking up the time of creative people with tests. (pp. 470–471).

Figure 1
The structure-of-intellect model, with three parameters (other parameters may need to be added).

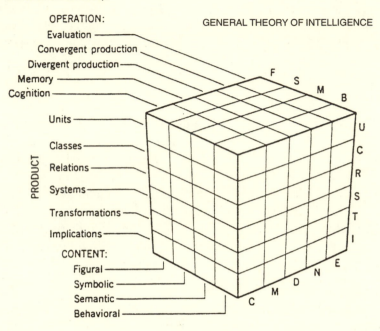

From Guilford, J. P. (1967). *The nature of human intelligence*, p. 63. New York: McGraw-Hill. Reproduced by permission of McGraw-Hill.

Guilford worked for three decades on his "structure of intellect" model of intelligence (Guilford 1967, 1970), a factor analytically generated theory of adult intellect that consists of at least 120 different factors (see Figure 1). Guilford and his coworkers set about devising test instruments to measure each of the factors his theoretical model had generated. At last count in the 1970s more than eighty such factors had been "operationalized" in tests, with a myriad of technical reports from the testing laboratory at the University of Southern California showing the monumental amount of work that went into the project. Eventually, with theoretical modifications incorporated, Guilford's model reached 180 separate abilities (Comrey, Michael, Fruchter 1988, p. 1087).

For the most part one looks in vain through the technical reports from Guilford's laboratory for evidence concerning the ability of the various factors in the structure of intellect model to predict real-world performance. This is not to say that no evidence whatever was collected, only that the clear emphasis was on filling out the model rather than on showing the usefulness of each of the tests as it was produced. Guilford seems to have been smitten with his own model and seen its fulfillment as depending upon the development of a battery of tests to assess each of the original 120 factors proposed.

Guilford's own agenda included little creativity research per se after the construction of his "model of intellect." Yet Guilford was well aware of validity issues; as one of the nation's leading psychometricians, Guilford knew well the technical as well as the practical importance of establishing adequate validity for any new test. He argued, though, that validity should not be a major concern until the factors of the model had been captured through tests designed for their specific requirements.

In Guilford's case, he seemed to have taken his own advice from 1950 so seriously that validity was relegated to a distant back burner, rarely to return in Guilford's own research. Nor was evidence for validity found much in the research of other investigators. The technique of factor analysis was accepted as sufficient validation during the initial years of study. But as Gould (1981) among others has pointed out, factor analysis is a technique of limited utility and is not a substitute for both theoretical and practical validation efforts.

Had Guilford and his colleagues in the early years of the creativity research movement actually produced tests that worked, that is, that predicted effectively the qualities of innovativeness and technological inventiveness that were so keenly desired by policymakers, the history of the field might have been different. Once begun, however, creativity research seemed to have a life of its own and became focused on the study of the "divergent thinking" capabilities proposed by Guilford.

The Yield from Creativity Research 1950–1970

Although the work fell far short of its promise, there were three noteworthy achievements of the creativity research movement through the early 1970s: the first is the demonstration that IQ is largely unrelated to divergent thinking (Wallach 1971, 1985); the second is that there seem to be certain personality traits that are characteristic of more creative individuals (Gardner 1988); and the third is that certain kinds of divergent thinking skills can be improved with training and practice (Barron 1988). While none of these sets of findings is revolutionary, and each has had to contend with methodological problems limiting its impact and generalizability, the findings have held up fairly well and have had some practical as well as research value (Wallach 1971, 1985).

More recently, work in the trait tradition has explored issues that help explain why some individuals are able to sustain the effort to produce original works. Amabile (1983, 1985, 1990) has shown in experimental work that intrinsic motivation, the desire to produce work for its own sake rather than some external reward, is more characteristic of creative individuals than those less so. And Albert (1969, 1990) has shown that individuals destined to become eminent in various fields share certain family and environmental experiences. These works have contributed to knowledge about the conditions that favor creativity. But of course they do not explain how creative work is actually done. Thus, although the trait tradition continues to make valuable contributions to our understanding of creativity, it has become less and less central to the field.

To repeat, what did *not* happen during the twenty years when major resources at the national level were invested in creativity research was an accumulation of new knowledge about how novel ideas are actually constructed. But it can be argued that it was never the intention of the sponsors of Guilford-inspired research to probe the processes of creativity. The initial aim of the creativity research movement was precisely as Guilford had described it in 1950: to better predict and thereby offer an improved chance of identifying and encouraging talent in areas of national interest (Amabile 1983, 1985; Csikszentmihalyi 1988a, b; Feldman 1974, 1980; Gruber 1982; Guilford 1950).

It is no less true in the 1980s than it was in the 1950s that the nation's security and well-being depend on the originality and productiveness of its most talented citizens. What seems to have happened is that the urgency to find better means of selecting promising scientists and technologists has diminished with the thawing of the Cold War. Perhaps the less apocalyptic tenor of the times has rendered the crisis in technology and science less an issue. For whatever reasons, by the middle-1970s the momentum that had been built up in the field of creativity research had all but dissipated, and little new work was appearing in the literature. But the seeds of a new direction for the field were being sown in the fallow fields of trait research.

Domain Specific Creativity

The most influential creativity trait researcher of the 1960s, Michael Wallach, proposed the new direction for the field in 1971. Wallach, lamenting the too-broad generalizations that had been made about creativity and the thin data base upon which such generalizations were built, suggested that more limited studies of specific fields would yield better insights into the nature of creative processes. Wallach wrote:

If we want to learn about the enhancement of creativity, we had better consider training arrangements that make a person more competent at creative attainments themselves—such as writing novels well, excellence in acting, skill as a musician, or quality of art work produced. In like manner we have seen that learning about what covaries with creativity differences requires us to consider correlates of creative attainments themselves. (Wallach 1971, p. 23)

Wallach was arguing that efforts to isolate a trait of "creativity" to complement the trait of "intelligence" had gone as far as was useful. The work had shown that intelligence test scores were only modestly related to creative accomplishment, and virtually unrelated in the above average range (although see Torrance 1988 for a dissenting view).

Recognizing that IQ would tell little about creative potential, and realizing that so-called creativity tests did not predict real-world creative accomplishments, Wallach urged that detailed studies of creativity in various specific fields might yield information about the development of talent in those fields.

This is, of course, not a great deal more than Guilford himself had claimed in 1950; the difference was that Wallach's claim was based on a goodly number of empirical studies, while Guilford's argument was based for the most part on informal experience in the testing program during the Second World War. With Wallach's review the hope of making a practical creativity test was dashed, but the hope of better understanding creativity in various fields was raised. Although few commitments (private or government) were made to support such research, a number of initiatives were started in this more "domain specific" direction.

There have been several groups of researchers who have done work in creativity along more domain specific lines, but four have had the most sustained research programs. These, briefly, are the case studies of individual development within various fields, carried out by Howard Gruber and his associates, with work in Charles Darwin being the most substantial (Gruber, 1981a, 1982; Wallace and Gruber 1989); studies of critical periods of productivity in various times and domains by Dean Keith Simonton (Simonton 1984); computer simulations of thinking processes, including the discovery of new theorems in science and mathematics by Herbert Simon and others (e.g., Simon and Newell 1971); and work on the development of artists over a twenty-year period by Mihalyi Csikszentmihalyi and colleagues (Getzels and Csikszentmihalyi 1976; Csikszentmihalyi and Robinson 1986; Csikszentmihalyi 1988 a,b, 1990).

It should, of course, be noted that work on domain specific creativity has been done since the beginning of the empirical research movement of the 1950s (Barron 1953, 1955, 1988). Barron, MacKinnon, and their associates, for example, selected architects, mathematicians, and other groups for intensive study. Their purpose, however, was not to understand the distinctive qualities of each of these fields itself, but rather to shed light on qualities of creative individuals in general. Much useful knowledge about creativity in various fields was gathered during these studies, but it tended to be interpreted in relation to the desire to define *the* creative personality. With Wallach's review in 1971, a shift to more limited goals was proposed.

Thus, creativity research began to reemerge during the mid-1970s with different sorts of concerns. Rather than trying to predict which individuals were in general more likely to do creative work, creativity researchers began to ask questions about the nature of creative thinking in various domains and how it develops. The "cognitive revolution" of the 1970s seems to have carried creativity research along with it. No longer were investigators so concerned with differential prediction; their interests turned more to developmental issues, cognitive processes, social context influences, and domain questions. The study of creativity had become once again an area of basic psychological science (Abra 1988; Horowitz and O'Brien 1985; Sternberg 1988).

Studies have begun to address questions that have perennially been asked about creativity, but which were less central during the psychometric era. For example, why is it that certain places during a given historical period seem to yield an outpouring of creative work? Simonton (1984, 1987, 1988, 1990), using a statistical approach called "historiometry," has examined the tendency of inventiveness to surge in relation to sequences of more controlling and less controlling government regimes. He has also found that certain social and historical conditions tend to favor creativity in specific fields: philosophical, literary, and musical genius tends to appear alongside scientific advance, suggesting a *zeitgeist* influence. On the other hand, eminent artists may or may not co-occur with the others, forming a sort of "second cluster" of creative individuals, affected perhaps differently by the conditions that favor the other fields.

Csikszentmihalyi (1988b) approaches the same issue at a more microscopic level of analysis, focusing on the first few decades of the fourteenth century in Florence, where an outpouring of artistic quality, perhaps unmatched in history, took place. Csikszentmihalyi found that many factors help explain why it was possible for such unprecedented artistic flowering to occur. Among these factors are such mundane matters as the fact that Florence was a very wealthy city-state that had a long tradition of involvement in the arts, and that it had a highly intricate infrastructure, built over several decades, in support of artistic endeavor. Included were patrons of sophisticated taste, artists willing and able to educate as well as satisfy those tastes, and competitions and awards for prized commissions. Several hundred individuals helped form an artistic community which welcomed and encouraged peak performance in the arts. The magnificent work produced during these years becomes more comprehensible in the light of the many forces that were at work to help bring it about, including several forces that were not directly part of the artistic production process itself. In this manner, Csikszentmihalyi has enlarged our understanding of the social and cultural context of artistic development, helping explain why and under what conditions certain locales have given rise to remarkable concentrations of creative work.

Howard Gruber, in his elegant studies of Charles Darwin and other unquestionably creative individuals, has helped show how the process of discovery is quite different, at least in biological science, from the romanticized version often accepted, even in the creativity research literature. Gruber found by examining primary sources, such as Darwin's notebooks, that novel insights are actually quite common and do not generally stand out from the flow of experience, at least not as much as most of us tend to believe. The famous Darwinian insight about Malthus, for example, does not appear to have been an earth-shaking experience for Mr. Darwin, at least from the evidence from his private notebooks. Rather, a different picture emerges, of a diligent, steady, searching curiosity, almost an obsession to solve a particular problem. Many models and solutions to the problem of physical evolution were tried, and when the most pleasing appeared, it was taken as much as a matter of relief as it was of triumph (Gruber 1981a).

An emphasis on developmental studies of how new thoughts are constructed, and under what conditions, within specific content areas and cultural contexts, can thus be said to mark a major shift in the field of creativity research during the past decade.

Toward a Useful Framework for the Study of Creativity

Michael Wallach had helped set the stage for a revitalized approach to creativity by shifting focus from trait to process and from broad generalities to a domain specific focus. But if such an approach is to be successful, it will have to be more coherent and focused than is currently the case. It is fair to say that in the past decade or so a number of promising lines of work have emerged, but that they are somewhat scattered and diverse, have different disciplinary identities, and lack a coherent framework within which to carry out a coordinated set of studies.

By proposing such a framework, we hope to show that it is possible to move toward a better understanding of how new ideas occur, how they are brought to expression, and how to comprehend the conditions that tend to favor such events. Seeing creativity as an expression of several sets of processes operating at several levels offers the opportunity to consider the interplay among and between such processes, a vital feature of the framework presented here.

As for the dimensions of analysis themselves, we see three as most promising. One of these is the *field*, which refers to the social and cultural aspects of a profession, job, or craft. A second is the *domain*, which refers to the structure and organization of a body of knowledge evolved to contain and express certain distinct forms of information. And finally, there is the *individual person*, the site of the acquisition, organization, and transformation of knowledge that has the possibility of changing domains and fields (Csikszentmihalyi, 1988b).

For each of the three dimensions of analysis, further differentiation into more specific topics could be achieved. For example, within individuals there are several possible levels at which creativity might be profitably studied. Howard Gardner (1982, 1983, 1988) has proposed that various combination of biologically influenced "intelligences" might very early dispose individuals toward one or another domain and afford them greater chance of productively transforming that domain. In a discussion of Freud's configuration of such intelligences, Gardner points out that Freud was aware of both his strengths and weaknesses, and was a master at exploiting the former and avoiding situations that necessitated the latter. Gardner writes:

> It is possible to pinpoint Freud's gifts. His memory was astounding. During his youth, photographic recall allowed him to glance at textbooks and then recall the wording exactly . . . From a "multiple intelligences" perspective, it appears that Freud was extremely gifted in linguistic intelligence . . . Freud [also] possessed logical-mathematical gifts, the kinds of abilities on which scientists characteristically rely. (Gardner 1988, pp. 305–306; see also Ch. 2, this volume)

And it is also of interest that Freud did not see himself as particularly intelligent. He complained that "my chief reproach to the Almighty would be that he had not given me a better brain" (Jones 1961, p. 26).

We will more fully review two other approaches to analysis of individual development in a later section of this essay; that of Howard Gruber and his associates who have described creativity as an expression of "evolving systems" of knowledge, feelings, and purposes or goals; and David Feldman's effort to describe the kinds of distinctive mental processes (as contrasted with more common ones) that are required to transform knowledge and extend its boundaries. All of the above (and others that could be mentioned) are individual-oriented approaches.

Before turning to these matters, we first wish to sketch the broad context for our framework, that of cultural evolution as a crystallization of creative processes, and move from there to the formation of new ideas, technologies, techniques, representations, and descriptions of the humanly crafted world.

CREATIVITY AND CULTURAL EVOLUTION

We will argue that the tendency of human beings to intentionally transform their physical and social worlds is a unique, exclusively human process. All species have their distinctive ways of adapting, from mating patterns, to markings, to tendencies to protect their young. This focus on what is uniquely true of human psychology puts our work squarely in the tradition best exemplified by the Soviet developmentalist Lev Vygotsky (Vygotsky 1962, 1978).

All animal groups vary in terms of their tendencies to produce variations in behavior. Peter Marler, a specialist in bird song, reports that certain species are not appropriate subjects for studying canonical bird song development because they continually transform their song patterns (Marler and Terrace 1984). Other species are more regular and consistent, making them more suitable for these biological research purposes.

Similarly, Jerome Bruner (1972) summarizes evidence from primate studies of monkeys in which species differ in their mode of adaptation. The Vervet requires precise conditions of habitat for survival, while the adaptable Rhesus survives under relatively widely varying conditions. There have been claims that certain monkey groups make changes in their environments to improve the quality of the food supply, but these claims are not completely documented. In any case, species can and do differ with respect to their characteristic tendencies toward behavioral continuity and behavior change. In humans, however, these tendencies have been taken to extremes that make them qualitatively different from those of other living things.

This way of characterizing human uniqueness does not make a claim for exempting humanity from the laws of organic life or of evolution; it only asserts that the special turns that evolution has taken in the human case render its ways of adapting to and transforming habitats quite unlike those of any other group.

For whatever historical reasons, psychological science has tended to focus its resources on the ways that species are similar, attempting to show that all living things are subject to the same physical processes and biological principles. Great strides have been made in this manner, but we are left with little knowledge about the special ways that (especially humans) have developed to deal with and change their world.

Perhaps humanity had to be first brought "down" by scientific psychology to the level of other living things before it was possible to erect a scientifically responsible effort to consider its uniqueness. For most of known history humanity has cast itself as either special in the eyes of the gods, as created in the image of a god or gods, or as having unique spiritual status. Darwin and Freud seem to have all but dispatched these self-serving illusions.

These facts, combined with the obvious fact that the natural landscape has been dramatically transformed by human beings, make it plain that the major force for change in human culture is humanity's creation of culture. In other words, human beings put ideas and artifacts into the world that become important elements of the environment. This proliferation of changes in the habitat of human societies goes beyond unintentional and unintended changes in the world such as are caused by animal behavior, like eating all the grass in an area and causing it to dry out, which in turn produces changes in habitats for other animals. With human change, the effects on environments are for the most part self-conscious efforts at *producing* advantageous conditions. Artifacts, technologies, tools, techniques, symbol systems, and the like are intended to make the world a different and better (or at least more interesting) place.

Three other facts about human experience bear noting. One is the overall rapid pace of change in human cultures: another is variations in rate of change that can be observed both within and across cultures. In biology the idea of "punctuated evolution" is gaining currency to account for more rapid variations believed to occur during certain periods (Gould 1981), but still the fact remains that the rate of change for human cultures has been greater and includes more different kinds of changes than any other life form. A third fact is the apparent reversibility or shift of direction that can be brought about by self-conscious efforts at innovation among human societies. Reducing air pollution is a recent example of self-conscious efforts to reverse an undesirable change in habitat. While many would also agree that nuclear weaponry should be removed from the habitat, there are conflicts about the wisdom of doing so that make it less likely to occur. In either case, there is a conscious awareness of the possibility of reversing an existing change in environment.

There are changes in culture without corresponding morphological changes in physical characteristics to accompany them. We have the self-conscious desire to bring into the world new conditions that will make it a more satisfactory place, at least for an individual or that individual's group. We have rapid rates of change in environment that exceed the most dramatic change mechanisms for any other living species by orders of magnitude, and we have the possibility of reversing the direction of change within and across cultural groups. Up to this point we are dealing with facts, facts not always as well recognized as they might be, but facts nonetheless.

Within the constraints imposed by the facts just reviewed, there are a number of points of view that might guide further inquiry. The framework we describe here seems like the most useful one for organizing efforts to understand how and under what conditions humans try to transform their world in positive ways. We recognize that our proposed framework is not the only way to go about organizing the field, but it does capture and provide a way of ordering the main lines of work on creativity. This framework, which we call DIFI (for Domain Individual Field Interaction) divides the problem into three main parts, and specifies that only by considering the three—domain, individual, and field—as a set of continuously interrelated issues will it be possible to move the field forward in a coherent manner.

The conceptualization of our framework was initially carried out by Mihaly Csikszentmihalyi (Csikszentmihalyi and Robinson 1986; Csik-szentmihalyi, 1988b). The SSRC group (see Preface) had been struggling with the fact that the field seemed to lack a coherent way of describing its new direction, and several ways of capturing it had been proposed to the committee. The response to Csikszentmihalyi's model in the committee was favorable, and its usefulness was immediately recognized. He then went on to write several papers based on the DIFI framework (although not with that name), and the summary presented in this chapter is based on those publications (Csikszentmihalyi 1988, a and b, 1990); cf. Csikszentmihalyi and Robinson, 1986).

The DIFI Framework

A number of scholars have emphasized that creativity can be approached from several perspectives: from that of the *person* carrying out the work; from that of the *product* that arises from the efforts of the person or people; from that of the *process* that brings about the novel idea or product; or from the *response* of others to the existence of a new product (Barron 1988; Jackson and Messick 1965; Rothenberg and Hausmann 1976). Each perspective brings with it the possibility of new insights into the nature of creativity. Along with greater insight, however, there is a tendency as well to discount the importance of the other perspectives (Feldman 1990).

In the framework proposed here, we recommend that each perspective be continuously considered even when one or another has been selected for emphasis. If the investigator is concerned with the personality or intellectual characteristics of creative persons, a perfectly legitimate interest, this purpose should be pursued in the context of an understanding that desired personality characteristics may vary with the field in which the work is done, with stylistic variations in process, with the response that one's work has received, and so on. By locating the work one is doing within a broader framework, there is greater likelihood that the work will not be distorted, inflated, or overgeneralized.

The basic form of our framework is presented in Figure 2. It has three primary subsystems: *individual, domain, and field*. Each of the subsystems interacts with the others: individuals acquire knowledge of challenging domains, eventually propose new knowledge for those domains, and have the potential new knowledge considered and evaluated by the field. If the proposed new knowledge is accepted by the field, it becomes part of it and is added to the domain. Then, when another individual acquires the knowledge of the domain, it will contain the new element contributed by individuals who have acquired the knowledge of the domain at an earlier point.

Let us briefly consider the meaning of each of the three primary parts of the model.

Domains. A domain is an organized body of knowledge about a particular topic. The term *domain* is one that is used in many ways in the psychological literature, and for widely differing purposes (Ennis 1989). Here we refer to a domain as the formally organized body of knowledge that is associated with a given field. How to identify domains is a matter of informed judgment at this point, since few formal criteria have been proposed for doing so (Feldman 1986, 1994).

For example, mathematics seems too large to be called a single domain (for the purposes of analyzing creativity), but the various branches of mathematics seem of appropriate size. Algebra, geometry, number theory, and topology are sufficiently distinct branches of mathematics to be reasonably separate from each other, yet all fall within the realm of mathematical reasoning. Mathematical reasoning would in our framework be seen as a level of analysis broader than is represented in Figure 2, and would be seen as part of the context for understanding how a particular domain might be related to others that are also called mathematical. When contributions are made to mathematics, they are actually made to one of its domains. Although not always as clear in other domains, the task in describing a domain is to

Figure 2
The Locus of Creativity.

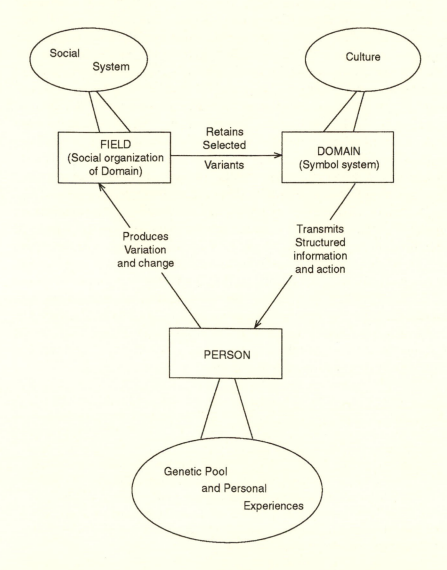

This "map" shows the interrelations of the three systems that jointly determine the occurrence of a creative idea, object, or action. The individual takes some information provided by the culture and transforms it, and if the change is deemed valuable by society, it will be included in the domain, thus providing a new starting point for the next generation of persons. The actions of all three systems are necessary for creativity to occur.

From: M. Csikszentmihalyi 1988, p. 329

choose a level of description that allows potential new knowledge to be evaluated in relation to existing knowledge.

A domain of knowledge exists before a person tries to master (or transform) it, and has a history that can be learned, to some degree, independently of the persons who constructed and distilled its contributions along the way. Typically, domains have representational techniques that uniquely capture the knowledge that is held in the domain, through specially constructed symbol systems, or special adaptations of other symbol systems, special terms, and technologies that are used only within that domain (Gardner 1983). The more tightly organized and coherent that knowledge is represented within a domain, the more readily will it be possible to evaluate possible transformations. In mathematics, it should be easier to determine if a proposed contribution is creative, and to what degree, than in ethics, or politics, or economics (Csikszentmihalyi, 1988b).

The person who masters the knowledge contained in a domain and who practices within the social constraints of a field will be the source of variations in the knowledge system of a domain. The processes that give rise to and shape variations intended to transform domains is a vital aspect of creativity research, but it is not sufficient without seeing these processes in the context of the domain and the field. Creativity in this sense is a contextual judgment rendered upon variations prepared by individuals. The contexts are provided by the domains, the fields which are the social support systems for domains, and the wider contexts of social system and culture.

Fields. A field is defined in this manner:

> It is the task of the "field" to select promising variations and to incorporate them into the domain. The easiest way to define a field is to say that it includes all those persons who can affect the structure of a domain. Thus, the field of art includes the following: art teachers and art historians, because they pass on the specialized symbolic information to the next generation; art critics, who help establish the reputation of individual artists; collectors, who make it possible for artists and works of art to survive; gallery owners and museum curators, who preserve and act as midwives to the production of art; and, finally, the peer group of artists whose interaction defines styles and revolutions of taste. (Csikszentmihalyi 1988b, p. 330)

Transforming domains is a kind of "boundary pushing" activity in which one or more individuals decides that change is called for (Perkins 1988; Robinson 1988). In order to make such a decision wisely, it is necessary to have a good sense of where the current boundaries of the domain reside and a feel for which ones are vulnerable to attack. Much of the activity within a field is intended to buttress current boundaries, to establish or consolidate new boundaries, or to make clearer why such boundaries must exist. A great deal less activity is spent trying to move boundaries, and probably relatively few individuals or groups see their primary role as boundary breaking (Feldman 1993; Perkins 1988).

Most examples of the transformation of a domain come from those who have mastered its principles thoroughly, but who are dissatisfied with one or another aspect of the domain as it exists. These are the individuals who understand best what the internal consistencies and inconsistencies of a domain are. Therefore, the people most likely to transform a domain are those who have perceived a problematic aspect and who are not so entrenched in the established knowledge and belief of the domain that they defend rather than extend its boundaries.

Often the resources necessary to transform a domain are imported from other, neighboring domains. When Piaget found no change mechanism in psychology adequate to account for what he observed in children's evolving behavior, he looked to biology for a process that could be adapted for the purpose and came up with the concept of equilibration, a modification of the physical science notion of equilibrium. When Watson and Crick were looking for a technique for cracking the genetic code, they realized that X-Ray crystallography might provide a key to its structure (Watson 1896).

Disciplines and crafts and technical fields are combined and recombined in various ways at various points, depending upon the success of the importation and its adaptation to new circumstances. There are several scholarly fields that now routinely involve more than one discipline: biochemistry, astrophysics, cognitive science, neuroscience, nuclear medicine, sociobiology, operations research, and chaos theory are just a few. And of course there are many fields which are inherently likely to draw upon several disciplines, trades, and crafts: architecture, business, education, medicine, law, politics, and many others. The point is that it is guaranteed that there will always be a fair amount of boundary establishing and boundary extending going on within an active domain (Thomas 1974). The rate of such activity may vary with varying circumstances, and this is of course a matter of great interest (Csikszentmihalyi and Robinson 1986; Csikszentmihalyi 1988b; Perkins 1988; Simonton 1984, 1987, 1988).

On much rarer occasions novel domains will be begun virtually from scratch. Psychoanalysis and computer programming are such domains, but there are no doubt others that we can no longer trace. At some time in history a person made marks in the sand with a stick, and perhaps noticed that the marks might represent a thought. That person may have tried to show this clever idea to someone else. The systematic tracking of movements among lights in the sky also had to begin somewhere at some time, as did the attempt to differentiate the sizes and intensities of such lights.

In our own time, the invention of a computing machine started a new domain and powerfully affected many others, as did the invention of the silicon chip. In each case, the motivation to transform a bit of the world catalyzed a process of change, whether part of an existing domain, a domain in need of infusion of new ideas, technologies, or techniques from neighboring domains, or the midwifing of a virtually new domain. There are also instances when a practitioner has no particular desire to change an existing domain or create a new one, and these instances place the responsibility for recognizing and using new ideas or products on those who appreciate what someone else has done, often at a later point than the work was completed. Gregor Mendel's work with bean plants is such an example, providing as it did the foundation for modern genetics.

As Brannigan (1981) has observed, Mendel had no intention of transforming the field of genetics, since the field did not exist as such when he carried out his famous studies of beans. Several decades passed before the findings of the inventive monk were perceived as relevant to the emerging field of genetics.

Persons. The person has traditionally been the focus of psychological research. When looking for creativity, we have tended to look for it in persons, assuming that it will be adequately explained by an account of the qualities of the person associated with a creative endeavor. In particular, the tendency to look for stable traits of intellect or personality characterized the first twenty or thirty years of creativity research. Although a number of such qualities seem to have emerged as associated with creative accomplishment, they fall well short of providing a satisfying explanation for how and why creative works are done (Feldman 1974, 1980; Gardner 1989).

More recently, researchers have begun to emphasize developmental aspects of persons and their relationship to creativity. Howard Gruber in particular has advanced a number of novel personological variables into the study of creative development. He has proposed, for example, that an examination of "networks of enterprise," interconnected sets of goals, purposes, projects, and preoccupations, are characteristic of creative individuals. The evolution of such networks may be key to understanding how a given individual organized and orchestrated a life of creative effort (Wallace and Gruber 1989).

Another notion introduced by Gruber is of "images of wide scope" such as the branching tree that Darwin included as the only illustration in *The Origin of the Species*. These images guide and inform the theorizing and speculating of the individual, and their changes too can be studied over time as developmental phenomena. How common they are, and how influential they become to the work of a given individual, are questions of great interest when studying creativity at the individual level (Gruber and Davis 1988; Wallace and Gruber 1989).

Interaction. Persons, domains, and fields therefore need to be studied in relation to each other, as well as independently. Since domains only exist as they are mastered, preserved, and transformed by individuals, they should be understood to have distinctive qualities that are independent of any person, but which require persons for their continued existence. Persons, however original or determined or skilled, make contributions to domains that have structure and yield to or transform constraints. It is only from knowing and confronting a boundary that they can be transformed. Setting and resetting the boundaries and accepting changes is the primary function of the field (Feldman 1993; Perkins 1988; Thomas 1974). As a set of interlocking systems, persons, field, and domain make up a reasonable context within which to carry out investigations of creativity: this can be the study of persons, of domains, of fields, or of various ways in which one or more systems interact with the others.

Using the framework. Howard Gardner (1988) has made a first effort to use a broad-gauged model such as that proposed by Csikszentmihalyi in the study of a single case: that of Sigmund Freud. By examining some of the qualities of Vienna near the turn of the century, the knowledge domains within which Freud worked, and his distinctive mix of talents, abilities, personality characteristics, Gardner has been able to add richness and texture to the knowledge we have about Freud's work in bringing the field of psychoanalysis into existence. For example, in examining his Viennese environment, Gardner suggests: "it can be argued that Freud had a symbiotically productive relationship with his home territory; living elsewhere, he might not have had the opportunity to make many of the observations that were key to his theory. Nor would he have felt that intense struggle between the expression of human instincts and the dictates of a repressive society that ultimately animated his theoretical edifice" (Gardner 1988, p. 314).

Of course, the proof of the value of an approach that looks at person, field, and domain simultaneously is whether new insights about the process of achieving something new and valuable will be forthcoming. Based on Gardner's initial attempt, the approach seems promising. And while efforts have begun to explicitly utilize the overall framework sketched earlier, other efforts, couched within that framework, have also been launched. The two we will describe both deal with individual creative processes, but do so with the larger context very much in mind.

Evolving Systems: A Broad Individual Approach

For the past two decades Howard Gruber and his associates have been developing a set of concepts and techniques for organizing research on the processes through which remarkable individuals have achieved major contributions to knowledge. For the most part, the research has been case study work, a technique with many pitfalls methodologically, but with unique advantages as well (Wallace and Gruber 1989). In 1974, Gruber published a major study of Charles Darwin, focusing on the two-year period (1836–1838) when he first formulated the theory of evolution based on random variation and natural selection.

The aim of Gruber's approach has been to better comprehend extreme and unequivocal instances of creative accomplishment through careful case analysis, typically based on primary source materials. For example, in the Darwin study, notebooks that had been ignored in previous scholarship were vital to the work of interpreting Darwin's thought processes during a critical period in his career. Gruber also used sources that added context and texture to the material, such as social and cultural analysis, developmental theory (especially Piaget's), and historical research. An account of the individual's life as purposeful, striving, and coherent was the outcome of Gruber's careful effort (Gruber 1981a,b; Gruber and Davis, 1988).

The most distinctive feature of Gruber's approach is the establishment of "middle level" concepts that organize but do not reduce the complexity of an individual's life (Strauss 1987). Gruber proposes that individual lives be analyzed in terms of three (three again!) interrelated systems: *knowledge, purpose, and affect* (Wallace and Gruber 1989). Each of these systems can be analyzed separately, and each is also enriched by its relations with the other systems in the individual's overall personality. Much of Gruber's work has been aimed at illuminating the nature of each of the above three systems as it operated in a given individual, such as Darwin or Piaget, and to examine how each system might have affected the others.

Formally, the three systems of Gruber are similar in structure to the three systems in Csikszentmihalyi's account. Three systems are proposed, each with independent status, each with implications for the others. Gruber's systems of knowledge, affect, and purpose are of course all internal to the individual, while Csikszentmihalyi's systems include domains and fields in addition to the individual, but as dynamic models, they share key features. The specific processes through which the three systems interact in the broader context are, of course, not proposed to be the same as those that operate within the individual's personality, but the assumption of interaction and joint influence resonates throughout both approaches.

Gruber has offered a number of other "middle level" concepts to guide research on individual creative processes. The term middle level in this context means that the concepts are placed between the most general notions that might be offered, such as traits of "incubation" or the like, and ones that are so specific that they offer little explanatory power; an example might be "memory capacity." The intent is to cut human nature at just the right level of generality to offer explanatory power, on the one hand, while not falling into such broad theorizing that the distinctiveness of the individual creator is lost. Gruber has been the leading researcher in this quest for middle-level concepts of creativity.

As mentioned earlier, another organizing principle for creativity research a la Gruber is the "network of enterprise" (Gruber 1981a, b; Gruber and Davis 1988; Abra 1988; Wallace and Gruber 1989). Gruber has observed that Darwin and other creators of the highest rank seem to have had a number of projects going simultaneously. In the individual creator's mind, there is typically a meaningful orchestration of these enterprises, a coherent set of guiding principles that select and organize the various activities she or he pursues. As is true of Darwin, the interrelations among his various projects were not known to the general scientific community, nor even to his closest associates. Having a set of scientific enterprises at various levels of difficulty, controversy, challenge, and duration, Darwin could move from one to the other as opportunity, inspiration, and internal timetables dictated, much as an artist moves from painting to painting in an atelier.

Gruber has begun to make explicit the relationships that might exist between the three broad systems, knowledge, purpose, and affect, and other concepts like networks of enterprise. One could see an array of projects as an expression of the three broad systems, perhaps most directly related to knowledge and purpose, with affect entering most decisively when frustration with progress occurs in one project, or a challenge intrudes from outside (as was the case when Alfred Lord Wallace wrote to Darwin about his work on evolution; see Gruber 1981a).

Gruber's work gives us concepts that are large enough to organize analysis over relatively long periods of time, to provide ideas that help reveal the distinctiveness of the creative individual without falling into the morass of uniqueness as a reason for not studying creativity as a process. Gruber's cases have a ring of reality about them, while at the same time they help shed light on general issues and point to certain processes that are implicated in all instances of creative work of the highest order. In other words, they make a positive contribution to the field of creativity research by attempting to chart critical patterns that must be understood without either reducing the distinctiveness of great creativity or render it bland through overgeneralization.

One of the specific topics taken up by Gruber and his colleagues has been the matter of "insight." By using their middle-level concepts as a guide, they have shown that the assumptions that are typically made about insight are not plausible. Although the "lightning bolt" suddenness of certain resolutions or solutions may occur (Feldman 1988a), Gruber sees insight as a relatively common occurrence, happening several times a week in Darwin's case and others that have been documented (Crovitz 1970). Seen in context, insight may or may not be crucial to major instances of creativity, and in any case, the interpretation of creativity as inspiration from unknown sources is highly misleading (Gruber 1981a, b). Using concepts such as duration, frequency, and magnitude as criteria, Gruber has been able to show that what are believed to be sudden, spontaneous solutions often turn out to be more protracted processes, guided by rational efforts and under at least partial conscious control. Insight may be better thought of as the end of a long process, the point of consolidation of a long-term project, a confirmation of mastery at a certain level rather than a moment of dramatic thrust into new and uncharted territory (see also Feldman 1988a, b for a somewhat different view; also this volume).

One need only contrast Gruber's central metaphor of the creative person at work with Guilford's (1950) definition of creativity as the set of traits that are possessed by the creative personality to see how different a conception is being pursued. Yet what is compromised in this shift is the possibility of generalizations across many individuals, so much a part of Guilford's initial research vision. What is gained in the comprehension of a unique accomplishment is perhaps lost to the goal of making valid generalizations. The value of Gruber's approach will therefore be best realized within the kind of framework that has been proposed by Csikszentmihalyi, and of course when many cases have been studied at a level of detail sufficient to permit comparative analysis.

Therefore, as richly informative as studies of the individual case are, we believe that efforts should continue to build models at both more molar and more molecular levels as well. One such more molecular model aims to provide accounts of how new thoughts themselves might be constructed. This is, after all, the sine qua non of creativity; plausible descriptions of the kind of system that could intentionally construct something new is an essential part of the story.

Thought Processes in Creativity: A Three-Part Model

Once again we find similarities with interacting systems as proposed in the two previous levels of description. Feldman proposes three interrelated internal systems (see Figure 3), each with a distinctive function and purpose that are coordinated in their contributions to the formation of novel ideas (Feldman 1988a, b, 1989). It is reasonable to view the various models as nested within each other, with Csikszentmihalyi's as the broadest, Gruber's nested within the Person component of Csikszentmihalyi's model, and Feldman's three-process thinking model nested with Gruber's knowledge system component, although perhaps less neatly so than the others. The particular model to be presented represents only one of several more individual-based approaches, one that emphasizes specific thought processes. Personal qualities such as motivational states (Hennessey and Amabile 1988) or physical capabilities would also be appropriate to examine at this level of analysis.

The uniquely human ability to reflect upon the state of the world and of one's own capabilities and make changes in them is perhaps the most dramatic way in which humans differ from other organisms. How such an ability might actually work in the human body is beyond the scope of this (or any other available) discussion, but that something like reflectiveness exists in humans is virtually beyond doubt (Campbell and Bickhard 1986; Piaget 1971a, b). The argument is not that no other organism has even a vestige of self-awareness; Premack (1976) and others have shown primitive capabilities of reflectiveness in certain primates. It is simply that reflectiveness (some would call it consciousness) is clearly the hallmark of the human mind (Dennett 1987, 1991).

This quality of reflectiveness seems to work toward inward as well as outward events. Humans are able to respond to their own thoughts and feelings with some kind of comprehension, to categorize and analyze them, and to modify them to some degree. There are even those who have given special status to the ability to be especially aware of one's own thoughts and feelings as an important dimension of human variability (Gardner 1983; Wilber, Engler, and Brown 1986). In addition, humans have the capacity to represent certain qualities of the external world around them, including things about other human beings, in ways that lead to their being represented and reflected upon in productive ways. For example, most adults in this culture are able to judge fairly well the degree to which a given physical space pleases them or does not please them. Through the use of language or some other symbolic representation, these reactions can be coded and manipulated, plans for changes can be generated, and perhaps implemented.

Again, some observers have distinguished among individuals in their inclinations toward and capabilities for analyzing and changing the world around them, but most human beings seem to possess these capabilities to a degree not found elsewhere in the animal world (Sternberg 1988). Some

Figure 3
Three Sets of Thought Processes Involved in Feldman's Model

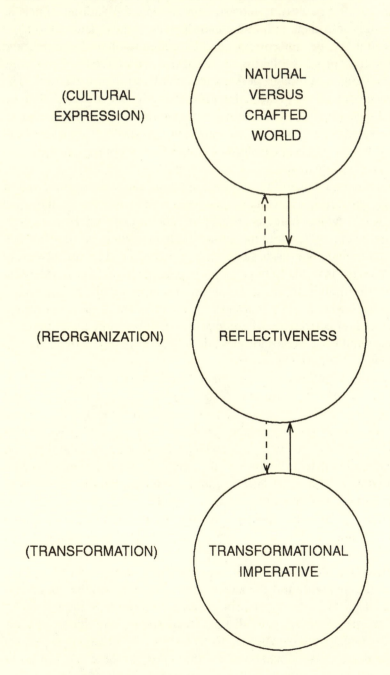

people seem more inclined to adjust themselves to fit the world that is perceived, others will go to extreme lengths to change their personal world if it deviates even slightly from their idea of what it ought to be (Erikson 1969). The kind of organism humans tend to be, to a greater or lesser extent, is the kind that reflects upon and makes changes in its world, even if change means simply picking up stakes and finding a more congenial place. No organism wanders like humanity wanders, toward the conditions that are satisfying and away from those that are not.

Purposefulness, then, also seems to be a unique quality of human thought and human behavior. This purposefulness or intentionality (Dennett, 1978, 1987, 1991), in turn, is born of an ability to reflect on experience, both from inside and from outside the skin, as well as a tendency to believe in the possibility of making changes to better achieve our ends. Reflectiveness alone, however, would not explain the tendency to modify the environment. Indeed, certain disciplines are designed to use reflection as the basis for accepting life as it is. Being aware of the fact that a habitat does not fulfill all of the desires and aspirations a person might conjure up would not necessarily lead to a commitment to try to change it. Indeed, the common tendency to persist in unhealthy situations or even dangerous ones reminds us of the variations in such abilities that continue to exist, even in the species that has developed pragmatic reflectiveness to such a marked degree.

As these tendencies have become widespread, their application has extended to groups small and large, so that purposefulness and reflectiveness have become indispensable to the formation and evolution of culture.

While all human beings develop the processes we are describing, they do not all develop them in similar ways. The input into them varies with the sensitivities and inclinations of the particular individual, and the circumstances that affect them are different in each case. In other words, while we wish to outline what seem to be fundamental human processes of understanding and transforming information and experience, processes that are used in distinct and varying ways to bring about newness, freshness, innovation, change that make a difference to others, we recognize the great variations that also exist (Vygotsky 1978).

At this point the three processes can only be described independently; it is obvious, however, that their interaction will provide the most revealing insights. Much the same could be said of the broadest level of the framework presented in this discussion, that of individual, domain, and field. But until the various components of the system are described adequately, interaction studies will not be feasible. To account for creative accomplishment, the systems will have to be integrated, and in terms that lead to sustained coordination for a sufficient duration to bring about a fresh construction. The first task, then, is to try to describe key processes.

Process 1: Reflectiveness. Of all the qualities that set human beings apart from other organisms, the quality of reflectiveness is probably the most important. It is an ability that makes possible the belief that we can know ourselves, can hold our experience and the experience of others up for examination, can build a sense of uniqueness and distinctiveness that we usually call a sense of self or identity. It is also of course a great deal of what we mean by consciousness, and makes possible virtually all of the symbolic and abstract activity that is the hallmark of human thought. How such a process of reflectiveness might have come about is a question for evolutionary biology and beyond the scope of this discussion (Churchland 1986; Simon 1990), but it is key to any theory of creativity (Dennett, 1987, 1991).

There must be some way of holding experience in mind in such a way that it is a "commentary" on what has happened. At this point all we can say is that the "second representation" must occur after the first. How much after, how many sense experiences must occur before a second representation is called forth, how the first set is related to the second set, these are matters beyond even our fairly loose speculation. But somehow, and in some fashion, it must be possible for the human mind to "reflect" on its experience, as well as to compare that experience with what it learns of the experience of others. As David Perkins (1988) has written, what is actual must also be possible. We must acknowledge that something like reflectiveness is actual; therefore, it must be possible.

Piaget (1982) and Bickhard (Campbell and Bickard 1986) in particular have been sensitive to a set of processes that examine experience at a more abstract or higher level. "Reflective abstraction" or "reflexive abstraction" is the term usually given for this tendency among human thinkers. Reflective abstraction is seen as the process through which all progress toward more powerful mental structures is achieved in both Piaget's and Bickhard's theories, although Bickhard's is more explicit as to just how such a process might work (Campbell and Bickhard 1986). Neither theorist has tried to locate reflective abstraction within a functional/physical/brain framework, but both implicitly assume such a model. Bickhard's "knowing levels" particularly are resonant with the approach taken here. Knowing levels are iteratively and recursively built from the "reflections" of the mind on its own experience.

Process 2: Transformational impulses from the unconscious. To imagine changes that might actually be brought into existence and placed into the crafted world of human culture is what must occur for creativity to be possible. This kind of thinking could only occur if it is pushed by a "transformational imperative" born of unconscious experiences of the power to bring about change beyond current reality constraints. It could also only occur if evidence of previous productive changes is available and accessible. The function we have been referring to as reflectiveness, which is built from awareness of experience in unconscious as well as external events, when catalyzed by awareness of previous efforts at self-directed change, may lead to further attempts to transform the external world, may lead, in other words, to innovativeness, novelty, and when highly successful, to creative products themselves.

It has been known for centuries that human beings have images and experiences that seem to come not from the outside but from the inside world. These have often been associated with creativity, but also with madness. Dreams, daydreams, fantasies, free associations, and the like are also likely to be unique human capabilities, or at least uniquely formed within the human nervous system. The "ideal" images of the Greeks, the gods and goddesses, demons, devils, monsters, fanciful and fateful myths, stories, and tales, all seem likely candidates to have originated in unconscious processes.

Although conscious awareness of such matters varies considerably, with most material quickly fading back into obscurity, especially in dreams, some of that material finds its way into awareness temporarily or even permanently. It is vital for our purposes that unconscious processes be understood both in their generative as well as their transformational tendencies. We must learn both how unconscious functioning forms and re-forms images, and how these tendencies might impact the other representations coming from more external sources.

This means that we must assume that there is "internal traffic" back and forth between and among conscious and unconscious functions. What is formed in the unconscious has to be in part constructed from material taken from representations based on sense experience. It also must become organized into images, events, objects, and processes. Otherwise, the unconscious forms would never include people and events from the real world, nor would familiar places appear in dreams.

We are far from the first to have speculated about reciprocal influences of conscious and unconscious processes. Freud, Jung, and other psychoanalysts did so seriously; analysts like Kris, Kubie, Rothenberg, Arieti, and Gedo have extended the general approach specifically to creativity (see Rothenberg and Hausmann 1976). In this respect we are simply placing the long-standing tradition of analysis of unconscious motivations and manipulations into a somewhat different context. We accept the possibility of images and impressions that originate in unconscious processes, as have many before, although we have little more to say about such matters in the present account. Our concern is with *how* the unique ways of forming and reforming ideas and images in different parts of the mind combine to make new thoughts possible.

What we wish to emphasize here is that any attempt to describe creativity must include explicit reference to the unconscious processes that are so clearly a part of human experience. Without trying to be more precise than is justified at this point, we can say that the most distinct features of unconscious processes for the present discussion are the following: first, that unconscious processing is fluid, continuous, active, and generative; second, that unconscious processing has contact with other sources of information going into the mind, particularly sense impressions, perceptions of humanly crafted ideas and things (detailed in the next section), and representations that become what we refer to as rational consciousness; and, finally, that unconscious processes can to some degree be brought into harness to serve various purposes directed at least in part by conscious goals. This must be the case if we are to in any sense believe accounts of insight that report sudden solutions coming "out of the blue." More likely they have come "out of the black" (Feldman 1988a, 1989).

Unconscious processes may be assumed to operate continuously, even when conscious processes are also underway. The two do not seem to ever be out of contact entirely; scary dreams do after all sometimes lead to awakening. Some people are even able to train themselves to be more skillful at monitoring dream content so that they "pull the alarm" if things get out of hand (Hartmann 1984). Artists and writers often report that they consciously use dream states, semidream states, states of reverie, and daydreams as sources of material. The ability to bring into conscious reference things which more typically come and go without record is one of the things that contributes to richness of expression, and also one of the ways that individuals differ from one another. Some people seem to have remarkable access to unconscious material, are able to hold that material in mind and memory indefinitely, and reflect upon that material for various reasons. Carl Jung was perhaps the individual of record who spent more of his life recording and analyzing the material sent from his unconscious, primarily dreams (Jung 1965): "I had the earliest dream I can remember, a dream which was to preoccupy me all my life. I was then between three and four years old." (p. 11) And later in the same work: "Consciousness is phylogenetically and ontogentically a secondary phenomenon. It is time this obvious fact were grasped at last. Just as the body has an anatomical history of millions of years, so also does the psychic system." (p. 348)

The key quality of unconscious thought in the context of the present discussion is that it seems to take liberties with whatever goes into it and whatever comes out of it. It seems to have little regard for "reality" or for the normal rules of thought or communication, and seems to operate with its own set of rules. We know all too little about just what these rules actually are, and we think it a high priority that efforts to discover these rules be pursued as vigorously as possible (Feldman 1989). In general, however, we believe that unconscious thought is motivated by a natural desire to transform, to change, to make things different from the way they were. It is a process that has certain tendencies to destabilize structures, to break them down and render them less organized. The means through which unconscious processes carry out their transformations are not well known, but dreams, drug states, hypnotic states, meditation, psychoanalyses, daydreams, and the like will all have something to tell us about them (Wilber, Engler, and Brown 1986).

Process 3: Changing the world. Somehow, the raucous disrespect for stability that seems to prevail in unconscious processes must be balanced against other tendencies to produce stable and predictable representations of the external world as well as the world of experience. It is in the interplay of processes of change and stability that innovative new ideas emerge. But in order for this to happen, there must be a special kind of awareness that is constructed (or is built) in the individual's mind. This awareness is not consciousness per se, but is a special kind of consciousness. It is a consciousness that includes the realization that the world as it is need not be the world forever (Feldman 1988a, 1989).

Human beings are unique in the ability to realize that they have the power to make the world into a difference place than it is. Through intentional efforts, things about the world can be changed (Dennett 1987, 1991). A roof can be made out of straw versus the traditional sticks. A river can be crossed on a fallen log, but perhaps better on a log that has its top surface flattened. An animal's flesh is good to eat, but easier when pulled away from the bone and dropped into a fire for awhile. Sand can be melted into something that stops the wind and yet can be seen through. There have been millions of instances in the history of human experience which have led to intentional changes in the world. Some of these, no doubt a small proportion, have proven to be of use and preserved, somewhat akin to the selection process that is brought to bear on variations in traits in physical evolution (Feldman 1980, 1986).

The importance of an awareness that the external world can be changed is no doubt at least partly a function of the fact that human beings experience internal change a good deal of the time. Combined with an ability to represent these internal experiences, to reflect on their occurrence along with a rational analytic ability to learn and organize complex information may have led to the realization that one can effect changes outside as well as witness changes on the inside in one's own mind.

How all of this could have occurred is not difficult to imagine, at least in outline. Suppose someone inadvertently acted in such a way as to make a change in the external environment, a change that had the potential to be useful. Once done, the ability to reflect on this experience is stimulated. This, combined with previous experience with transformed reality arising in unconscious thought, might move the individual to try to bring about further change, particularly if the effect of a change was in some way advantageous, say, led to catching an animal versus losing it.

In the present discussion, domains of knowledge and skill are evolving sets of cultural artifacts that reflect past creative activity. They also provide the existing context into which novel possibilities are introduced, some to be accepted and incorporated into the domain and others to be rejected or ignored. Culture also plays a dynamic role of support and organization through its fields of endeavor, which can be more or less loosely structured. Fields encompass the domain with sources of support, instruction, socialization, tradition, evaluation, and recognition. The existence of a well-organized and subtly structured field is a good indicator that creative activity has been valued in a domain for a long time. Music is perhaps the most venerable of fields, while computer science is perhaps the most rapidly evolving and transforming field of the past several decades.

We see important opportunities for research through the study of both domains and fields, selected for their particular features and developmental status. For example, if a field has existed as an organized entity for centuries, as has music, then certain questions may be more fruitfully addressed by studying that domain. It would make sense to study levels of instructional resources and how they are connected, or how institutions select, prepare, and channel talent into various roles in the field. For such questions, fields at earlier periods of their development may be more opportune as objects of study. For questions about legitimization of a newly emerging field, or about how fields become differentiated from other already existing fields, computer science may be a more appropriate subject. Without arguing that the study of domains and fields should be separated from the study of the individuals who are part of them, it should be clear that a great deal of work can be done to better comprehend how domains evolve and how fields function to support their development. Work along these lines is underway, some being pursued by the present authors.

As much as creativity depends on disrespect for the status quo, it must also be true of human beings that they value stability, that they do not want to change the world all the time. Here again is a dimension along which individuals no doubt vary; some want to reduce change to an absolute minimum, others are messing about trying to change things all the time. Even the most radical transformers must desire at least a minimum of stability, and even the most reactionary conservers must from time to time recognize the need for or are at least willing to accept some minimal changes. When one goes beyond these tolerances, it is likely that we have entered the zone of psychopathology: inability to prevent continuous trans- formation on the one hand, and uncontrollable fear of change on the other; schizophrenic tendencies on the one hand, obsessive tendencies on the other.

It is in the interplay between desire for preserving important features and qualities of experience and desire to transform experience that creativity takes place. Creativity requires the ability to comprehend that the internal and external environments can be intentionally transformed, within limits that have been evolved from the processes of representation, and with unconscious and conscious perceptions of change informing and shaping each other. Representation, organization of experience, skills, and analytic capabilities, including a sense of self, lie in between the two (internal and external) kinds of change. Representation and reflectiveness have as their fundamental purposes to organize and categorize and make useful the information that finds its way there. As Keil (1984, 1986), Gelman (1991), and others have argued, representations of experience form structures that reflect deep biological design and demand characteristics, which can in turn be reflected upon and transformed.

Both the internal urge to change reality and the external nature of constructed reality need to find their way into consciousness, to be repre- sented and thought about. As for the former, we have already indicated their likely source as dreams, reverie, meditation, and so on, which can be cultivated through practice, instruction, and the like. External changes can be directly observed but can also be transmitted through the efforts of other people through the symbol systems and artifacts that have already been created (Carroll and Campbell 1989).

Language is of course the transmitter of experience par excellence for human beings, but crystallized knowledge, including information about changes in knowledge, comes in numerous forms. The most important piece of information to be understood about change is that people have brought about many changes through their own self-conscious efforts. It need not occur spontaneously to the developing person that it is within his or her power to make the world a little different; this possibility can be helped along by innumerable examples throughout culture, brought to conscious awareness by mentors, teachers, and more experienced practitioners in the many fields that human beings have collectively constructed (Csikszentmihalyi 1988a, b, 1990; Gardner 1982, 1983).

When one gazes out at the world, some of what is perceived is natural, including natural change. The sun goes up, the sun goes down; leaves fall from trees; animals are born and animals die; stars move about in the sky. Some of what gets represented and reflected upon and comprehended as change is based on natural processes, including perhaps random or unconnected change processes. But much of what is observed is in the world because of the activities of human beings going about their business, including the business of intentionally changing things.

There is a "crafted world" that exists as well as a natural world (Chen, Goldsmith, and Feldman 1989). The two are constrained by each other and influence each other (consider the presence of acid in rainfall because of human industrialization). Human beings can observe and/or be shown how the activities of humanity have changed the environment, fostering the realization that other people may be able to also bring about change. They can also be shown and/or discover the ways in which change is represented, fostered, curtailed, or controlled in human symbol systems and human institutions, contributing to a distinctive set of understandings about change. A sense of what has been done helps lead to a sense of what might be done, as well as an appreciation for the kinds of established constraints that might affect imagined changes.

The presence of arrays of humanly crafted objects and the ability to control events through humanly created systems for comprehending organization of time, space, and causality profoundly affect what is perceived and organized in the human mind. It is true that time has always existed, but it is not true that time has always been understood in units like seconds, minutes, hours, days, weeks, months, years, decades, centuries, and millennia, let alone that time and space are relative to the perspective one takes. The overlay of human organization and categorization on natural events changes the form and meaning of the information in the environment. For an older person to say to a younger person that the family will move when the snows come is vastly different from saying that it will happen in three months and four days.

In 1946 the biologist R. W. Gerard wrote:

Imagination, not reason, creates the novel. It is to social inheritance what mutation is to biological inheritance; it accounts for the arrival of the fittest. Reason or logic, applied when judgment indicates that the new is promising, acts like natural selection to pan the gold grains from the sand and insure the survival of the fittest. Imagination supplies the premises and asks the questions from which reason supplies the conclusions as a calculating machine supplies answers. (In Ghiselin 1952, p. 227)

Conclusion: Productive balance. In the study of creativity, culture has been implicitly or explicitly taken to be the result of creative processes, but rarely has culture itself been given a dynamic role (Csikszentmihalyi, 1988b); Robinson 1988; Rogoff 1990). In extreme interpretations of changes in behavior, as in Skinner's radical environmental determinism, creativity is interpreted to be *nothing else but* a result of external events occurring in precise sequence. This point of view, however far afield it may be in other ways, has nevertheless proven useful in bringing to attention the fact that creative work is not simply the playing out of individual drives, desires, efforts, and interpretations. It all takes place in a context of already existing circumstances, which themselves bear upon and, to a degree (but far from completely), control the process. To be fair, Skinner acknowledged that individuals differ in their genetic makeup, and that these biologically conditioned differences affect the ways that environment impacts that person (Skinner 1968). But in keeping with his emphasis on the power of external forces to control events, almost nothing is made of these biological differences.

Not addressed explicitly in the present account are the many issues that need to be tackled if specific instances of creative work are to be understood. We are still left with many questions about the distinctive talents, qualities, and dispositions of an individual who decides to devote a life to solving a particular kind of problem, or pursuing an art form of unique challenge. It should be clear from the foregoing account that it is unlikely that a single formula or even a small set of prototypes will emerge as capturing the person who makes a creative contribution in the myriad fields in which they may potentially occur (Gruber and Davis 1988; Sternberg 1988).

What the framework described in this chapter does is provide an organized set of concepts and issues to address when dealing with the purposeful processes of change in human minds and human cultures. By specifying what these issues are at a level of generality that does not, on the one hand, distort them by reducing them to microprocesses, or raise them to such an abstract level as to render them true but vapid, we believe that research and theory can proceed in a reasonably guided manner. Were this to be the case, we could look forward to knowing more about creativity as both an individual and a broader contextual matter. As the human process par excellence, understanding creativity is worthy of our best efforts—and will probably require them.

REFERENCES

Abra, J. (1988). *Assaulting Parnassus: Theoretical views of creativity*. Lanham, MD: University Press of America.

Albert, R. (1969). Genius: Present-day status of the concept, and its implications for the study of creativity and giftedness. *American Psychologist, 24,* 743–753.

———. (1990). Identity, experiences, and career choice among the exceptionally gifted and eminent. In M. A. Runco and R. S. Albert (eds.), *Theories of creativity* (pp. 13–34). Newbury Park, CA: Sage Publications.

Amabile, T. (1983). *The social psychology of creativity*. New York: Springer-Verlag.

———. (1985). Motivation and creativity: Effects of motivational orientation on creative writers. *Journal of Personality and Social Psychology, 48,* 393–399.

———. (1990). Within you, without you: The social psychology of creativity, and beyond. In M. A. Runco and R. S. Albert (eds.), *Theories of creativity* (pp. 61–91). Newbury Park, CA: Sage Publications.

Barron, F. (1953). Complexity-simplicity as a personality dimension. *Journal of Abnormal and Social Psychology, 48,* 163–172.

———. (1955). The disposition toward originality. *Journal of Personality and Social Psychology, 51,* 478–485.

Barron, F. (1988). Putting creativity to work. In R. Sternberg, Ed., *The nature of creativity* (pp. 76–98). New York: Cambridge University Press.

Barron, F., and G. S. Welsh. (1952). Artistic perception as a possible factor in personality style: Its measurement by a figure preference test. *Journal of Psychology, 33,* 199–203.

Brannigan, A. (1981). *The social basis of scientific discoveries*. New York: Cambridge University Press.

Bruner, J. S. (1972). The nature and uses of creativity. *American Psychologist, 27,* 1–22.

Campbell, R. L., and M. Bickhard. (1986). *Knowing levels and developmental stages*. Basel, Switzerland: Karger.

Carroll, J. M., and R. L. Campbell. (1989). Artifacts as psychological theories: The case of human-computer interaction. *Behavior and Information Technology, 8,* 247–256.

Chen, J. C., L. T. Goldsmith, and D. H. Feldman. (1989, June). *The crafted world: Children's understanding of the distinction between natural objects and artifacts*. Paper presented at the Jean Piaget Society, Philadelphia, PA.

Chomsky, N. (1968). *Language and mind*. New York: Harcourt, Brace, Jovanovich.

_____ . (1980). *Rules and representations*. New York: Columbia University Press.
Churchland, P. (1986). *Neurophilosophy*. Cambridge, MA: MIT Press.
Clifford, G. J (1964). A culture-bound concept of creativity: A social historian's critique centering on a recent American research report. *Educational Theory, 14*, 133–143.
Comrey, A. L., W. B. Michael, and B. Fruchter. (1988). J. P. Guilford. *American Psychologist, 43*, 1086–1087.
Crovitz, H. (1970). *Galton's walk: Methods for the analysis of thinking, intelligence, and creativity*. New York: Harper & Row.
Csikszentmihalyi, M. (1988a). Motivation and creativity: Toward a synthesis of structural and energistic approaches to cognition. *New Ideas in Psychology, 6*, 159–176.
Csikszentmihalyi, M. (1988b). Society, culture, and person: A systems view of creativity. In R. J. Sternberg (ed.), *The nature of creativity* (pp. 325–339). New York: Cambridge University Press.
_____ . (1990). The domain of creativity. In M. A. Runco and R. S. Albert (eds.), *Theories of creativity* (pp. 190–212). Newbury Park, CA: Sage Publications.
Csikszentmihalyi, M., and R. Robinson. (1986). Culture, time, and the development of talent. In R. Sternberg and J. Davidson (eds.), *Conceptions of giftedness* (pp. 264–284). New York: Cambridge University Press.
Dennett, D. C. (1978). *Brainstorms: Philosophical essays on mind and psychology*. Montgomery, VT: Bradford Books.
_____ . (1987). *The intentional stance*. Cambridge, MA: MIT Press.
_____ . (1991). *Consciousness explained*. Boston: Little-Brown.
Ennis, R. H. (1989). The extent to which critical thinking is subject-specific: Further clarification. *Educational Researcher, 19*, 13–16.
Erikson, E. (1968). *Young man Luther*. New York: Norton.
_____ . (1969). *Gandhi's truth*. New York: Norton.
Feldman, D. H. (1974). Universal to unique: A developmental view of creativity and education. In S. Rosner and L. Abt (eds.), *Essays in creativity* (pp. 45–85). Croton-on-Hudson, NY: North River Press.
_____ . (1980). *Beyond universals in cognitive development*. Norwood, NJ: Ablex.
_____ . (1982). A developmental framework for research with gifted children. In D. H. Feldman (ed.), *Developmental approaches to giftedness and creativity* (pp. 31–45). San Francisco: Jossey-Bass.
_____ . (1986). How development works. In I. Levin (ed.), *Stage and structure: Reopening the debate* (pp. 284–306). Norwood, NJ: Ablex.
_____ . (1988a). Creativity: Dreams, insights, and transformations. In R. Sternberg (ed.), *The nature of creativity* (pp. 271–297). New York: Cambridge University Press.
_____ . (1988b). Universal to unique: Toward a cultural genetic epistemology. *Arvhives de Psychologie, 56*, 41–49.

_____. (1989). Creativity: Proof that development occurs. In W. Damon (ed.), *Child development today and tomorrow* (pp. 240–260). San Francisco: Jossey-Bass.

_____. (1990). Four frames for the study of creativity. *Creativity Research Journal*, 2, 104–111.

_____. (1994 2d ed.). *Beyond universals in cognitive development.* Norwood, NJ: Ablex.

Fodor, J. (1983). *The modularity of mind.* Cambridge, MA: MIT Press.

Gardner, H. (1982). Giftedness: Speculations from a biological perspective. In D. H. Feldman (ed.), *Developmental approaches to giftedness and creativity* (pp. 47–60). San Francisco: Jossey-Bass.

_____. (1983). *Frames of mind.* New York: Basic Books.

_____. (1988). Creative lives and creative works: A synthetic scientific approach. In R. Sternberg (ed.), *The nature of creativity* (pp. 298–324). New York: Cambridge University Press.

_____. (1989). Creativity: An interdisciplinary perspective. *Creativity Research Journal*, 1, 8–26.

Gelman, R. (1991). Epigenetic foundations of knowledge structures: Initial and transcendent constructions. In S. Carey & R. Gelman (eds.) *The epigenesis of mind - Essays in biology and cognition* (pp. 293–322). Hillsdale, NJ: Erlbaum.

Getzels, J., and M. Csikszentmihalyi. (1976). *The creative vision: A longitudinal study of problem finding in art.* New York: John Wiley.

Getzels, J., and P. Jackson. (1962). *Creativity and intelligence: Explorations with gifted students.* New York: Wiley.

_____. (1963). The highly intelligent and the highly creative adolescent: A summary of some research findings. In C. W. Taylor and F. Barron (eds.), *Scientific creativity: Its recognition and development* (pp. 161–172). New York: Wiley.

Ghiselin, B. (ed.) (1952). *The creative process: A symposium.* New York: Mentor.

Gordon, W.J.J. (1961). *Synectics.* New York: Harper & Row.

Gould, S. J. (1981). *Mismeasure of man.* New York: Norton.

Gruber, H. (1981a). *Darwin on man.* Chicago: University of Chicago Press.

_____. (1981b). On the relation between "aha experiences" and the construction of ideas. *History of Science*, 19, 41–59.

_____. (1982). On the hypothesized relation between giftedness and creativity. In D. H. Feldman (ed.), *Developmental approaches to giftedness and creativity* (pp. 7–29). San Francisco: Jossey-Bass.

Gruber, H., and S. Davis. (1988). Inching our way up Mount Olympus: The evolving-systems approach to creative thinking. In R. J. Sternberg (ed.), *The nature of creativity* (pp. 243–270). New York: Cambridge University Press.

Guilford, J. P. (1950). Creativity. *American Psychologist*, 5, 444–454.

_____. (1967). *The nature of human intelligence.* New York: McGraw-Hill.

_____ . (1970). Creativity: Retrospect and prospect. *Journal of Creative Behavior*, *4*, 149–161.

Hartmann, E. (1984). *The nightmare: The psychology and biology of terrifying dreams*. New York: Basic Books.

Hennessey, B., and T. Amabile. (1988). The conditions of creativity. In R. Sternberg, (ed.), *The nature of creativity* (pp. 11–38). New York: Cambridge University Press.

Horowitz, F. and M. O'Brien (eds.) (1985). *The gifted and the talented: developmental perspectives* (pp. 99–123). Washington, DC: American Psychological Association.

Jackson, P. W. and Messick, S. (1965). The person, the product, and the response: Conceptual problems in the assessment of creativity. *Journal of Personality*, *37*, 309–329.

Jones, E. (1961). *The life and work of Sigmund Freud*. New York: Basic Books.

Jung, C. (1965). *Memories, dreams, reflections*. New York: Vintage Books (Translated by Richard and Clara Winston).

Keil, F. (1984). Mechanisms in cognitive development and the structure of knowledge. In R. Sternberg (ed.), *Mechanisms of cognitive development (pp. 81–100)*. San Francisco: W. H. Freeman.

_____ . (1986). On the structure-dependent nature of stages in cognitive development. In I. Levin (ed.). *Stage and Structure* (pp. 144–163). Norwood, NJ: Ablex.

Mackinnon, D. (1962). The personality correlates of creativity: A Study of American Architects. *Proceedings of the Fourteenth Congress on Applied Psychology*, *2*, 11–39.

Marler, P., and H. S. Terrace. (1984). *The biology of learning*. Berlin, Germany: Springer-Verlag.

Parnes, S. (1967). *Creative behavior guidebook*. New York, NY: Scribners.

Perkins, D. (1988). The possibility of invention. In R. J. Sternberg (ed.), *The nature of creativity* (pp. 362–385). New York: Cambridge University Press.

Piaget, J. (1971a). *Biology and knowledge*. Chicago: University of Chicago Press.

_____ . (1971b). The theory of stages in cognitive development. In D. Green, M. Ford, and G. Flamer (eds.), *Measurement and Piaget* (pp. 1–11). New York: McGraw-Hill.

_____ . (1982). Creativity. In J. M. Gallagher and D. K. Reid (eds.), *The learning theory of Piaget and Inhelder* (pp. 221–229). Monterrey, CA: Brooks/Cole.

Premack, D. (1976). *Intelligence in ape and man*. Hillsdale, NJ: Erlbaum.

Robinson, R. (1988). Project and prejudice: Past, present, and future in adult development. *Human Development*, *31*, 158–172.

Rogoff, B. (1990). *Apprenticeship in thinking*. Cambridge, MA: Harvard University Press.

Rothenberg, A., and C. Hausman. (1976). *The creativity question*. Durham, NC: Duke University Press.

Simon, H., and A. Newell. (1971). Human problem solving: The state of the theory in 1970. *American Psychologist, 26*, 145–159.

Simon, H. (1988). Creativity and motivation: A response to Csikszentmihalyi. *New Ideas in Psychology, 6*, 177–181.

———. (1990). Invariants of human behavior. *Annual Review of Psychology, 41*, 1–19.

Simonton, D. K. (1984). *Genius, creativity, and leadership: Historiometric inquiries*. Cambridge, MA: Harvard University Press.

———. (1987). Multiples, chance, genius, and zeitgeist. In D. N. Jackson and J. P. Rushton (eds.), *Scientific excellence* (pp. 98–128) Beverly Hills, CA: Sage Publications.

———. (1988). Creativity, leadership, and chance. In R. Sternberg (ed.), *The nature of creativity* (pp. 386–426). New York: Cambridge University Press.

———. (1990). *Scientific genius*. New York: Cambridge University Press.

Skinner, B. F. (1968). *The technology of teaching*. New York: Appleton-Century-Crofts.

Sternberg, R. (ed.) (1988). *The nature of creativity*. New York: Cambridge University Press.

Sternberg, R., and J. R. Davidson (eds.) (1986). *Conceptions of giftedness*. New York: Cambridge University Press.

Strauss, S. (1987). Educational-developmental psychology and school learning. In L. Liben (ed.), *Development and learning: Conflict or congruence?* (pp. 133–158). Hillsdale, NJ: Lawrence Erlbaum.

Thomas, L. (1974). *The lives of a cell: Notes of a biology watcher*. New York: Bantam Books.

Torrance, E. P. (1962). *Guiding creative talent*. Englewood Cliffs, NJ: Prentice-Hall.

———. (1988). The nature of creativity as manifest in its testing. In R. J. Sternberg (ed.), *The nature of creativity* (pp. 43–75). New York: Cambridge University Press.

Vygotsky, L. (1962). *Thought and language*. Cambridge, MA: M.I.T. Press (First published in 1934).

———. (1978). *Mind in society: The development of higher psychological processes*. (Edited by M. Cole, V. John-Steiner, S. Scribner, and E. Souberman). Cambridge, MA: Harvard University Press.

Wallace, D. and H. Gruber. (1989). *Creative people at work*. New York: Oxford University Press.

Wallach, M. (1970). Creativity. In P. H. Mussen (ed.), *Carmichael's manual of child psychology, Vol. 1* (3rd ed., pp. 1211–1272). New York: Wiley.

———. (1971). *The creativity-intelligence distinction*. New York: General Learning Press.

_____. (1985). Creativity testing and giftedness. In F. Horowitz and M. O'Brien (eds.), *The gifted and talented: Developmental perspectives* (pp. 99–132). Washington, DC: American Psychological Association.

Wallach, M. and N. Kogan. (1965). A new look at the creativity-intelligence distinction. *Journal of Personality, 33,* 348–369.

Watson, J. D. (1968). *The double helix: A personal account of the discovery of the structure of DNA.* New York: Signet Books.

Weisberg, R. (1988). Problem solving and creativity. In R. Sternberg (ed.), *The nature of creativity* (pp. 148–176). New York: Cambridge University Press.

Wilber, K., J. Engler and D. P Brown. (1986). *Transformations of consciousness: Conventional and contemplative perspectives on development.* Boston: New Science Library.

2

The Fruits of Asynchrony: A Psychological Examination of Creativity

Howard Gardner
Constance Wolf

A "POTTED HISTORY" OF PICASSO AND CUBISM

The name "Pablo Picasso" and the founding of cubism are virtually synonymous. According to the widely known story, Picasso was a preternaturally gifted young artist who was drawing like a master at a young age (for biographical details, see Barr [1946], Gilot and Lake [1964], and Penrose [1958]). The sketches of his childhood, and even the scribbles in his school notebooks, showed enormous skill and imaginativeness. By early adolescence, Picasso had already exhausted the art educational resources of his native Spain. Indeed, according to the legend—and this particular legend has the ring of truth—young Pablo was so accomplished that his father, also an artist, ceased to paint after his son had reached the age of fourteen.

Visiting Paris while still a teenager, Picasso soon had mastered the various styles of Western painting that had been developed by 1900. He was able to imitate the great masters of the past with fidelity, and his paintings and drawings reflected the trends and schools that characterized *la Belle Epoque*. The periods of his art at that time merited and have come to be known by special names: the Blue Period of 1901–1904, when he concentrated on figures, using monochrome blue toning; and the Rose Period of 1904–1906, when terra-cotta tonalities brightened canvases full of circus themes or figures in a "classical" repose. While not yet famous, Picasso was already recognized as a phenomenon. As his close friend Gertrude Stein once observed, "Picasso wrote painting as other children wrote their a.b.c. . . . his drawings were not of things seen but of things expressed, in short they were words for him and drawing was his only way of talking and he talks a great deal" (Burns 1970, p. 4).

By 1905, at age twenty-four, Picasso had clearly surpassed his contemporaries in Spain and in France. His portrait of Gertrude Stein (1906) and his self-portrait (1906) revealed the first traces of an emerging new style. The faces appeared masklike and reflected his growing interest in Iberian sculpture. As he himself later put it, "We were trying to move in a direction opposite to Impressionism. That was the reason we abandoned color, emotion, sensations and everything . . . to search again for an architectonic basis in the composition, trying to make an order of it" (Gilot and Lake 1964, p. 69). Then there was a landscape painting (1907) and other portraits in which he embodied Paul Cezanne's lapidary formula. "You must see in nature the cylinder, the sphere, the cone" (quoted in Barr 1936, p. 30). Above all, there was his early masterpiece *Les Desmoiselles d'Avignon*, a hauntingly powerful portrait of five prostitutes. This "battlefield of trial and experiment" (Barr 1946, p. 57) portrayed figures that were fragmented in a way never before attempted in Western painting. So iconoclastic was this work that some of Picasso's own friends were horrified, and, for years, Picasso hesitated to display it in public. The sketches for this path-breaking painting were folded over in his notebook; perhaps Picasso himself was overwhelmed by his revolutionary creation.

In the next few years, Picasso saw his experiments to their logical conclusion. In 1908–1909, analytic cubism was launched. In his works from this period, sometimes undertaken in close collaboration with Georges Braque, Picasso broke down familiar objects, like faces or tableware, into their component elements so that all the facets of these objects could be apprehended on a single canvas in a single glance. It was said by Guillaume Apollinaire that Picasso "studies an object as a surgeon dissects a corpse" (quoted in Penrose 1958, p. 188). Some five years later, the synthetic cubism phase began. In this mode of painting, the tactile aspects of the dissected objects were highlighted, and collages were created pictorially or with parts of the actual objects themselves. While the cubist movement as such had begun to dissipate by 1915 or so, significant cubist canvases were painted for the rest of the decade. Picasso continued to include cubist features in his paintings for the rest of his lengthy career; for example, they are visible in the monumental *Guernica* (1937).

What we were presented thus far is familiar to any casual observer of the arts in the twentieth century. To use a literary phrase, it is "potted history," but, we must stress, it is potted history of a definite sort. Put directly, in this history of cubism, we have focused almost exclusively on the creative genius of a single prodigious painter, Pablo Picasso. Such an account, the sort with which psychologists are traditionally most comfortable, highlights the contributions of a single individual, attributing a new movement chiefly to his efforts and thoughts. The clear implication is, without Picasso, no cubism—or, at the very least, no cubism until many years later.

A PSYCHOLOGIST'S APPROACH TO CREATIVITY

Scratch a psychologist, or turn the pages of a psychology textbook, and you encounter an account something like that just presented. Individuals differ from one another in many respects, and one of the chief ones is intelligence. Some individuals are, from the first, brighter than others, and, so long as there are no drastic unexpected events, the brighter individuals will perform more successfully in this world. Intelligence tests are paper-and-pencil instruments that provide at least a rough estimate of the intelligence of a given individual.

There is at least a modest relation between intelligence and creativity. Indeed, while the intelligent person arrives at the correct answer more or less quickly, the creative individual is more likely to be fluent, to come up with many plausible answers and, perhaps, even with some answers of striking originality. The testing of creativity is not so advanced as the testing of intelligence—quite possibly because creativity is a more elusive trait. Nonetheless, by asking individuals how many uses they can think of for a brick or by requesting that they interpret a squiggle in as many ways as possible, psychologists can achieve a reasonable estimate of the creative potential of an individual.

Unfortunately, Picasso antedated creativity tests, and it is not self-evident that he would have agreed to sit for one. But any psychologist sympathetic to the account presented above would have to argue as follows: had Picasso taken a creativity test, he would have achieved an extremely high score on this measure. It was this creative trait, working in conjunction with at least reasonably high intelligence and perhaps some other talents as well, that permitted Picasso to be so innovative and that led, ultimately, to the founding of cubism.

Of course, not all psychologists would repeat exactly the same tale. Those influenced by Gestalt psychology might point to a special ability to "see" a solution to a problem, while others do not discern the crucial pattern. Those of a behaviorist persuasion would underscore a certain pattern of reinforcement (first explicit rewards from other individuals and perhaps later the anticipation of recognition or money) that drove Picasso to ever greater attainments. Those of a more contemporary cognitive bent might suggest that creative individuals are capable of a special kind of information processing, can process information with great speed, or are particularly supple at producing powerful mental models (Johnson-Laird 1983; Perkins 1981; Sternberg, 1988). But all would agree that the occasion of creative output is the thought and behavior of a single individual.

CUBISM AS SEEN THROUGH OTHER LENSES

There is no imperative to view cubism as the psychologist would. Indeed, just as success has a thousand parents, so, too, a movement as influential as cubism has spawned explanation drawn from a range of disciplines (N. Stahler, personal communication, 1985; see also Goldwater 1938; Gopnik 1983; and Teuber 1982). Picasso himself was skeptical of such efforts. He once declared, "Mathematics, trigonometry, chemistry, psychoanalysis, music, and whatnot have been related to Cubism to give it an easier interpretation. All this has been pure literature, not to say nonsense, which brought bad results, blinding people with theory" (quoted in Barr 1946, p. 74). But not even this caution from the founder himself has muted the efforts of researchers to discover the key to cubism.

Consider, as a start, the art historian. From his or her perspective, there was an inexorable trend away from realism at least since the mid-nineteenth century. This trend, no doubt aided by the invention of photography, gave rise first to impressionism, then to postimpressionism, and then to expressionism and fauvism. Each of these movements-in-reaction represented a further step away from faithful rendering of nature and another step toward a more direct treatment of light, emotional content, or form. Inevitably, the object itself would begin to fragment—as it did in cubism—destined eventually to disappear entirely in abstract expressionism, a movement with which Picasso never associated himself.

The art historical approach can center around individuals. In such an account, a key figure is Cezanne, who stressed the importance of ferreting out the geometric shapes that underlie familiar objects. Once Cezanne had thought and painted in this vein, the advent of cubism was inevitable. But the story can be related with a focus on other individuals as well. Some would highlight the intimate relationship between Picasso and Braque, which stretched out over several years and, as Braque said, made them feel "rather like two mountaineers roped together" (quoted in Berger 1965, p. 73). Still others would stress the artistic breakthroughs of Henri Matisse and the intense rivalry between Matisse and Picasso that followed. Once

Picasso saw that his chief peer, Matisse, had turned his back on realistic portrayal in favor of the wild colors and forms characteristic of fauvism, he was determined to go even further.

Enter the anthropologist or the Africanist. From such a perspective, a decisive influence on contemporary Western painting was the accumulation, in the late nineteenth century, of many works of tribal art from Africa and the South Seas (Goldwater 1938; Rubin 1980). These masks and sculpted pieces, collected first for their scholarly interest, soon struck observers by virtue of their simplicity, elegance, directness, and expressive power. Many artists were fascinated by them, and some collected them. Picasso's fascination with Iberian sculpture led him to purchase sculptured heads. Subsequently, he visited the Louvre on many occasions and the Palais du Trocadero as well to look at African objects (Goldwater 1938). Perhaps it was just a short step from the prizing of these highly abstracted forms to the attempt to recreate them in the plastic artistic language of Europe.

There may be no limit to the list of contributing factors. Scientists and historians of science point to the almost simultaneous emergence of the theory of relativity and the field of cubism. Musicians cite Stravinsky's flight from tonality, and literary critics note the breakdown of classic forms in the poetry of T. S. Eliot and in the novels of Virginia Woolf and James Joyce. Even scholars of childhood have their say: many (including Picasso) have commented on the childlike quality of some cubist art, and one commentator suggests that the breakdown of forms began in Picasso's high school notebooks (N. Stahler, personal communication, 1985). Finally, those involved in documentary history note the emergence of cubist forms in the popular caricatures of the late nineteenth century (Gopnik 1983) and in the geometric illusions that came to populate not only psychology textbooks but also popular magazines (Teuber 1982).

A SYNTHETIC-SCIENTIFIC APPROACH TO CREATIVITY

How can one make one's way among these competing definitions, particularly when it is likely that some combination of the aforementioned factors fomented the rise of cubism? Our own belief is that there is no need to favor one line of investigation to the exclusion of others and that, indeed, creative lives and creative works can come about only in the wake of numerous interacting factors. In the pages that follow, we will sketch out some of these factors and indicate the ways in which they interact. Rather than claim that all these factors must interact in a seamless manner, however, we shall suggest an alternative account. In our view, creative efforts are more likely to arise when there is a certain tension or asynchrony among the principal factors that underlie human behavior. It is this tension that ultimately gives rise to creative works.

Our working definition of creativity is rather heterodox. We view the creative individual as one who can regularly solve problems or fashion products in a domain in a way that is initially original but that ultimately is accepted in one or more cultural settings. The controversial aspects of the definition include the following. (1) To begin with, we do not see creativity as accidental; an ordinary individual will not suddenly produce a creative product. Rather, creative products or solutions can be expected with some regularity, in virtue of the kind of life led by the creative individual. (2) Just as a person is unlikely to be intelligent "across the board," so, too, individuals are not creative in all areas. Creativity tends to be domain specific. The fact that an individual may be highly creative in language predicts nothing about his or her creativity in such other domains as music, science, or social interaction. Nor does excellence in any of these other areas have any greater predictive power. (3) It is useful, and sometimes creative, to solve problems, but such solutions are, perhaps, the less compelling examples of creative capacity. It is the ability to find new problems and to fashion products of scope and power that especially marks the creative individual (Getzels and Csikszentmihalyi 1976). It is unfortunate that, because of limits of time and technology, psychologists have had to shy away from assessing the fashioning of products—for here lies the heartland of creative functioning. (4) Nearly all observers would agree that creativity combines novelty and acceptance. The question of how acceptance occurs is usually left vague, however. In our view, it is acceptance within one or more cultural settings that is crucial to a judgment of creativity. There is no time limit to such acceptance. Still, no matter how potentially creative a product may be, if it is nowhere apprehended as such, one may not consider it to be creative.

Let us mention some of the features that fail to appear in our definition. We include nothing about creativity as a trait, nothing about its being inborn (or acquired), nothing about creativity as occurring in an isolated moment or as a capacity that pervades all of an individual's activities. Whether creative potential or achievement can be assessed by a psychologist using any of the current methods is dubious, though of course one cannot ever prove that such psychometric methods are inappropriate or inadequate.

What, then, does the student of creativity do? In our view, the student's mission is to discover the rules or principles that govern the behaviors of those individuals who work productively within a domain and within a given culture. To the extent that the creative biographies of a Beethoven or a Mozart, a Rembrandt or a Picasso, a Freud, a Darwin, or an Einstein, are completely idiosyncratic, hopes for a science of creativity are misguided.

If, however, one can find some principles or themes at work in disparate creative lives, there remains some hope for a science of creativity.

Two methodological guidelines are preliminary to such an undertaking. To begin with, as already suggested, the study of creativity ought to begin with unambiguous cases (Gruber 1981; John-Steiner 1985). If we can explain those individuals who most clearly merit the epithet "creative," we have some confidence that our model is apt. (Conversely, if we were to develop a model for "ordinary" creative individuals, we risk the possibility that a Freud or a Picasso may operate in a qualitatively different way from our standard case.)

The second methodological precept reflects our belief that creativity will never reveal its secrets to a single discipline. The biologist or the geneticist who claims to have discovered the "secret" of creativity is as misguided as the psychologist or anthropologist who utters a similar boast. Rather, as Medawar (1969) suggests, creativity is the discipline par excellence for an interdisciplinary or "synthetic science" approach: "The analysis of creativity in all its forms is beyond the competence of any one accepted discipline. It requires a consortium of talents: psychologists, biologists, philosophers, computer scientists, artists and poets would all expect to have their say. That 'creativity is beyond analysis' is a romantic illusion that we must now outgrow" (p. 47).

If, then, we adopt a synthetic science approach, it is necessary to indicate which disciplines ought to be brought to bear in a study of a creative individual. In our view, it is necessary to incorporate at least five different perspectives. In what follows, we introduce these five perspectives. To give a feeling for their application, we will apply them to the case of Pablo Picasso. For a contrast, we will cite evidence from another creative individual to whom we have devoted study: the psychoanalyst Sigmund Freud (see Gardner 1986).

FIVE PERSPECTIVES ON PICASSO AND FREUD

The Subpersonal Level: A Neurobiological Perspective

In examining creative individuals from a neurobiological perspective, one seeks to determine the influences of genetics as well as the structure and functioning of a particular nervous system (Gardner and Dudai 1985). In the cases of Picasso and Freud, it is easy, but ineffectual, to apply this perspective—for, of course, nothing is known about the neurobiology of either individual.

Still, there are two reasons for insisting on the importance of this perspective. First, there already exists considerable technical paraphernalia whereby the neurobiological features of an individual can be assessed. It is no longer in the realm of science fiction to think of a creative individual being studied in vivo, with measures being made of brain waves, cerebral blood flow activity, neuromorphological features, and so on. Of course, the brains of creative people who have died can also be examined, as has already happened in the case of Einstein (Diamond 1985; Reich 1986). To be sure, there is no guarantee that the brains of creative individuals will turn out to differ in either structure or function from those of "uncreative mortals"; but, certainly, this question deserves to be investigated.

There is another reason for invoking a neurobiological perspective. It is in the neurobehavioral laboratory that one encounters individuals with anomalous cognitive profiles (Gardner 1975; Sacks 1986). Sometimes these individuals have unusual nervous systems from birth, while at other times these anomalies are the result of brain injury. In those cases in which an unusual behavioral profile can be linked to an anomalous brain structure, one achieves powerful evidence that comparable behavior in the extraordinary individual may also be yoked to characteristic neural structure. So, for example, the incredible drawings of a single autistic child like Nadia (Selfe 1977) may yield information about the kinds of neural structures that allow facile modeling and drawing without the benefit of formal tutelage. Perhaps such studies can suggest something about the brain of a prodigious young Picasso—an individual who might be thought of as a "Nadia with concepts."

The Personal Level: A Cognitive Perspective

When one moves to the level of the person, or, if one likes, the psychological level, one option is to focus on the cognitive capacities of the creative individual. Indeed, as we have already observed, many, if not most, psychologists focus on the cognitive characteristics of a creative individual. Such a focus can be undertaken in many ways. For present purposes, it will suffice to comment on the kinds of distinctive mental strengths—or intelligences—displayed by our two subjects (see Gardner 1983).

In the case of Picasso, it is clear that one is dealing with an individual who had superlative spatial and bodily kinesthetic intelligence. As can be seen in his works, his notebooks, and in the movie *The Mystery of Picasso*, Picasso was able effortlessly to form visual-spatial "images in his head," to manipulate them at will, and to record every manner of transformation of probable, possible, and "impossible" forms. By the same token, thanks to virtuoso bodily ability, he was able to render these forms with rapidity and accuracy. Whatever other intelligences or combinations of intelligences may have characterized Picasso, he certainly had these two in abundance.

Paradoxically, Freud was notoriously weak in both the spatial and the bodily intelligences (Jones 1961). Moreover, he himself confessed to ineptitude in and dislike of music. However, Freud displayed a remarkable combination of three intelligences that were of much lesser import to Picasso. He possessed quite powerful abilities in the logical-mathematical areas; his knowledge of persons (both himself and others) was highly unusual for a scientist; and his linguistic genius was virtually unprecedented for a scientist. It is probably in his ability to yoke the linguistic and logical talents, which are necessary for scientific work, with superlative sensitivity to the world of other individuals that his special scientific aptitude lay.

The Personal Level: Personality and Emotion

Creative individuals, then, seem to differ dramatically from one another in the kinds of intelligences that they possess in abundance and in the ways in which they deploy these intelligences. They prove far more similar to one another in noncognitive areas—in personality, motivation, social relationships, and emotional status. Indeed, those psychologists who claim that creative individuals exhibit common traits are on much firmer grounds in the noncognitive areas.

Like other creative individuals, both Picasso and Freud were individuals of great self-confidence; each was convinced from a young age that he knew what he was doing and that it was right. Rarely were they shaken from a course of action simply because of negative feedback. They were fantastically ambitious and hardworking, willing to neglect everyone and everything in order to accomplish their goals. Indeed, they identified quite explicitly with conquest, Picasso seeing himself as the matador taming the bull, Freud thinking of himself as a military leader, a conquistador, and an intellectual incarnation of his boyhood hero, Hannibal.

This extreme self-absorption can have its costs. Both Freud and Picasso made great demands on those about them. Both had complex relationships with both sexes, but Freud can be seen as working out much of his professional life with reference to other men in the psychiatric and medical communities, while Picasso's paintings can be viewed with reference to the many women with whom he had relations (Gedo 1980). Each man was quite capable of forming an intense relationship with another human being, exploiting it for some period of time, and then rejecting the other quite peremptorily because of an imagined wrong or because of the need for some other form of human support. On occasion, after the termination of these intense relationships, suicides followed, for which such creative individuals bore at least a tangential (or a symbolic) responsibility.

In view of our interest in asynchronous conditions, it is worth noting that both Picasso and Freud felt distinctly marginal for much of their lives. When Picasso was still very young, he left his native Spain. While he became attached to his adopted homeland of France, he always maintained extremely strong (if ambivalent) ties to Spain and was distraught by the rise of fascism there. Picasso saw himself as a Spaniard among Frenchmen, as an uneducated painter among writers and other intellectuals, and, at least initially, as a social "naïf" who painted for a Continental aristocracy. As a Jew living in Vienna, Freud always felt vulnerable; and as a maverick physician, he felt estranged from the medical profession and eventually attracted his own group of peers via the mystique of psychoanalysis. Presumably, these feelings of marginality served to motivate our two creative heroes to "prove themselves."

The Impersonal Level: Domains of Knowledge

While the first three levels—subpersonal, personal cognitive, and personal noncognitive—are familiar to biologists and psychologists, the latter two levels are less well known and merit separate introduction. In explicating these concepts, we rely heavily on the works of two colleagues: David Feldman, a developmental psychologist at Tufts University, and Mihaly Csikszentmihalyi, a social psychologist at the University of Chicago.

The notion of domain is an epistemological one (see Feldman 1980). The term "domain" refers to the structure of knowledge within a particular area, craft, or discipline. Domains run the gamut from standard academic disciplines (such as physics or history) to cultural practices that are conveyed chiefly by example (such as sailing or baseball). Crucial to the existence of a domain as an end state of knowledge/competence is a set of steps through which individuals will ordinarily pass, from novice to expert status.

While domains necessarily involve human beings, they are best thought of apart from human beings—bodies of knowledge that can be described in the abstract and that would in some sense continue to exist even if all individuals disappeared. One can think of a domain as the information that could be contained in a textbook or in a series of lessons or demonstrations.

Turning to our two creative individuals, a domain perspective yields quite different pictures. In the case of Picasso, he was involved from an early age in the domain of painting. Initially, like any young student, he was strongly influenced by the state of the domain as it existed at the end of the nineteenth century. He soon mastered the extant domain and then, in the succeeding fifty years, made a series of fresh contributions to the evolving domain. The structure of knowledge of painting—what it is—has changed appreciably, thanks to his daunting example. Picasso did make contributions to other domains as well—from sculpture to ceramics to play writing—but it is in the domain of painting that his niche is most firmly established.

Freud's life can be seen as a passage through numerous domains until he finally devised his own. He began with an attraction to philosophy—an attraction that he ruthlessly suppressed for many decades—and then turned to scientific medicine. Within medicine, he studied, and made contributions in, neurology, neuroanatomy, psychiatry, and psychology (Sulloway 1983). He also practiced clinically on the border of neurology and psychiatry. Perennially dissatisfied, however, Freud kept searching for a domain to which he could make a unique and indispensable contribution. Eventually, he invented psychoanalysis as both theory and clinical practice; so successful was this invention that it has since become a domain itself to which others can make contributions. Following the invention of psychoanalysis, Freud naturally devoted much attention to the fostering of its development—but he continued to contribute to, and exert influence on, a wide range of domains, including literary history, political science, sociology, and the visual arts. These contributions continue posthumously, as his successors continue to modify the contemporary structure of domains.

The Multipersonal Level: The Perspective of the Field

While "domain" is a distinctly epistemological notion, "field" is inherently a sociological concept (Csikszentmihalyi, 1988; Csikszentmihalyi and Robinson 1986). The field consists of the teachers, judges, institutions, agencies, reward systems, and other entities that allow or thwart the development of a career and the production and recognition of creative works. Acknowledgment of the field entails a recognition that no individual can work in a vacuum—that, ultimately, every action must stand judged by the community.

To convey a feeling for the concepts of domain and field, it may help to offer some examples. For contrast, let us consider mathematics and the visual arts. In the case of mathematics, there is an entire discipline that has evolved over the centuries, whose contents can be summarized in textbooks and monographs. Anyone who would wish to become a mathematician must master the contents of the domain, a slowly but ever changing set of facts, concepts, and theories. However, contributions to mathematics cannot occur simply as a result of an individual intelligence wrestling with an impersonal domain. Rather, the individual must pass through an educational process during which he or she works with teachers, takes courses, discusses proofs, writes articles, has them judged by peers, and, eventually, either wins or fails to win acceptance, authority, and prizes. All these latter factors constitute the field at work. By a nice irony, the prize awarded periodically to the outstanding mathematician under the age of forty is called the Field's Medal.

If the field is obtrusive even in so apparently objective a discipline as mathematics, it is overwhelmingly evident in the visual arts. There, the envelope within which individual creation occurs consists of gallery owners and gallery spaces, curators and museums, newspaper and magazine reviewers, collectors and other "art lovers," agents, publicity experts, and the like. Some skeptics would even claim that, in the current climate in the visual arts, only the field is evident. This would be an exaggeration, however. Any artist creates with reference to—even if in reaction to—the works and the methods that have been developed by predecessors, and this is the point at which the impersonal domain exerts its effect.

Books have been written about the fields within which Picasso and Freud worked, over roughly the same historical epoch. It is difficult to think of Freud apart from the scintillating but somewhat decadent atmosphere of Vienna at the turn of the century (see Janik and Toulmin 1974; Schorske 1973). While Picasso retained much of the Spaniard within him, the environment of Paris at the turn of the century was certainly critical in his formation and his innovation. So crucial were these milieus, in fact, that one cannot readily conceive of cubism emanating from Tokyo or Los Angeles or of psychoanalysis being born in London.

The field, however, extends far beyond the city or the country in which an artist or a scientist happens to work. Field factors begin with one's family, friends, and relatives. Ultimately, they extend to the educational institutions or apprenticeships, to the set of peers with whom one begins one's career, and, in the end, to one's relationships with the leaders of a discipline, the opinion makers, the general public, and posterity.

Both Picasso and Freud lived long lives, during which they were subjected to many field forces and exerted their own force on fields. In Picasso's case, he had an intimate relationship with Braque but also a somewhat wider support system among the artists and intellectuals of Paris. Having achieved worldwide fame while still young, he spent much of his life in a kind of flirtation with many fields, alternatively teasing, tormenting, and embracing his wide public. By the end, he had isolated himself almost entirely from the rest of the world, seeking satisfaction from solitary creation. In Freud's case, the field was once as small as his correspondence with a single friend, Wilhelm Fliess. For many years, he felt alone and isolated, bitterly disposed toward the medical community of Vienna, which did not appreciate his accomplishments. Ultimately, this situation changed dramatically; fields that he had invented came to encompass much of the civilized world.

SYNTHESIZING THE FIVE PERSPECTIVES

We have described five different vantage points from which one can (and, in our opinion, should) view the creative lives of outstanding individuals. These cover a wide range, from the gene and the neuron to the community and, indeed, the world of ideas. While such a catholic approach may seem comprehensive, it is not immediately evident how such a range of perspectives could usefully be combined; nor is it evident how one proceeds from individual case studies to the construction of a science.

We would suggest the following investigative strategy. To begin with, it is important to carry out detailed case studies of many individuals and to determine how our several levels of analysis help to illuminate the careers and products of the individuals under investigation. Only if we have carried out studies—and ones far more detailed than those adumbrated here—can we begin to determine which factors seem to characterize all creative individuals, which characterize some set (either within or across a discipline), and which seem either idiosyncratic to a few or unique to a given individual. For instance, even our extremely modest comparison here indicates that blends of intelligence can differ widely across creative individuals; that aspects of personality and motivation may be more similar across persons, at least within a given epoch and a given civilization; and that there were certain pockets within turn-of-the-century Europe where radical departures from earlier practice were to be expected.

One ally in this line of study is the potential for pointed comparisons. It should be possible to compare unambiguous cases of creativity—the Picassos and the Freuds—with other individuals of their epoch who were drawn from the same "general population" but who differed from them in an instructive way. For example, in the case of Picasso, one could compare his life course with that of Georges Braque or Juan Gris, two other early cubists. For a more radical comparison, one could contrast his life with that of his much less successful father or with a more recent and still largely unrecognized artist such as Harold Shapinsky (Weschler 1985). Freud could be contrasted with the dominant French psychiatrist of his era, Pierre Janet, a man who had anticipated some of Freud's major discoveries but is now largely forgotten outside the French-speaking world (Ellenberger 1970).

Again, for a more radical comparison, Freud could be contrasted with his contemporaries Josef Breuer or Wilhelm Fliess, who are remembered chiefly because of their early associations with Freud.

One must still ask, however, about the ways in which the various levels of analysis come together, in a description of lives and in the lives of the individuals themselves. Do the genes, the intelligences, the personality, the structure of the discipline, and the surrounding field exist as five separate entities, united only in a scientific taxonomy—or are there important and systematic interactions among and conjunctions of these analytic levels?

A promising beginning on this issue comes from the work of Csikszent-mihalyi (1988). Raising questions about the classical formulation; "What is creativity?" Csikszentmihalyi suggests instead the felicitous rewording, "Where is creativity?" In his reformulation, he locates the possibility for creativity in an interaction among a number of these factors. In particular, he envisages a three-way dialectic obtaining among the personal level (individual talents), the impersonal level (various domains of knowledge), and the multipersonal level (the surrounding fields within which careers and lives unfold).

Again, a concretization can be helpful. Consider, for example, the operation of a discipline like physics. One has a point of departure a collection of talented individuals, gifted in logical-mathematical thinking, who begin to study the physical world itself as well as the ways in which earlier scientists have thought about it. This collection of individuals in 1900 included not only the likes of Albert Einstein and Niels Bohr but also many others whose names are known only to specialists or who are completely forgotten.

These talented individuals mastered the knowledge in the domain as it existed in 1900 and attempted to add to the body of knowledge called "physics." They proposed various schemes, and these were, in turn, examined by the "high priests" of the field—those who edit journals, make appointments, publish critiques and refutations, and award prizes. A small set of individuals emerged in a single generation as worthy of special attention, and, of these, an even smaller number actually came to change the delineation of the domain. (It is said that over half the Nobel Prize winners in physics have received the accolade for work executed in subdisciplines that did not even exist when they were in graduate school.)

The cycle continues, for, in the next generation, students confront a revised physics, one that has changed fundamentally because of the work of Einstein, Bohr, Heisenberg, and other exceptional scientists. Indeed, the field may also change, as factors other than those that were important around 1900 may become relevant to the shape of a career. Also, while the individual intelligences of human beings do not themselves change, those relevant to physics may. It has been said (A. Miller, personal communication, 1985) that, before 1927, possession of strong visual-spatial skills was an important prerequisite for contributing to physics but that thereafter such skills were no longer at a premium and might even have interfered with a physics that became more purely mathematical and posited entities that were difficult to envisage.

On the Csikszentmihalyi analysis, then, it no longer makes sense to think of creativity as a process that occurs in a lone individual's head. There cannot be a hermit creator. Instead, creativity is more properly thought of as a process in which individual minds struggle to master and, ultimately, change a domain; in which field forces determine which individuals are picked out and recognized; in which, over time, certain contributions come to affect the actual definition of the domain (and, perhaps, of the field as well); and in which succeeding generations of students must master a somewhat different domain and be prepared to face a somewhat altered field.

So far, we have spoken chiefly about the ways in which a multilevel perspective should change the study of creativity. But can this new perspective also affect the ways in which we think of creative lives themselves?

One possibility is that the creative individual is the one in which all these levels work together in perfect harmony, in complete synchrony. On this analysis, it is the individual whose genetic inheritance, neurobiological functioning, blend of intelligences, and type of personality match perfectly with one another and, moreover, are ideally suited to a domain within his society. Such an individual is most likely to master the domain to conceive of new contributions, and to be recognized as innovative by the caretakers of the field.

This is a credible story and, in fact, probably the correct one for certain cases—but not for the cases that we are considering here. In his studies of prodigies, Feldman (1986) proposes the concept of "co-incidence"—a simultaneous coming together of a whole range of factors that allow a few individuals to become prodigies. Indeed, a prodigy—a youngster performing in a domain at the level of a competent adult—is virtually unthinkable in the absence of exemplary synchronies among a genetic inheritance, a highly supportive family, an excellent collection of teachers and mentors, a domain that is ready to be absorbed by a young mind, and a surrounding culture that chooses to honor gifted youngsters—at least so long as they are young.

But prodigiousness is not creativity. Indeed, as Bamberger (1982) has suggested, precocious superiority may ultimately cause difficulties and get in the way of ultimate achievement. Hector Berlioz quipped of the precocious Camille Saint-Saëns, "He knows everything but he lacks inexperience" (Schonberg 1969, p. 17). If all factors are unfolding and interacting too smoothly, there may be enormously rapid growth, but the ultimate level of achievement may be unimpressive or even nonexistent (Wallace 1986).

We are, therefore, stimulated to propose an alternative hypothesis. On this rival account, the creative individual is marked, but by synchrony, but by asynchrony—not by a perfect match within or across levels, but rather by strategic mismatches or asynchronies. Only through such asynchronies does the possibility arise of new creations, of new visions, ones that may initially be seen as aberrant or idiosyncratic but that ultimately come to be accepted in one or more cultural settings—our definition of creativity.

It is easy to find support for this "asynchrony hypothesis." We can begin with the two cases on which we have been focusing. Both Picasso and Freud exhibited unusual blends of intelligence. Picasso had uniquely powerful visual-spatial skills but was unremarkable in most other intelligences and was reportedly not even able to master his numbers in school. Freud complained of his inferior spatial and bodily intelligence but was able to yoke extraordinary personal intelligences to the linguistic and logical intelligences more typically associated with scientific work. Surely, it is plausible that these uneven cognitive profiles helped our heroes to see the world in an unaccustomed way.

Even as their own intellectual profiles were unusual, so, too, both Picasso and Freud failed to blend in easily with the communities in which they lived. Picasso was too talented and too driven to remain in his native Spain, so he somehow found his way to Paris. (One may well ask how so many young talents found their way to Paris in 1900 or to New York in 1940). He remained on the margins of the French and Spanish cultures for the remainder of his life. Freud lived in Vienna for most of his life (he seemed to hate other locales even more) but was never comfortable there. As a Jew in the medical profession, he felt estranged; in fact, his ambition seems to have been fueled by his consistent clashes with the gentile establishment.

Numerous instances of asynchrony can be found within these two lives. Moreover, the literature of creativity abounds with other classic asynchronies: the homosexuality of many artists; the clashes of Mozart and of Beethoven with members of their families; Einstein's and Churchill's early difficulties in school; the childhoods of sickness and loneliness that seem almost de rigueur for writers of the Romantic era.

But here, of course, is the problem. Asynchrony is too easy to find. Given a complex life, and even a minimally competent biographer, one can dredge up multiple instances of asynchrony. What is needed are definite objective ways in which to assess asynchrony, to ascertain whether there are certain kinds of asynchronies that stand out and which are particularly likely to mark the lives of creative individuals. At the same time, it is important to document the lack of asynchrony in those who do not attain the same level of creativity.

Coming up with a metric of synchrony, asynchrony, and (perhaps) productive and unproductive asynchrony is by no means a straight forward task. How much must a youth clash with a parent, a young worker with his peers, an ambitious researcher with his community, before the requisite level of asynchrony is reached? When does asynchrony become counter-productive? Should these measures be pursued primarily in a case-study manner (as we have proposed here), or is it better to use statistics drawn from large populations, as Simonton (1984) has done in his studies of eminent individuals? These and many other questions need to be tackled if our asynchrony hypothesis is to be reasonably assessed.

Even if we do find convincing support for the asynchrony hypothesis, a further troubling consideration arises. Perhaps creative individuals are marked by asynchrony not because it plagues them but rather—and pre-cisely—because they seek it. Perhaps their temperament is such that, constitutionally dissatisfied with the status quo, they are perennially predis-posed to up the ante, to stir up troubles, to convert comfortable synchrony to tension-producing asynchrony. Should this be the case, the asynchrony hypothesis would be confirmed but for an unanticipated reason—certain individuals seek asynchrony, and, if they do not readily find it in sufficient quantity, they create it or exacerbate it.

Perhaps, indeed, creative individuals find asynchrony where others de-tect only harmony. It is told that, when Freud returned to Vienna after his only trip to the United States, his then associate Carl Jung remained in the States. Jung had a wonderful time touring the salons of the Eastern seaboard and finally sent back to his mentor an enthusiastic telegram—"Psychoanaly-sis great success." Ever vigilant and perhaps searching again for asyn-chrony, Freud immediately wired back—"What did you leave out?"

CONCLUSIONS: THE INEVITABILITY OF THE FIELD

From a psychological perspective, it is bracing, but somewhat distressing to conclude that creativity can no longer be thought of, at least exclusively, as the purview of the individual. There may come to be an individual of the greatest potential in one or more domains, but, if he or she fails to come into contact with that domain, misconstrues the domain too radically, or fashions products that cannot be assimilated by the field, such work will not be considered creative by our definition. Enlarging the disciplinary realm within which one must consider creativity may be scientifically necessary, but, for those researchers accustomed to working at the level of the person, it makes the task much more difficult. Still, it is useful, at least as an exercise, to consider creative processes in the absence of the field. Is it possible to create in the absence of the field, and, if so, what form does such creativity assume?

We may consider three instances of apparently "fieldless" creativity. There is, first of all, the accomplished master—say, a Picasso—who continues to engage in creative work while paying little or no attention to the reactions of the field. This instance proves not to be problematic from the point of view of our analysis. In the course of his development, Picasso internalized the standards of the field and could, even in the privacy of his atelier, bring to bear the kinds of considerations that others had earlier presented to him in a more direct manner. Actual contact with the field was for him no longer necessary. Of course, in the long run, the field will still determine the merit of Picasso's work. In fact, in the case of his later works, those produced in virtual isolation from the rest of the artistic world, there is at present considerable controversy. Perhaps Picasso would have done well, in his later years, to remain in closer contact with his various publics.

Picasso and the field were inevitably intertwined. But what of the solitary individual, the one who continues to work in an area in apparent ignorance of, or indifference to, the external field? There is Emily Dickinson, unpublished in her lifetime but afterward discovered to be a major poet. There is the aforementioned Harold Shapinsky, who painted in total obscurity for thirty years but who has recently been promoted as a significant abstract expressionist of the second generation and whose canvases now earn considerable sums. There are no doubt thousands of amateur writers, artists, musicians, scientists, and mathematicians who either continue to produce for their own satisfaction or have tried and failed to exert an influence on the field—or even to be noticed at all.

Are not these individuals creative as well? Is the field really necessary? As a start, it is important to point out that these individuals have not created in complete isolation from the field. They have all been formed on the basis of earlier work produced in a domain/field, and, in that sense alone, they are not complete isolates. Still, it is true that the interaction has been unidirectional: they may have learned from the field, but the field has—at least so far—proved indifferent to them.

We could discern here a kind of indeterminacy principle at work. Of course, in one sense, Dickinson or Shapinsky remain the same kind of person, whether or not the field ultimately decides to award them the accolade of "creativity." But, unless the field's standards are brought to bear on their work, the status of that work remains completely indeterminate. Moreover, once the field is brought to bear, then it *has* been brought to bear. It is no longer sensible to talk of a Dickinson or a Shapinsky in the absence of the field. Thus, in a manner analogous to Heisenberg's principle in particle physics, the very act of determining whether something is creative immediately and inevitably involves the invocation of the field: to ask whether something is creative is to introduce the field irrevocably into what might hitherto have been viewed as a relatively fieldless endeavor.

Neither Picasso nor Dickinson, then, can be thought of as individuals outside a field, even if they themselves worked in splendid isolation. There are individuals who do create largely outside the field, however. These are young children. In every culture, young children play with the symbol systems of their milieu. They make graphic depictions, they sing, they tell stories, and they tinker with objects. And they undertake this activity with sublime indifference to the domain, the structure of knowledge in a particular discipline, and with equivalent indifference to the field, the roles and institutions that determine the paths of careers. To be sure, in the course of socialization, these youngsters will be introduced to the relevant domains and fields, and they will thus enter into the process—the dialectic—of creativity. But, at least at the outset, their protocreative activities occur outside the field, if not beyond the pale.

For the most part, this distancing from the field is a two-way process. The child ignores the field, and the field ignores the child. In nearly all societies, and for nearly all human history, the protocreative products of young children have been of essentially no interest to anyone except the children themselves. If the insightful developmental psychologist Piaget (1962) is to be believed, children themselves would never think to raise such questions. Only in our time, and in no small measure because of the rise of such fields as child psychology and psychoanalysis, the works of young children have begun to arouse interest and to be assessed in terms of the criteria of creativity. To the extent that this trend continues, the field of artistic production will have entered the realm of childhood creativity and may even be transformed by it.

This coming together of childhood activity and the study of creativity is appropriate. Even if, in the final analysis, creativity cannot be assessed apart from the Csikszentmihalyi dialectic, there remains a sense in which it begins in the activities of young children (Gardner, Phelps, and Wolf, in press). Here, we believe, children first begin to toy with the boundaries around them, to engage in novel activities, to gain pleasure from the manipulation of symbolic forms. It is this activity—often long suppressed during latency years—that resurfaces in the more competent hands of the master and seems to constitute an important part of the thrill of the creative life. Childhood creativity is not equivalent to the creativity of the master—but it is difficult to envisage the possibility of adult creativity without the experience of childhood. In this sense, it is fitting that our modest study of creativity has focused on two individuals who have helped to form the sensibility of our time: Sigmund Freud, who first underscored the extent to which later mental life is dictated by the experiences of childhood, and Pablo Picasso, whose work had such deep links to the simple forms favored in childhood and who recognized the deep truth, "Once I drew like Raphael but it has taken me a whole life to learn to draw like a child" (quoted in de Meredieu 1974, p. 13).

NOTES

This paper has been adapted from oral remarks presented to the Conference on Creativity and Adolescence, American Society for Adolescent Psychiatry, Philadelphia, September 1986. Some of the work described in this chapter was supported by the MacArthur Foundation and the Spencer Foundation.

1. For a representative set of readings in the psychology of creativity, see Vernon (1970).

REFERENCES

Bamberger, J. 1982. Growing up prodigies: the midlife crisis. In D. H. Feldman, ed. *New Directions for Child Development*, vol. 17. San Francisco: Jossey-Bass.

Barr, A. 1936. *Cubism and Abstract Art*. Cambridge, Mass.: Harvard University Press, 1986.

Barr, A. 1946. *Picasso: Fifty Years of His Art*. New York: Museum of Modern Art, 1974.

Berger, J. 1965. *The Success and Failure of Picasso*. New York: Pantheon.

Burns, E. 1970. *Gertrude Stein on Picasso*. New York: Liveright.

Csikszentmihalyi, M. 1988. Society, culture and person: a systems view of creativity. In R. Sternberg, ed. *The Nature of Creativity*. New York: Cambridge University Press.

Csikszentmihalyi, M., and Robinson, R. 1986. Culture, time, and the development of talent. In R. Sternberg and J. Davidson, eds. *Conceptions of Giftedness*. New York: Cambridge University Press.

de Meredieu, F. 1974. *Le dessin d'enfant*. Paris: Editions Universitaires Jean-Pierre de Large.

Diamond, M. 1985. On the brain of the scientist: Albert Einstein. *Experimental Neurology* 88:198–204.

Ellenberger, H. 1970. *The Discovery of the Unconscious*. New York: Basic.

Feldman, D. H. 1980. *Beyond Universals in Cognitive Development*. Norwood, NJ: Ablex.

Feldman, D. H. 1986. *Nature's Gambit*. New York: Basic.

Gardner, H. 1975. *The Shattered Mind*. New York: Knopf.

Gardner, H. 1983. *Frames of Mind: The Theory of Multiple Intelligences*. New York: Basic.

Gardner, H. 1986. Freud in three frames. *Daedalus* 115 (Summer): 105–134.

Gardner, H., and Dudai, Y. 1985. Biology and giftedness. Items 39:1–6.

Gardner, H.; Phelps, E.; and Wolf, D. In press. The roots of creativity in children's symbolic products. In C. Alexander and E. Langer, eds. *Beyond Formal Operations*. New York: Oxford University Press.

Gedo, M. 1980. *Picasso—Art as Autobiography*. Chicago: University of Chicago Press.

Getzels, J., and Csikszentmihalyi, M. 1976. *The Creative Vision*. New York: Wiley.

Gilot, F., and Lake, C. 1964. *Life with Picasso*. New York: McGraw-Hill.

Goldwater, R. 1938. *Primitivism in Modern Art*. Cambridge, Mass.: Harvard University Press, 1986.

Gopnik, A. 1983. High and low: caricature, primitivism and the cubist portrait. *Art Journal* (Winter), pp. 371–376.

Gruber, H. 1981. *Darwin on Man*. Chicago: University of Chicago Press.

Janik, A., and Toulmin, S. 1974. *Wittgenstein's Vienna*. New York: Simon & Schuster.

Johnson-Laird, P. N. 1983. *Mental Models*. Cambridge, Mass.: Harvard University Press.

John-Steiner, V. 1985. *Notebooks of the Mind*. Albuquerque: University of New Mexico Press.

Jones, E. 1961. *The Life and Work of Sigmund Freud*. Edited and abridged by Lionel Trilling and Steven Marcus. New York: Basic.

Medawar, P. 1969. *Induction and Intuition*. Philadelphia: American Philosophical Society.

Penrose, R. 1958. *Picasso: His Life and Work*. 3d ed. Berkeley and Los Angeles: University of California Press, 1981.

Perkins, D. N. 1981. *The Mind's Best Work*. Cambridge, Mass.: Harvard University Press.

Piaget, J. 1962. *Play, Dreams and Imitation*. New York: Norton.

Reich, W. 1986. The stuff of genius. *New York Times Magazine* (July 25), pp. 23–25.

Rubin, W. 1980. *Pablo Picasso: A Retrospective*. New York: Museum of Modern Art.

Sacks, O. 1986. *The Man Who Mistook His Wife for a Hat and Other Clinical Tales*. New York: Summit.

Schonberg, H. 1969. It all came too easily for Camille Saint-Saëns. *New York Times* (January 12).

Schorske, C. 1973. *Fin-de-Siècle Vienna*. New York: Knopf.

Selfe, L. 1977. *Nadia*. London: Academic Press.

Simonton, D. K. 1984. *Genius, Creativity, and Leadership*. Cambridge, Mass.: Harvard University Press.

Sternberg, R., ed. 1988. *The Nature of Creativity*. New York: Cambridge University Press.

Sulloway, F. 1983. *Freud: Biologist of the Mind*. New York: Basic.

Teuber, M. 1982. *Formvorstellung und Kubismus oder Pablo Picasso und William James in Kubismus: Kuenstler, Themen, Werke, 1907–1920*. Cologne: Josef-Haubrich-Kunsthalle.

Vernon, P. 1970. *Creativity*. London: Penguin.

Wallace, A. 1986. *The Prodigy: William James Sidis, America's Greatest Child Prodigy*. New York: Dutton.

Weschler, L. 1985. A strange destiny. *New Yorker* (December 16), pp. 47–48.

3

The Creators' Patterns

Howard Gardner

In the human sciences, a useful distinction has often been drawn between idiographic and nomothetic research (Allport 1961). In idiographic work, the focus falls sharply on the individual case study, with its peculiar emphases and wrinkles. In nomothetic work, the focus falls instead on a search for general laws; such work, by its very nature, overlooks individual idiosyncracies, searching instead for those patterns which appear to apply to all, or to the vast majority of cases.

One can readily find this distinction echoed in research in the human sciences that has been centered on creative individuals, works, and processes. Since, as it is usually construed, "the creative" is an unusual occurrence, there have been several efforts to study a creative entity in great depth. In recent times, this work has been epitomized by Gruber's important studies of Charles Darwin and Jean Piaget (Gruber 1981; Gruber and Davis 1988). Befitting the fact that such case studies have been done in a social-scientific rather than humanistic spirit, there have been efforts to tease out more general principles at work (Langley et al. 1986; Perkins 1981; Wallace and Gruber 1990). In contrast to this idiographically tinged work, there have been frank efforts to go beyond the individual, to examine the processes at work in large numbers of creative individuals, texts, or processes. This line of study has been pursued most rigorously and vigorously by Dean Keith

Simonton (1984, 1988a, 1988b) and by others working in this historiometic tradition, such as Martindale (1990).

In this chapter I seek to begin the construction of a bridge that spans the usually separate realms of idiographic and nomothetic lines of work on creativity. I report on a set of case studies that examine the creative lives of seven individuals who lived around 1900 and who have deliberately been drawn from disparate domains of accomplishment. These case studies are detailed in a forthcoming book, entitled *Creating Minds* (Gardner 1993). My focus falls on those patterns that seem to characterize all, or at least a sizeable majority of these individuals. As such, the essay constitutes a modest effort to tease out generalizations that may obtain more generally to highly creative individuals in our time.

APPROACHES TO CREATIVITY

Until recently, social-scientific work in the area of creativity has been dominated by psychology, and particularly by two subdisciplines within psychology. On the one hand, there is an extensive amount of work in the psychometric tradition. Since the Second World War, much effort has been expended in an attempt to measure creative processes in normal and in unusually talented individuals (Guilford 1950, 1967). The basic model has been to administer creativity tests that are loosely modelled after intelligence tests. While some useful information has been gleaned from this research (Torrance 1988), it has failed to establish itself as sufficiently valid and has been abandoned by some of its strongest supporters (Wallach 1976, 1985).

Complementing the psychometric work have been efforts to determine the psychological traits of creative individuals. Some of this work has been empirical, as creative individuals have described themselves or been described by close peers (Barron 1969; MacKinnon 1962). Other work has come more directly out of the psychoanalytic tradition; such work has stressed the neurotic or sublimatory foundations of creative efforts (Freud 1958; Kubie 1958). From this line of work has emerged one or more descriptions of the creative personality; as in the case of psychometric efforts, some useful generalizations have emerged but only limited understanding of creative efforts in their fine structure.

My own review identifies two promising approaches in recent years. From the point of view of motivation, important research has been carried out on the centrality of intrinsic, as compared to extrinsic motivations, in the conduct of creative work (Amabile 1983; Hennesey and Amabile 1988). In related work, Csikszentmihalyi (1988a, 1988b, 1990) has highlighted the reinforcing character of "flow states"; those pleasurable periods of complete immersion in the activity of creation that come to characterize the creative individual. Fresh energy has also been conferred upon creativity research by the efforts of individuals drawn from cognitive psychology, developmental psychology, and cognitive science (Feldman [with Goldsmith] 1986; Langley et al. 1986; Perkins 1981; Simon 1988). This latter group of researchers has highlighted the rule-governed nature of much creative work; provided a detailed information-processing approach to the delineation and solution of problems; identified intriguing parallels between "ordinary" and "exceptional creativity" and between problem solving as carried out by human beings and by artificial computational systems. These lines of work have been recently reviewed in a number of publications (Boden 1990; Briggs 1989; Gardner 1988; Ochse 1991; Runco and Albert 1990; Sternberg 1988; Weisberg 1986).

THE PRESENT APPROACH

In my own work, I have sought to build upon the strengths of recent work in creativity. Reflecting my own training, the stress has fallen particularly on cognitive and developmental psychological approaches, but I have sought to take into account as well social and motivational aspects of creation and perspectives taken from the other human sciences.

According to my definition, a creative individual solves problems, fashions products, or poses new questions within a domain in a way that is initially considered to be unusual but is eventually accepted within at least one cultural group. In its mention of problem solving, and its contrast between initial novelty and ultimate acceptance, this definition conforms closely to that put forth by other researchers. Its somewhat different accent is conveyed by a few phrases:

1. I focus equally on problem solving, problem finding, and the creation of products, such as scientific theories, works of art, or the building of institutions.

2. I emphasize that all creative work occurs in one or more domains. Individuals are not creative (or noncreative) in general; they are creative in particular domains of accomplishment, and require the achievement of expertise in these domains before they can execute significant creative work.

3. No person, act, or product is creative or noncreative in itself. Judgments of creativity are inherently communal, relying heavily on individuals expert within a domain.

This definition also has implications with respect to methodology. In my view, the study of creativity is inherently interdisciplinary; in addition to being rooted in psychology, the student of creativity must be informed about epistemology (the nature of knowledge in different domains) and about sociology (the ways in which judgments are reached by experts in different domains).

Moreover, this perspective on creativity draws attention away from the questions of *who* and *what* is creative and instead to the question of *where is creativity*. As formulated by Csikszentmihalyi (1988b), creativity emerges by virtue of a dialectical process among *individuals* of talent, *domains* of knowledge and practices, and *fields* of knowledgeable judges. If one wants to understand phenomena of creativity, one cannot simply focus on the individual—his brain, her personality, their motivations. Instead, one must broaden one's focus to include a study of the area in which that creative individual works and the procedures by which judgments of originality and quality are rendered.

To this general position, I bring two further perspectives. The first perspective posits the existence in human beings of a number of separate faculties or intellectual strengths, that I have labeled the seven human "intelligences" (Gardner 1983, 1992). It is my claim that all normal human beings can develop at least seven different intelligences, and that individuals differ from one another in the strengths and configurations of these intelligences.

The second perspective involves the claim that creative individuals are characterized particularly by a tension, or lack of fit, between the elements involved in productive work—a tension that I have labeled *fruitful asynchrony* (Gardner and Wolf 1988). This concept is best illustrated by a contrast with the case of the prodigious individual. In the case of a prodigy, a talented individual fits very well with a domain that exists in his society and his work is immediately recognized as highly competent by members of the relevant field (Feldman with Goldsmith 1986). In contrast, the creative individual is marked by one or more asynchronies: an unusual configuration of talents, and an initial lack of fit among abilities, the domains in which the individual seeks to work, and the tastes and the prejudices of the current field. Of course, in the end, it is the conquering of these asynchronies that leads to the establishment of work that comes to be cherished.

Against this background of assumptions, I launched my study of the seven "creators of the modern era." I chose to work with seven individuals, each an acknowledged creator, each exemplifying at least one of my seven intelligences: Sigmund Freud was the exemplar of intrapersonal intelligence; Albert Einstein represented logical-mathematical intelligence; Pablo Picasso, spatial intelligence; Igor Stravinsky, musical intelligence; T. S. Eliot, linguistic intelligence; Martha Graham, bodily-kinesthetic intelligence; and Mahatma Gandhi, interpersonal intelligence. And I deliberately elected to work with individuals who were roughly contemporaries of one another, so that any differences observed could not be attributed simply to their existence at a different historical moment.

In what follows, I begin with a sketch of E. C., an Exemplary Creator. E. C. is exemplary in the sense of Weber's "ideal type": that is, E. C. captures several of the powerful generalizations that obtained across all or the majority of my seven creators. I then mention some of the more striking findings that emerged when I focused on the specific elements of the creative process. I conclude by indicating the two most surprising results of the investigation and by noting some limits of, and some future directions for, this line of work that seeks to close the idiographic-nomothetic gap.

E. C. An Exemplary Creator: E. C. comes from a zone somewhat removed from the actual centers of power and influence in her society, but not so far away that she and her family are entirely ignorant of what is going on elsewhere. The family is not wealthy, but neither is it in dire financial circumstances; and life for the young creator is reasonably comfortable in a material sense. The atmosphere at home is better described as correct than warm; the young creator often feels a bit estranged from her biological family. Even when there are close ties to one or another parent, these are laced with ambivalence. Intimate ties are more likely to obtain between E. C. and a nanny, nursemaid, or more distant member of the family.

The family of E. C. may not be highly educated, but it values and has high expectations with respect to learning and achievement. Usually, the child's area of strength (her dominant intelligence) emerges at a relatively young age, and the family encourages these interests, though there may be ambivalence about a career which falls outside the established professions. There is a moral, if not religious, atmosphere around the home, and the child develops a strict conscience, which can be turned against herself but also, and especially in later life, against others who do not adhere to desired behavioral patterns.

There comes a time when the growing child—now an adolescent—seems to have outgrown her home environment. Often, the adolescent has already invested a decade of work in the mastery of a domain and is near its forefront; she has little to learn from her family and from local experts, a quickened impulse to test herself against the leading young persons in the domain. And so, the adolescent or young adult ventures toward that city which is seen as a center of vital activities. (Around 1900, London, Paris,

Berlin, and Zürich were favorites.) With surprising speed, the future creator discovers a set of peers who share the same interests; and together, these "young Turks" explore the terrain of the domain, often organizing institutions and issuing manifestos, stimulating one another to new heights. Sometimes E. C. proceeds directly to work in a chosen domain; not infrequently, there are flirtations with a number of different career lines until a crystallizing moment occurs.

Experiences within domains differ from one another, and there is no point in glossing these over. Still, with greater or lesser speed, E. C. discovers a problem area or line of production of special interest, one that promises to take the domain into uncharted waters. This is a highly charged moment. At this point E. C. generally becomes isolated from peers and must work on her own. She senses that she is on the verge of a breakthrough that is as yet little understood, even by her. At this point, some kind of support from others is crucial.

In the happy circumstances that I studied, E. C. succeeds in effecting at least one major breakthrough, one which is recognized with relative rapidity by the relevant field. E. C. finds herself to be different from others and goes to extraordinary lengths to retain this difference. E. C. works nearly all the time, making tremendous demands on herself and on others, constantly raising the ante. She is self-confident, able to deal with false starts, proud and stubborn, reluctant to admit mistakes to others, though usually willing to shift course when such a tack seems indicated.

In general, given such enormous energy and commitment, the opportunity arises for at least one more breakthrough. That breakthrough occurs about a decade after the first. As I shall show, the possibility for future breakthroughs is closely tied to the nature of the domain. In any event, E. C. seeks to retain her creativity; she will seek marginal status, or heighten the ante of asynchrony, in order to maintain freshness and to secure the "flow" that accompanies formidable challenges and exciting discoveries. In cases where there is an outpouring of works, a few of them will stand out as *defining*, both for E. C. herself and for members of the encompassing field.

Inevitably, with the onset of advanced age, limits emerge in the powers of the creative individual. Younger persons are sometimes cultivated or exploited as a means of rejuvenation. Often, even if original new works prove elusive of production, an important role as critic, commentator, or sage remains. Some creators die young, but in the case of E. C., she lives on until late in life, gains many followers, and continues to make significant contributions until the time of her death. Moreover, because her life's work has transformed the domain and the field, her effect continues to be felt for many years afterward.

Of course, no single creator, let alone the seven that I've studied, conforms exactly to this pattern. The patterns proposed here are illustrative rather than definitive; one would need larger samples, and more precise measures, to establish the validity of any proposed pattern—to effect the course from idiographic to nomothetic. Nonetheless, the "ideal-type" portrait at least conveys the kinds of generalizations that one hopes to obtain from studies of these kinds. I turn now to some of the more specific patterns that emerged from the intensive studies that I have carried out.

Cognition

Each of my creators was selected because of a suspected strength in a particular intelligence, and so, not surprisingly, each of them has a distinctive cognitive profile. What I had not suspected was that the creative individual is characterized as much by an unusual combination of intelligences as by a single outstanding intelligence. Thus, for instance, Freud had the combination, unusual for a scientist, of linguistic and personal intelligences, Stravinsky combined musical with other artistic intelligences, Einstein featured a strong spatial intelligence to complement his logical-mathematical strengths. With the possible exception of Stravinsky, each of the creators also had definite areas of intellectual weakness, though it remains speculation whether that form of asynchrony contributed to their specific creative course.

It has been appreciated for some time that it takes approximately a decade for an individual to master a domain, to come to the level of technical expertise that is expected of an adult professional (Hayes 1981). Generally the most pronounced breakthrough occurs within a decade after this initial mastery: I speak here of such works as Freud's account of the unconscious processes in dreams, Einstein's theory of relativity, Gandhi's *Satyagraha*, and the breakthroughs captured in Picasso's *Les desmoiselles d'avignon*, Stravinsky's *Le sacre du printemps*, Eliot's *The Waste Land*, and Martha Graham's *Frontier*.

Not infrequently, a second breakthrough occurs, about a decade later. While still radical, this additional breakthrough involves a reconciliation between creator and the broader traditions of the domain. I cite here Freud's work in social psychology, Einstein's general theory of relativity, Gandhi's well-orchestrated, large-scale protests, Picasso's *Guernica*, Stravinsky's *Les Noces*, Eliot's *Four Quartets*, and Graham's *Appalachian Spring*. Some creators continue to have breakthroughs over several more decades, but

Einstein and Eliot did not. I speculate that the possibility for breakthroughs beyond the first is a function, on the one hand, of the nature of the domain (arts being more susceptible than the sciences), and, on the other, of the personality of the creator (some content to rest on the laurels of their first breakthrough, others determined to surpass themselves).

Other Psychological Dimensions

It has always been known that creative individuals are highly energetic and extremely demanding of themselves and others. Their work stands above all else. I had not fully appreciated, however, the extent to which these individuals are frankly difficult. All of them were quite prepared to use individuals and then to discard them when their utility was at an end. A legacy of destruction and tragedy surrounds those who enter into the orbit of the creative individual; the excitement of being in the company of such individuals is great but the decompression afterwards can be quite trying. There is also much self-promotion and, often, a concomitant deprecation of others.

Two other personal dimensions are worthy of comment. The first is the distinct marginality of creative individuals. In most cases, the marginality was there from the start—by place of birth, by religion, by gender. But even when it was not there initially—as in the case of T. S. Eliot—it becomes possible to lead one's life so as to become and to remain determinedly marginal. And this is what each of our creators was determined to do. Indeed, when acceptance appears at hand, there is a temptation—usually accepted— to raise the ante so that one's marginal status is again firmly established.

The second dimension concerns the extent to which creative individuals retain features of their childhood. Sometimes, this retention stresses some of the less appealing aspects of childhood—such as selfishness, self-centeredness, intolerance, silliness, stubbornness. But even when these traits are not salient, the creative individual retains a ready access to what might be called childlike traits—the ability to ignore convention, to follow a lead where it goes, to ask questions that adults usually have stopped asking, to go directly to the essence of an issue. It is not surprising that, whether or not they had children themselves, each of the creators was quite fascinated by childhood and actively sought to retain some of the cognitive, affective, emotional, and social strands of their own childhood.

Domain

Many investigators of creativity, including myself, have been attracted by the possibility of creating a scheme that pertains to all creative activity

(Gardner and Nemirovsky 1991; Wallas 1926). Indeed, when I first began this study, I sought such an integrative framework. I have become convinced, however, that there exist at least five different kinds of creative activity. It is important to understand the dimensions of each activity, before one searches for generalizations that may obtain across these varieties:

1. *The solution of a well-defined problem.* This kind of work is often pursued in the course of training, as when Stravinsky was asked by his teacher to orchestrate well-known melodies. However, it has the potential to be highly creative, when the problem is important and has not yet been solved. A modern example is the discovery of the double-helix by James Watson and Francis Crick. In their early scientific work, both Freud and Einstein exhibited this form of creativity several times.

2. *The devising of an encompassing theory.* We see the development of a widely incorporative theory in the example of Freud studying the unconscious, and of Einstein pondering the riddles of relativity. In creating such a theory, the scholar not only reconfigures existing data and concepts but points the way to future lines of research. Certain important artistic movements, such as cubism or twelve-tone music, bear something of an analogy to what is usually achieved in this kind of scientific work.

3. *The creation of a "frozen work."* Most artists, working alone or in collaboration, create some kind of a work in a symbolic system. That work can then be examined, performed, exhibited, evaluated by others who are knowledgeable in the domain. In any event, there is a distance between the occasion of creation and the times when the work is encountered and evaluated. In this respect, the work differs from the fourth variety of creation.

4. *The performance of a ritualized work.* Some works can only be apprehended in performance, and the creativity inheres chiefly in the particular characteristics of the specific performance. The prototypical example is the performance of a dance by Martha Graham. While the dance can in principle be notated and performed by someone else, in fact Graham's creativity adhered significantly in her capacity to perform in a distinctive and valued way. In art forms where notations do not exist, or where the notations fail to capture important aspects of the performance, the performance *is* the work.

5. *A "high-stakes" performance.* In the fifth variety, an individual actually carries out a series of actions in public in order to bring about some kind of social or political change. Our prototypical instance here is the protests, fasts, and nonviolent confrontations engaged in by Gandhi and his followers. In contrast to ritualized artistic performances, where the steps can be worked out in advance, this performance is determinedly "high-stakes." It is not possible to work out the details of the performance in advance

because much of it depends upon the reactions of the audience or the combatants.

There is clearly a relationship between the kinds of creative activities outlined here and the domains in which creative work can be achieved. Scientific domains highlight the first two kinds of activity; the second pair of activities are particularly associated with artistic work; and the final kind is most likely to occur in the political domain. Anyone who wishes to enter into the space of creative individuals needs to take into account these domains, these kinds of activities, and the overlap and nonoverlap among them.

One further significant aspect of domains is the extent to which they are paradigmatic. This notion, building on the well-known concept of Kuhn (1970), calls attention to the extent to which individuals working in a domain agree about the delineations of problems and solutions within that domain. In the case of well-developed sciences, there is generally agreement about what constitutes appropriate problems, methods, and solutions; and in art forms where practices have been well-established, such as classical painting or the 19th-century novel, a similar consensus can obtain. However, at certain times in the sciences, and currently in the arts, one encounters a situation where there obtains little agreement about paradigms. Such moments are particularly ripe for breakthroughs, and yet the dispersed nature of the domain makes it less likely that the breakthroughs can be immediately appreciated.

Field

In some respects, the concept of field is the social counterpart to the concept of the domain. The domain is a set of practices associated with an area of knowledge; the field consists of the individuals and institutions that render judgments about work in the domain. An important feature of the field is the extent to which it is hierarchical: that is, the extent to which a few powerful individuals can render influential judgments about the quality of work.

Such hierarchical domination occurred, for example, in the area of physics early in the century, when the editors of the leading physics journals played a major role in determining which ideas were published and which received attention. Einstein owed much to the support of Max Planck and a few other powerful figures. But it occurred equally prominently in modern dance in the 1930s, when a few powerful critics brought attention to the performance of Martha Graham. To the extent that the field is hierarchical, it is possible to be quickly recognized and to gain influence; the costs of this hierarchization is that one runs the risk more quickly of becoming "dated," as younger figures master the art of addressing the field appropriately.

Another dimension of the field involves the relation of aspiring creators to others who are pursuing the same line of work. I have been impressed by the rapidity and ease with which aspiring creators locate their peers at an early age and, at least for awhile, work together cooperatively with them. However, competition and isolation eventually become powerful factors, and the recognized creator generally searches for followers and for promoters rather than for challenging competitors. And in the case of our titans, they often come to identify with great figures from other eras, or from distant domains, rather than with the few peers in their own chosen area of specialty.

Fruitful Asynchrony

My study of creators provided ample evidence in support of the notion of fruitful asynchronies. One could almost plot out the seven target lives in terms of the numbers and types of "lacks of fit" which characterized them. These include powerful tensions with the nodes (Picasso's strong spatial intelligence in contrast to his weak scholastic intelligences; the tension in the domain of physics between an approach that was built upon the concept of the ether and one that questions its utility; the tension within the musical field between supporters of Stravinsky's chromatic music and devoteés of Schoenberg's twelve-tone music). And it includes powerful tensions among the nodes: the lack of fit between Freud's intelligences and those that were usually honored in the sciences; the tensions between Picasso's Cubist works and the earlier dominance of representational works; the tensions between the poetry that was prized in the nineteenth century and the contrasting pulls of élite and mass literary taste in the twentieth century.

The problem with the concept of fruitful asynchrony is not, then, a question of locating support for it; rather its very ubiquity in the lives of human beings becomes a problem. Perhaps asynchrony is everywhere potentially fruitful and it is only a question of making use of it. My study does not resolve this question, but it raises two interesting possibilities.

First of all, it seems that creators, more so than other mortals, search for asynchronies, thrive on them, receive flow from them. This is exemplified by the findings on that type of asynchrony termed *marginality*: when marginality is not given to creators, or when it appears to be disappearing, the creators—unlike many others—actually attempt to reestablish the asynchrony.

The second point has to do with amount of asynchrony. It is possible to have too much asynchrony. Indeed, all of our creators seem to have suffered some kind of breakdown when they were still relatively young; this dysfunction suggests a degree of asynchrony that was beyond endurance. The creator may stand out for the *amount* and *type* of asynchrony that she can endure and exploit without being overwhelmed in the process.

Two Unexpected Findings

Though all have their pet hypotheses, researchers usually are most grateful if their studies turn up a result that is a surprise for them and will, hopefully, constitute a surprise for others as well. In the case of my study of creators, two findings stand out.

1. Cognitive and affective support systems. First of all, at the time of the greatest breakthrough, our creators were in one sense very much alone. Often they had physically withdrawn from other individuals; and, at least in their exploration of the farthest reaches of their domain, they were venturing into areas where no one had gone before.

Somewhat paradoxically, however, it was precisely at these times that our creators needed, and were fortunate enough to be able to secure, strong support from other individuals. The support needed to be both cognitive—from someone who could understand the nature of their breakthrough; and affective—from someone who could assure them that they were alright as human beings and that they had not departed from their senses. In the majority of the cases, the support came from the same individual—for example, Louis Horst provided both forms of support for Martha Graham, just as Wilhelm Fliess provided both forms for Sigmund Freud. However, a division of labor is also possible: Einstein received cognitive support from a group called the Olympiad and from his friend Michelangelo Besso, affective as well as some cognitive support from his wife Mileva.

2. A Faustian bargain. Another unexpected finding concerns the extent to which creators are willing, so to speak, to sell their souls in order that their creative juices can continue to flow. In the cases of each of the creators, I found evidence that they had made bargains with themselves—and with their Makers—which struck me as quite extreme. Sometimes the arrangements were ascetic, almost masochistic in nature; at other times, they were frankly exploitative, even sadistic in character. But in either instance, these arrangements seem to have been made so that the creator had the best opportunity to continue to work in her domain.

On the masochistic side, one finds Freud and Gandhi taking vows of celibacy at a young age; Eliot, Graham, and Gandhi pursuing extremely ascetic kinds of existences. More exploitative forms of bargains were struck by Picasso, who ruthlessly exploited those about him, and especially "his" women; and Stravinsky, who engaged in tireless litigation against nearly everyone in his personal and his professional circle, as if determined that no advantage ever be taken of him. In some cases, one can find evidence of both forms of bargain—Freud was as severe with reference to other individuals as he was to himself. And even the individual least involved in the world of other human beings, Albert Einstein, essentially gave up family life and intimate relations so that he could pursue his work—though, paradoxically, he retained a keen if distanced interest in the broader world of other human beings.

FINAL REFLECTIONS

In the course of this whirlwind tour of a set of case studies about the founders of the modern era, I have conveyed a set of impressions and trends. Each of these, it should be stressed, arises from the idiographic study of a well-documented life; yet it is only by examining such lives together that one begins to discern those patterns that may strain toward, and perhaps even reach, the status of a nomothetic finding: the "creators' patterns" of my title.

The limitations of such a study are evident. I have selected but seven individuals for study, all living within the same time compass, and all influenced primarily by Western Europe; the very factors that make for some comparability at the same time constrain the reach of the generalizations. We simply do not know to what extent similar patterns would have obtained if I had selected other exemplars from the era—say Henri Matisse, Virginia Woolf, or Mao Zedong; individuals drawn from other domains, such as Thomas Edison, Ludwig Wittgenstein, or Barbara McClintock; let alone individuals drawn from a different historical era, such as Mozart, St. Augustine, or Dante. Above all, generalizations obtained on the basis of five, six, or seven cases can easily be undone by the next dozen cases, or, for that matter, by a somewhat different set of criteria or scoring decisions than the ones that I have chosen to employ.

A more delicate issue concerns the kinds of creativity that I have examined. Clearly there is a bias toward individuals who have been revolutionary rather than evolutionary—individuals who took the dramatic steps of *Le sacre du printemps* or *Les Noces*, rather than the more evolutionary changes associated with a Bach from another era, or a less radically oriented composer, like Béla Bartók or George Gershwin from our own era. There is a possible confound with the factors of success and of self-promotion: Pierre Janet made many of the same discoveries as Freud, Braque contributed as much to Cubism as did Picasso; Doris Humphrey was possibly a more outstanding choreographer than Martha Graham; and yet relatively few studies have been carried out of the less illustrious of each pairing. In a sense each of the individuals that I studied became an icon of the domain during the modern era; that decision was made as much by the field, for its own purposes, as by the "objective" factors of the creators' achievement.

Although case studies have their limitations, I believe that the present ensemble of cases in particular helps to illustrate two possibly important phenomena of a more general nature. First of all, I believe that creative individuals of each era make some kind of a raid upon their childhood, preserving certain aspects of their own earlier life in a way that advances their own work and makes sense to their peers. In the case of the creators of the modern era, each of them seems to me to have made contact with the years of early childhood—the preschool years. Whether it is Einstein peering at the erratic behavior of the needle of a compass, Stravinsky experimenting with the rhythms that had struck him when he was barely capable of speaking, or Freud looking at the dreams and wishes of early childhood, the creators of the modern era seem drawn to the same basic, elemental, simple forms that attract the mind of the child before it has been too influenced by the conventions of his society.

Second, and finally, in considering creative work, it is important to be sensitive to two contrasting trends: a tendency to question every assumption and to attempt to strike out on one's own as much as possible, and a countervailing tendency to exhaust a domain, to probe more systematically, deeply, and comprehensively than anyone has probed before. One can distinguish cultures and eras that are determinedly iconoclastic, such as the high Renaissance; and one can counterbalance these instances with the work produced during the medieval era or with the traditions that are so valued in China. From my vantage point, the changes that took place in Europe around the turn of the century represent an extreme in the challenging of given assumptions about life, work, progress, value; even compared to the succeeding postmodern era, that heroic and epoch-making time continues to stand out. In that sense, at least, it may signal some of the outer limits of which human beings are capable during the very few years that each of us has been allotted.

NOTES

This paper summarizes some of the major themes of a recently completed book, entitled *Creating Minds*. (New York: Basic Books, 1993). Portions of the paper were discussed at the Workshop of the Achievement Project, Ashford, Kent, England, January 13–15, 1992. I am grateful to Margaret Boden, Penelope Gouk, and the others in attendance at the conference for their helpful feedback.

REFERENCES

Allport, G. (1961). *Patterns and growth in personality*. New York: Holt, Rinehart and Winston.

Amabile, T. (1983). *The social psychology of creativity*. New York: Springer-Verlag.

Barron, F. (1969). *Creative person and creative process*. New York: Holt, Rinehart and Winston.

Boden, M. (1990). *The creative mind*. New York: Basic Books.

Briggs, J. (1989). *Fire in the crucible*. New York: St. Martin's Press.

Csikszentmihalyi, M. (1988a). Motivation and creativity: Toward a synthesis of structural and energistic approaches to cognition. *New Ideas in Psychology*, 6, 2, 159–176.

———. (1988b). Society, culture, and person: A systems view of creativity. In R. J. Sternberg (ed.), *The nature of creativity*. New York: Cambridge University Press, pp. 325–338.

———. (1990). The domain of creativity. In M. A. Runco and R. S. Albert (eds.), *Theories of creativity*. Newbury Park, CA: Sage Publications, pp. 190–212.

Feldman, D. (1980). *Beyond universals in cognitive development*. Norwood, NJ: Ablex.

Feldman, D. (with L. Goldsmith) (1986). *Nature's gambit*. New York: Basic Books.

Freud, S. (1958). *On creativity and the unconscious* (edited by B. Nelson). New York: Harper and Row.

Gardner, H. (1983). *Frames of mind*. New York: Basic Books.

———. (1988). Creativity: An interdisciplinary perspective. *Creativity Research Journal*, 1, 8–26.

———. (1992). *Multiple intelligences: The theory in practice*. New York: Basic Books.

———. (1993). *Creating minds*. New York: Basic Books.

Gardner, H., and R. Nemirovsky. (1991). From private intuitions to public symbol systems: An examination of creative process in Georg Cantor and Sigmund Freud. *Creativity Research Journal*, 4 (1), 1–21.

Gardner, H., and C. Wolf. (1988). The fruits of asynchrony: A psychological examination of creativity. *Adolescent Psychiatry*, 15, 106–123. (see chapter 2)

Gruber, H. (1981). *Darwin on man*. Chicago: University of Chicago Press.

Gruber, H., and S. N. Davis. (1988). Inching our way up Mount Olympus: The evolving systems approach to creative thinking. In R. J. Sternberg (ed.), *The nature of creativity*. New York: Cambridge University Press, pp. 243–270.

Guilford, J. P. (1950). Creativity. *American Psychologist*, 5, 444–454.

———. (1967). *The nature of human intelligence*. New York: McGraw-Hill.

Hayes, J. (1981). *The complete problem-solver*. Philadelphia: Franklin Institute Press.

Hennessey, B., and T. Amabile. (1988). The conditions of creativity. In R. J. Sternberg (ed.), *The nature of creativity*. New York: Cambridge University Press, 11–38.

Kubie, L. (1958). *The neurotic distortion of the creative process*. Lawrence, KS: University of Kansas Press.

Kuhn, T. S. (1970). *The structure of scientific revolutions*. (2d ed.) Chicago: University of Chicago Press.

Langley, P., H. Simon, G. L Bradshaw, and J. Zytkow. (1986). *Scientific discovery: Computational explorations of the creative process*. Cambridge, MA: MIT Press.

MacKinnon, D. (1962). The nature and nurture of creative talent. *American Psychologist*, 17, 484–495.

Martindale, C. (1990). *Clockwork muse*. New York: Basic Books.

Ochse, K. (1991). *Before the gates of excellence*. New York: Cambridge University Press.

Perkins, D. N. (1981). *The mind's best work*. Cambridge, MA: Harvard University Press.

Runco, M., and R. Albert (eds.) (1990). *Theories of creativity* Newbury Park, CA: Sage Publishers.

Simon, H. (1988). Creativity and motivation: A response to Csikzentmihalyi. *New Ideas in Psychology*, 6, 2, 177–182.

Simonton, D. K. (1984). *Genius, creativity, and leadership*. Cambridge, MA: Harvard University Press.

———. (1988a). *Scientific genius*. New York: Cambridge University Press.

———. (1988b). Creativity, leadership, and chance. In R. J Sternberg (ed.), *The nature of creativity*. New York: Cambridge University Press, pp. 386–426.

Sternberg, R. J. (ed.) (1988). *The nature of creativity*. New York: Cambridge University Press.

Torrance, E. P. (1988). The nature of creativity as manifest in its testing. In R. J. Sternberg (ed.), *The nature of creativity*. New York: Cambridge University Press, pp. 43–75.

Wallace, D., and H. Gruber. (1990). *Creative people at work*. New York: Oxford University Press.

Wallach, M. (1976). Tests tell us little about talent. *American Scientist*, 64, 57–63.

———. (1985). Creativity testing and giftedness. In F. Horowitz, and M. O'Brien (eds.), *The gifted and talented: Developmental perspectives*. Washington, DC: American Psychological Association.

Wallas, G. (1926). *The art of thought*. New York: Harcourt, Brace.

Weisberg, R. (1986). *Creativity, genius, and other myths*. New York: Freeman.

4

Creativity: Proof That Development Occurs

David Henry Feldman

We appear to be in the midst of a resurgence of radical nativism, a viewpoint that attributes much of human experience and activity to innate factors. This resurgence has gone so far as to raise questions about the viability of the concept of development itself (Chomsky, 1980; Fodor, 1980, 1983; Liben, 1987). Although there are now strong counterresponses in the literature to the claim that development is yet another human illusion, like self or God or progress, the need still remains to put the antidevelopmental claims to rest once and for all (Bickhard, 1979, 1980; Campbell and Bickhard, 1986, 1987; Feldman and Benjamin, 1986; Liben 1987). The purpose of this chapter is to provide another argument against the radical nativist position by showing that, because it is impossible to ignore the reality of human creativity, development must perforce exist.

There are, however, a number of preliminaries to be attended to before tackling the main points in the argument. First, it must be acknowledged

Note: The work reported here was supported by grants from the Andrew W. Mellon Foundation, the Jesse Smith Noyes Foundation, and the Spencer Foundation. Grateful acknowledgment is also given to those who read and responded to earlier drafts of this chapter, especially Robert Campbell, William Damon, Howard Gardner, Lynn T. Goldsmith, and the members of the Developmental Science Group at Tufts University.

that an argument for development does not require a denial that biological factors play a significant part in the process. As we shall see, natural human qualities are vital aspects of the overall account. Second, it is essential to be explicit about what is meant by creativity and development in the context of the present discussion. Finally, it must be recognized that the argument put forward here is substantially conceptual and theoretical in nature and, by virtue of this, must be taken as preliminary to the establishment of a firmer empirical base on which to make (and test) its claims.

DEFINITIONAL ISSUES

For the past thirty years, creativity has most often been taken to mean the ability to generate infrequent or unusual ideas, and it typically has been assessed by standardized tests (Guilford, 1950; Torrance, 1962). Unfortunately, there has been little evidence that these tests actually assess anything resembling the ability to make truly creative contributions, such as establishing a new theorem, producing a remarkable work of art, or discovering a new sub-atomic particle (Feldman, 1970; Gardner, 1988; Wallach, 1971, 1985).

I use the term *creativity* here to mean the purposeful transformation of a body of knowledge, where that transformation is so significant that the body of knowledge is irrevocably changed from the way it was before. This kind of transformation can be accomplished conceptually, as in the case of proposing a new theory, or by making new products or representations, developing new technologies, or proposing innovative practical techniques. This notion of creativity emphasizes high-level functioning brought to bear on specialized problems, in contrast to notions of creativity that argue for a generic life force (Maslow, 1972) or quality of mind (Guilford, 1950). There is a place for such notions in an overall account of creativity, but that is not the best place to start. As Gruber (1981) has argued, it is best to begin with unambiguous cases of creativity, such as Darwin's theory of biological evolution, Einstein's ideas about the physical universe, or Mozart's great operatic works. From there we can move, if we wish, toward establishing common qualities among more widespread transformational uses of mind.

Obviously, the definition proposed here assumes a quality of human purposefulness, an unusual set of talents, and probably optimal circumstances for developing those talents in a distinctive direction. This point will be discussed further later in this chapter. For now, it is sufficient to note that, as used here, creativity refers to relatively rare events that are marked by their transforming effect on existing bodies of knowledge. When domains are reorganized in ways that can reasonably be described as qualitative and irreversible, then creativity of the sort defined here has occurred. It is itself a formidable problem to judge when a change is sufficiently powerful to be considered qualitative and irreversible, but criteria do exist and have been tested empirically with some success (Feldman, Marrinan, and Hartfeldt, 1972; Jackson and Messick, 1965).

The relationship between creativity and development, then, is based on the importance of transformations to both of these processes. The concept of development is of course the broader of the two, referring to any internal transformation of a body of knowledge that yields a qualitatively advanced (for that person) reorganization of knowledge. Developmental changes may be as common as the periodic systemwide reorganizations of each individual's intellectual structure, as described by Jean Piaget, or as idiosyncratic as the achievement of a more advanced level of mastery of an esoteric body of knowledge, such as chess or juggling (Feldman, 1980; Walton, Adams, Goldsmith, and Feldman, 1987). Creativity is a particularly strong and powerful instance of development, in which a personal, internal reorganization also leads to a significant change in the external form of a domain. A given instance of development may or may not contain the possibility for creative reorganization, but it always sets the stage for such a possibility (see Feldman, 1980, 1982, and Feldman and Benjamin, 1986, for discussions of the relation between creativity and development).

By emphasizing purposefulness in the creative process, I do not mean to deny the importance of natural biological factors, for they are vital in at least two senses. Some people are more naturally gifted and/or inclined toward representing experience through various domains than are others. Individuals also differ naturally in the personal, emotional, and social qualities that co-occur with their cognitive strengths and weaknesses (Gardner, 1982, 1988; Wexler-Sherman, Gardner, and Feldman, 1988). The sources of such individual variations are numerous to be sure, but at least some of that variation is undoubtedly a direct function of biological processes.

The second sense in which biology is central to the account proposed here is Piagetian. Development is assumed to be a universal human process, which means that it must be strongly supported by a biological substrate (Bringuier, 1980; Piaget, 1971a). Creativity, being a special case of development, must also be based on biological processes, but less directly so. Understanding creativity therefore requires understanding development, including the biological aspects of development (Feldman, 1974, 1980, 1982; Gardner, 1982).

However, biological processes alone are not a sufficient source of explanation for creativity, let alone development. To argue that innate capabilities determine in every important detail all that an individual will ever accomplish is to legislate against the existence of a problem, but it fails to provide any better an explanation for the phenomenon than any other radically reductionist scheme. To "explain" that a fire attributable to arson started because of a reaction between flammable material and a heat source is to miss the point, even if (and this is closer to the mark) the nature of the material can be specified and the heat source can be identified.

That there are biologically programmed processes that are common across individuals is no reason to assume that such processes adequately explain why individuals differ from one another in what they accomplish, and it is certainly no warrant for denying the existence of such phenomena as development or creativity. Turning away from complex issues like creativity in favor of explaining other phenomena at other levels—even if those explanations turn out to be an important part of the story—is not a satisfactory response to the issue of development and the implications of assuming a nondeterministic view of human development and change.

The main purpose of this discussion is to begin to glimpse the form that an explanation of development and creativity must take. The best place to start is with what we already know about the process, and what we already know about development comes largely from the work of Piaget and his collaborators.

DEVELOPMENT AS CONSTRUCTION: THE INFLUENCE OF PIAGET

The most important advance of this century for understanding development and, by virtue of this, for understanding creativity was Piaget's constructivist theory (Feldman, 1985; Piaget, 1971a, 1971b, 1975, 1979 [1972] 1982). Piaget knew that it was vital to the achievement of his epistemological goals to be able to account for creativity, although he was never able to do so to his own satisfaction (Bringuier, 1980; Feldman, 1982, 1988; Feldman and Benjamin, 1986; Piaget, 1971b). What he was able to do was to provide the fundamental breakthrough in epistemology upon which an adequate explanation of creativity might be built.

The central problem in understanding creativity is understanding change—how it is experienced and how it is controlled: How much change is there in the real world of experience? How do changes occur? Can there be changes in knowledge or experience that go beyond what already exists? What is the relationship between the individual's experience of change and a decision to create changes that alter aspects of the world?

Piaget argued that, while change is inevitable, it has order and can be comprehended. He saw individuals during their life spans going through a series of lawful changes both large (the four stages of thought) and small (local accommodations). Bodies of knowledge also change, and even the physical world changes, although the principles upon which it does so change slowly, if at all. For Piaget, the goal of epistemology was to describe the various systems that people construct for describing and explaining changes in their world. This way of thinking about change places the human mind (Piaget's "epistemic subject") at the center of the process, in control of the mental structures developed to bring stability and order to systems for understanding the world. In this respect, Piaget's developmental psychology was the first distinctly psychological theory of intellectual change.

Instead of being driven to explaining development on the basis of the external world alone, as behaviorist approaches had done, or to supporting nativist explanations of innate biological unfolding. Piaget held to a "constructivist" position. He argued that changes in experience and in the interpretation of experience are inevitable but that the source of such interpretation lies in individuals' building and revising theories based on their experiences with the world rather than in the individual alone or in the environment alone. Piaget posited that there were laws to be discovered and revised regarding how such cognitive changes take place, and establishing such laws was the central goal of his epistemology.

Piaget attempted to provide an explanation of change in knowledge structures through a process termed *equilibration*. His formulation was revolutionary in at least two respects. First, his change mechanism led to transformations not only in the individual's store of knowledge but in the very mental structures that are the sources of knowledge. Thus not only does knowledge change, but knowledge-gathering capabilities also change. Second, Piaget proposed that changes in knowledge come about not just from mental reflection but also from action, which he defined as the desire to understand the world through activity, exploration, and interpretation (Feldman, 1985; Flavell, 1963; Piaget, 1975, 1979).What makes Piaget's epistemology so much more powerful than its predecessors' is this distinctly constructivist character.

Finally, since the principles of knowledge formation change as a function of the individual's own epistemological purposes, Piaget gave new substance and status to the self: "Free will" can exist as biological adaptation and psychological epistemic reality. The most remarkable examples of individually rendered changes in thought processes are often called "creative" because they not only change a person's understanding of a domain but lead to changes in the codified structures of knowledge in that domain as well—that is, they change existing bodies of knowledge (Feldman, 1974, 1980, 1988; Feldman and Benjamin, 1986).

Despite these extraordinary advances, Piaget was unable to account for how creative changes come about. He did understand that his theory would be incomplete until he was able to explain adequately how truly new, qualitative changes can be achieved through the conscious, directed efforts of individuals. Near the end of his life, he reiterated a point he had made many times before: "The central problem of constructivist epistemology is the problem of the construction or creation of something that did not exist before" (Piaget and Voyat, 1979, p. 65). It was his failure to fully recognize the importance of differences between universal and nonuniversal domains that left him unable to posit a satisfying account of novel, creative thought (Piaget, [1972] 1982).

Limitations of Piaget's Theory

As concerned as Piaget was about the systems people create for understanding the world, he failed to see any theoretical importance in differences between universal reorganizations of knowing systems (the famous four "stages" of development) and nonuniversal reorganizations such as we are considering here (Feldman, 1980). Nonuniversal reorganizations are those transformations in knowing systems that apply to a particular domain of knowledge but are not universally attained. Such changes are not guaranteed to occur in all individuals or for mastery of all bodies of knowledge, but they nonetheless are developmental in all other essential senses of the term (Feldman, 1980; Vygotsky, [1934] 1962).

In both universal and nonuniversal development, the individual struggles to interpret the world. But because development in nonuniversal domains is not guaranteed, there is more of a role for individual talent or inclination, on the one hand, and for specific, domain-related influences, on the other. While Piaget frequently used examples from mathematics and other nonuniversal domains to illustrate what he meant by qualitative shifts in knowing, he failed to exploit important differences between universal and nonuniversal shifts in knowing systems (Feldman, 1980).

The key problem with Piaget's account of individual change, then, is that it does not deal systematically with the humanly crafted aspects of a changing world. The world that Piaget's system deals with best is a stable, natural, physical world, with durable underlying logical principles governing its functioning. The child's challenge is to discover these immutable principles. These discoveries lead to mental changes that are more than quantitative, as, for example, when a child "solves" the integration of number and order in a seriation problem. What does not change either qualitatively or quantitatively in such a situation is the domain, the body of knowledge itself. Even the term that Piaget uses to describe individual changes—*accommodation*—signifies that change is in the child's mind, not in the external world as represented by the body of knowledge. Creative changes that require the domain to "accommodate" along with the individual are simply not well integrated into Piaget's universalist framework.

Piaget believed that the same principles of change that account for universal knowledge development could also account for change in bodies of knowledge (Bringuier, 1980). This idea offered a productive point of departure, and it has led to efforts to describe creativity as a cognitive-developmental phenomenon governed by equilibration processes (Feldman, 1974, 1980, 1982; Gruber, 1981). But it eventually led to an impasse, since it is not obvious where to look within the Piagetian framework for the reasons why some individuals and some reorganizations lead to changes in the domain while others do not. The universalist assumption virtually prevents serious consideration of other processes that might be called into play to help explain unique reorganizations as distinguished from universal ones (Feldman, 1980).

It seems clear, despite these criticisms, that Piaget was moving toward considering nonuniversal bodies of knowledge and their role in development. Indeed, as early as around 1970, he began to wonder if his most mature stage of Formal Operations was truly as universal as he had originally thought (Piaget, 1972). He mused that perhaps individuals did not display Formal Operational thinking in all domains but rather manifested the tendency toward this form of thought only through a particular domain, with different domains accessible to different individuals. While never giving up his belief in the underlying unity of the development of mind, he began to consider the possibility that identifying universal processes in different minds might require accessing them through different, specific knowledge domains. This line of thought brought Piaget as close as he was to get to the crucial distinction between universal and nonuniversal bodies of knowledge (Feldman, 1974, 1980, 1982, 1988; Feldman and Goldsmith, 1986).

What is of central importance for understanding creativity is that the processes that govern such changes, while sharing much in common with the universals of Piaget's theory, are also different in certain important respects. For Piaget, the creation of Boolean algebra was a novelty in need of an explanation. For deep epistemological reasons, Piaget was tied to the centrality of universal qualities of mind, the application of which might lead to both universal and nonuniversal reorganizations of thought. When applied to particular bodies of knowledge, universal cognitive achievements might indeed lead to specific changes in nonuniversal domains such as Boolean algebra, but just *how* they might do so cannot be explained within

Piaget's universalist framework. The phenomenology of change in the two situations—trying to better comprehend an existing body of knowledge versus trying to transform its deep structure—is a different sort of activity and requires a different epistemology.

Although Piaget's own epistemology prevented him from accounting for truly creative accomplishments, he was still extremely close to the mark. Piaget wrote that: "The whole of human history is a history of *inventions* and creations which do not stem simply from the potentialities of the human race as a whole" (Piaget, 1971b, p. 212, emphasis original). Having come this close, Piaget characteristically fell back on biology, saying that the answer to how such inventions could arise would come from studies of the evolution of the nervous system. Yet he was very close to a plausible psychological explanation of novelties, including nonuniversal ones.

In spite of Piaget's monumental contributions to our understanding of mental development, and in spite of the truly revolutionary nature of his theory, he was unable to propose a plausible explanation for major examples of human creativity. This was no small piece of unfinished business. And Piaget was aware that he had failed to resolve a central issue: "[The] crux of my problem is to try to explain how novelties are possible and how they are formed" (Piaget, 1971b, p. 194).

THE CRAFTED WORLD: SOURCE OF A DIFFERENT EPISTEMOLOGY

Piaget assumed that the same epistemological purposes that accounted for universal changes in thought would account for nonuniversal ones. It is no doubt true that the child's inherent curiosity about the world and efforts to comprehend it through equilibration processes are key factors in the desire to know. These qualities are necessary, to be sure, but are they sufficient? Beyond an inherent curiosity, individuals must come to believe that bodies of knowledge, disciplines, and fields of endeavor are not immutable but in fact can be changed. The distinctive feeling necessary for creativity in the larger sense is the belief that the knowledge structures existing in the world—its disciplines and technologies— have been changed by consciously directed human efforts and can continue to be changed when necessary. This is a vastly different epistemological position from the one Piaget explored, and it is essential to creativity (Bruner, Olver, and Greenfield, 1966).

Piaget's framework requires individual accommodation to an existing system for comprehending the world, a powerful but ultimately limiting source of new knowledge. Creativity, in the form of major new transformations of knowledge, occurs when a different stance is taken—a stance that questions the adequacy of existing domains for comprehending the world and that requires the world itself to accommodate. Although subtle, this shift in expectation and orientation is essential if creativity is to occur. Where does the feeling come from that the world must accommodate? It comes at least in part from the world itself—from clear evidence that other people have already made significant changes in the world and have forced it to accommodate. This kind of evidence, which is virtually everywhere, may not be obvious to the growing mind without assistance from those who have gone before. It also comes from culturally held beliefs that intentional changes are, at least some of the time, desirable and that those people who can facilitate valuable changes are given special recognition (Csikszentmihalyi and Robinson, 1986).

The world is therefore made up of fundamentally different sorts of things, those that are "natural" and those that are "humanly made." There is increasing evidence that children are inherently aware of certain distinctions among properties of objects, such as alive/not alive (Carey, 1985; Keil, 1986). These ontological distinctions are natural divisions of the young mind. Although the matter has not been empirically tested, it seems plausible to propose that children might also make a distinction at an early age between natural and humanly crafted aspects of the world: things that have "always been there or were put there by God" and things that are there because other people made them. Although it may take some time for children to refine this distinction, it is vital to the process of creative transformation that such a distinction be deeply appreciated by the developing mind.

When creativity occurs, it occurs in part because a person is motivated by the belief that, through his or her individual efforts, the world can be changed. Certain features of the world seem less changeable, and it is the understanding of these features that Piaget sought to capture in his universal stages: the logic underlying knowledge about space, time, causality, and morality. Most of the environment, however, particularly in urban, industrialized cultures, is in fact of human construction and human design. Awareness of this distinction is one of the most powerful sources for understanding that it is possible to transform the world—to make it a different place. The perception of this possibility is essential to all major forms of creativity.

This last point touches upon the crux of the nativist/constructivist debate (Piattelli-Palmarini, 1980): Is it possible to create something genuinely new with a mind that does not inherently already contain that new thing? Antidevelopmentalists argue that in principle it is impossible to create a more powerful mind from a less powerful one (Chomsky, 1980; Fodor, 1980, 1983). Yet recognizing the importance of the crafted world allows us to show that the mind can indeed create something new without already possessing a preformed version of the new idea. The crafted world offers myriad examples of new ideas and products, as well as cultural prosthetics that encode the techniques and provide the tools for making other new things (Bruner, Olver, and Greenfield, 1966; Olson 1970). The crafted world provides the opportunity for a developing mind to access the accumulated knowledge of a culture, perceive selected and preserved examples of human efforts at transformation, and learn about the techniques for bringing about such changes. It is upon the crafted world that the possibility of creativity depends, not the preexistence of new ideas in the mind.

The error of earlier analyses, including Piaget's, was the assumption that every new idea and product of importance had to be invented in its entirety by an individual. In fact, this is not true. Know-how, tradition, and example after example of the fruits of earlier creative activity are available to the growing mind. From these sources, in conjunction with the individual's own disposition toward novel activity, will emerge the makings of genuinely new things. Without accepting the strong form of the behaviorist argument, I would argue that new possibilities can be catalyzed in the developing mind from the outside, interacting with and influencing the individual's future course of understanding.

It is indeed possible for there to be something new under the sun. One need only consider how much of what is now under the sun would not be there if the humanly crafted world were to suddenly disappear (Csikszentmihalyi and Robinson, 1986; Feldman, 1988; Gardner, 1988). The implications of this argument are that development and creativity do occur—indeed they must occur—since the evidence for their occurrence is all around us in the form of the crafted world of human cultures.

The antidevelopmentalist argument is false because its assumptions are false; development is from the outside in as well as from the inside out. The potential for using outside information must be inherent in the human mind, of course, but a more powerful nonuniversal mental structure can be constructed from a less powerful mental structure through the use of externally available information, prosthetics, and instruction (Bruner, Olver, and Greenfield, 1966; Olson, 1970). All that must be assumed is the potential to use such information, not its presence in some preformed state.

THE TRANSFORMATIONAL IMPERATIVE: A MECHANISM FOR CHANGE

Having just proposed that creativity (and, in fact, most nonuniversal development) depends upon the existence and availability of both humanly crafted environments and techniques for changing them, the question remains as to where the principles of change themselves come from. The crafted world provides numerous examples of significant, radical transformations in bodies of knowledge, as well as an appreciation for the fact that what is now "the state of the art" can be changed again. The actual capabilities for effecting such changes, however, must come from individual minds. I have called this tendency of mind to produce novel constructions "the transformational imperative" (Feldman, 1988).

The transformational imperative differs quite substantially from the equilibration mechanism proposed by Piaget, because it is intended to account for the tendency to transform away from stable knowledge states—in direct contrast to the Piagetian emphasis on transformation toward more logically mature structures and greater stability. In my own reflections on and speculations about transformation, I have found it helpful to distinguish between knowledge processes that seek to preserve reality and those that seek to change it. For the most part, the study of cognitive development has dealt with processes whose primary function is to construct a stable, coherent, internally consistent view of reality. The processes traditionally studied represent conscious, rational, logical, and categorical efforts to establish and preserve a stable and unchanging interpretation of experience. Piaget was of course a preeminent contributor to this line of thought.

Yet anecdotal accounts and self-reports from individuals who have made creative contributions strongly suggest that such rational thought processes are complimented by nonrational, noncategorical, fluid, and transformational thinking that often goes on outside of conscious awareness (Feldman, 1988; Freud, 1958; Gedo, 1983; Ghiselin, 1952). Creators themselves maintain that this sort of transformational thinking contributed in critical ways to the eventual form of their work—be it poems, mathematical equations, musical compositions, or scientific theories. When asked to reflect on the process of inspiration, Jean Cocteau wrote: "We indulge ourselves like invalids who try to prolong dream[ing] and dread resuming contact with reality; in short, when the work that makes itself in us and in spite of us demands to be born, we can believe that the work comes to us from beyond and is offered us by the gods" (Ghiselin, 1952, p. 82).

Piaget's preoccupation with the consciously directed aspects of transformation may have kept him from explicitly including within his system these more primitive tendencies to transform. Yet it is precisely these processes that are necessary to the appearance of the "novelties" that Piaget so earnestly wanted to explain. This has of course been clear to the psychoanalytic community for many years (Arieti, 1976; Freud, 1958; Gedo, 1983; Kris, 1952). Any explanation of creativity that does not include some kind of inherent nonrational tendency to take outrageous liberties with reality is likely to fall short of the mark (Feldman, 1988).

Granting, then, that a powerful tendency to change reality occurs naturally in human mental functioning, there remains the formidable challenge of specifying the principles upon which such a tendency might operate. Kurt Fischer (Fischer and Pipp, 1984) has proposed a set of transformation rules for rational thought; a complementary set for nonrational thought could prove useful to the further understanding of creative thought. Perhaps further studying transformations in a variety of other states of consciousness, such as dreaming, daydreaming, drug states, or meditation, will make it possible to build a plausible set of such principles (Hartmann, 1984; Wilber, Engler, and Brown, 1986).

At the very least, it makes sense to consider the very real tension between the competing tendencies to preserve a constructed reality and to change it (Arieti, 1976). It is almost certain that such tendencies vary in intensity from person to person and within persons across domains. So far as we know, Einstein lived a quiet and conservative life; it was only in his thoughts about the forces governing the physical universe that his ideas were radically transformational. It is virtually certain that individuals also vary in how readily or in what domains they are inclined to transform knowledge; understanding these differences should help account for why some individuals seem more prepared to change things in various realms than others.

ESSENTIALS FOR CREATIVITY

Based on the previous discussion, an adequate explanation of creativity would seem to require a tripartite set of processes: (1) something like Piaget's equilibration process, which is a rational, conscious, intentional tendency to construct systems of order; (2) the perception of the external world of crafted objects and ideas as a changeable reality; and (3) a powerful innate tendency to change reality outside the bounds of stable, ordered experience. All three seem to be critical ingredients for an adequate account of change, particularly for changes that substantially transform the world.

The third ingredient, the transformational imperative, is intended to contrast with the conscious, rational preference for assimilation to an already known reality. Accommodation has always seemed awkward within Piaget's system, performed only reluctantly and grudgingly by the epistemic subject. I suspect that this is because accommodation runs counter to the purposes of a system dedicated to preserving itself, whereas the opposite is true of a system whose purpose is to transform itself. It would seem that a framework invoking assimilation, accommodation, *and* transformation as equal components in a balanced system would yield a better rendering of the equilibration process, all operating within the context of a world of both cultural and natural objects (Feldman, 1988). Were such an expanded version of Piaget's change process adopted as a heuristic to guide inquiry, it would be better suited to the purpose of building a satisfying explanation of major reorganizations in thought.

ANTIDEVELOPMENTALISM RECONSIDERED

This chapter began with the observation that radical nativism has challenged the viability of the concept of development. I hope it is clear by this point that, while this challenge needs to be met head on, it need not discourage developmentalists interested in articulating major qualitative transformations in thinking. The basic premise of the nativist charge is false: It *is* possible for something more developed to emerge from something less developed without resorting to preformist explanations. The existence of the crafted world in all its manifestations, including techniques and technologies for making qualitatively different things from other things, ensures that development can and does occur.

The clearest examples of development are those changes in the crafted world that we identify as "creative." By so labeling the fruits of certain human efforts to transform, we give objective credibility to the existence of qualitative, irreversible transformations, both in various objects in the world and in our understanding of them (Jackson and Messick, 1965). In other words, we have demonstrated that development, in the sense that the term is usually meant, exists. By interacting with domains that are available in the world of humanly created culture, individuals are able to transcend constraints and extend systems. When such interactions lead to significant changes in the domains themselves, then the individuals who created these external reorganizations have concurrently created internal changes in their own systems for understanding and interpretation.

Not all significant reorganizations in thought can be considered creative in the sense of leading to transformations in a body of codified knowledge. Strictly speaking, we have only proven that development occurs in those instances in which the label "creative" can be conferred on the outcome of an effort to transform. It is much more difficult to support a claim that qualitative reorganization has taken place in a person's mind when that person is only able to do what others have done before. This is why Piaget's theory was so vulnerable to the nativist attack, a vulnerability that is avoided in the present discussion.

TOMORROW

To have shown—at least in the extreme situation of creative accomplishment—that development exists is surely a step forward. But it leaves a great deal to be done. If development *only* occurs in extreme situations such as those we have called creative, then the argument for development still lacks sufficient force to refute the nativist logic entirely; the strong form of the present argument rests on an unproven assumption that all qualitative reorganizations in thought—creative and noncreative alike—rest on similar principles. What must be done is to show in what senses more common forms of reorganizations in thought also transcend constraints and establish qualitative advances in thought. But note how far we have come toward constructing a positive framework for guiding efforts to comprehend developmental change and how little this framework depends on innate structures.

That events occur that are genuinely developmental should now be clear; that they can be achieved by processes that do not require preexisting structures or innate knowledge should also be clear. The question now is to understand *how* development works and, in particular, how development works when it changes the world in ways that become part of the crafted human culture (Feldman, 1988). However sufficient or insufficient the processes proposed in the present account turn out to be for explaining development, they do not describe *how* such processes might be used in the construction of a qualitatively new thought or idea. This seems to be the next step in understanding development, and a giant step it will be.

REFERENCES

Arieti, S. *Creativity: The Magic Synthesis*. New York: Basic Books, 1976.

Bickhard, M. "On Necessary and Specific Capabilities in Evolution and Development." *Human Development*, 1979, 22, 217–224.

Bickhard, M. "A Model of Developmental and Psychological Processes." *Genetic Psychology Monographs*, 1980, 102, 61–116.

Bringuier, J. C. *Conversations with Jean Piaget*. Chicago: University of Chicago Press, 1980.

Bruner, J., Olver, R., and Greenfield, P. *Studies in Cognitive Growth*. New York: Wiley, 1966.

Campbell, R. L., and Bickhard, M. *Knowing Levels and Developmental Stages*. Basel, Switzerland: Karger, 1986.

Campbell, R. L., and Bickhard, M. "A Deconstruction of Fodor's Anticonstructivism." *Human Development*, 1987, 30, 48–59.

Carey, S. *Conceptual Change in Childhood*. Cambridge, Mass.: MIT Press, 1985.

Chomsky, N. "On Cognitive Structures and Their Development." In M. Piatelli-Palmarini (ed.), *Language and Learning: The Debate Between Jean Piaget and Noam Chomsky*. Cambridge, Mass.: Harvard University Press, 1980.

Csikszentmihalyi, M., and Robinson, R. E. "Culture, Time and the Development of Talent." In R. Sternberg and J. E. Davidson (eds.), *Conceptions of Giftedness*. New York: Cambridge University Press, 1986.

Feldman, D. H. "Faulty Construct-ion: A Review of Michael Wallach and Cliff Wing's *The Talented Student.*" *Contemporary Psychology*, 1970, 15, 3–4.

Feldman, D. H. "Universal to Unique: A Developmental View of Creativity and Education." In S. Rosner and L. Abt (eds.), *Essays in Creativity*. Croton-on-Hudson, N.Y.: North River Press, 1974.

Feldman, D. H. *Beyond Universals in Cognitive Development*. Norwood, N.J.: Ablex, 1980.

Feldman, D. H. (ed.). *Developmental Approaches to Giftedness and Creativity*. New Directions for Child Development, no. 17. San Francisco: Jossey-Bass, 1982.

Feldman, D. H. "The End of a Revolution or the Beginning? A Review of Christine Atkinson's *Making Sense of Piaget: The Philosophical Roots.*" *Contemporary Psychology*, 1985, 30, 604–605.

Feldman, D. H. "How Development Works." In I. Levin (ed.), *Stage and Structure: Reopening the Debate*. Norwood, N.J.: Ablex, 1986.

Feldman, D. H. "Creativity: Dreams, Insights and Transformations." In R. Sternberg (ed.), *The Nature of Creativity*. New York: Cambridge University Press, 1988. (see also chapter 5)

Feldman, D. H. "Universal to Unique: Toward a Cultural Genetic Epistemology." *Archives de Psychologie*, 1988, 56, 41–49.

Feldman, D. H., and Benjamin, A. C. "Giftedness as a Developmentalist Sees It." In R. Sternberg and J. Davidson (eds.), *Conceptions of Giftedness*. New York: Cambridge University Press, 1986.

Feldman, D. H., and Goldsmith, L. T. *Nature's Gambit: Child Prodigies and the Development of Human Potential*. New York: Basic Books, 1986.

Feldman, D. H., Marrinan, B., and Hartfeldt, S. "Transformational Power as a Possible Index of Creativity." *Psychological Reports*, 1972, 30, 491–492.

Feynman, R. "The Pleasure of Finding Things Out." *NOVA* episode on Public Television (WGBH, Boston), January 25, 1983.

Fischer, K., and Pipp, S. "Processes of Cognitive Development: Optimal Level and Skill Acquisition." In R. J. Sternberg (ed.), *Mechanisms of Cognitive Development*. New York: W. H. Freeman, 1984.

Flavell, J. H. *The Developmental Psychology of Jean Piaget*. New York: D. Van Nostrand, 1963.

Fodor, J. "Fixation of Belief and Concept Acquisition." In M. Piattelli-Palmarini (ed.), *Language and Learning: The Debate Between Jean Piaget and Noam Chomsky*. Cambridge, Mass.: Harvard University Press, 1980.

Fodor, J. *The Modularity of Mind*. Cambridge, Mass.: MIT Press, 1983.

Freud, S. "The Relation of the Poet to Day-Dreaming." In B. Nelson (ed.), *On Creativity and the Unconscious*. New York: Harper & Row, 1958.

Gardner, H. "Giftedness: Speculations from a Biological Perspective." In D. H. Feldman (ed.), *Developmental Approaches to Giftedness and Creativity*. New Directions for Child Development, no. 17. San Francisco: Jossey-Bass, 1982.

Gardner, H. "The Fruits of Asynchrony: A Psychological Examination of Creativity." In R. Sternberg (ed.), *The Nature of Creativity*. New York: Cambridge University Press, 1988. (see also chapter 2)

Gedo, J. E. *Portraits of the Artist: Psychoanalysis of Creativity and Its Vicissitudes*. New York: Guilford Press, 1983.

Ghiselin, B. (ed.). *The Creative Process*. New York: Mentor, 1952.

Gruber, H. *Darwin on Man: A Psychological Study of Scientific Creativity*. (2nd ed.) Chicago: University of Chicago Press, 1981.

Guilford, J. P. "Creativity." *American Psychologist*, 1950, 5, 444–454.

Hartmann, E. *The Nightmare: The Psychology and Biology of Terrifying Dreams*. New York: Basic Books, 1984.

Jackson, P., and Messick, S. "The Person, the Product, and the Response: Conceptual Problems in the Assessment of Creativity." *Journal of Personality*, 1965, 33, 309–329.

Keil, F. "On the Structure-Dependent Nature of Stages of Cognitive Development." In I. Levin (ed.), *Stage and Structure: Reopening the Debate*. Norwood, N.J.: Ablex, 1986.

Kris, E. *Psychoanalytic Explorations in Art*. New York: International Universities Press, 1952.

Liben, L. (ed.). *Development and Learning: Conflict or Congruence?* Hillsdale, N.J.: Erlbaum, 1987.

Maslow, A. "A Holistic Approach to Creativity." In C. W. Taylor (ed.), *Climate for Creativity*. Elmsford, N.Y.: Pergamon Press, 1972.

Olson, D. *Cognitive Development: The Child's Acquisition of Diagonality*. Orlando, Fla.: Academic Press, 1970.

Piaget, J. *Biology and Knowledge*. Chicago: University of Chicago Press, 1971a.

Piaget, J. "The Theory of Stages in Cognitive Development." In D. R. Green, M. P. Ford, and G. B. Flamer (eds.), *Measurement and Piaget*. New York: McGraw-Hill, 1971b.

Piaget, J. "Intellectual Evolution from Adolescence to Adulthood." *Human Development*, 1972, 15, 1–12.

Piaget, J. *The Development of Thought: Equilibration of Cognitive Structures*. New York: Viking Penguin, 1975.

Piaget, J. "Correspondences and Transformations." In F. Murray (ed.). *The Impact of Piagetian Theory on Education, Philosophy, Psychiatry, and Psychology*. Baltimore, Md.: University Park Press, 1979.

Piaget, J. "Creativity." In J. M. Gallagher and D. K. Reid (eds.), *The Learning Theory of Piaget and Inhelder*, Monterey, Calif.: Brooks/Cole, 1982. (Originally published 1972).

Piaget, J., and Voyat, G. "The Possible, the Impossible, and the Necessary." In F. Murray (ed.), *The Impact of Piagetian Theory on Education, Philosophy, Psychiatry, and Psychology*. Baltimore, Md.: University Park Press, 1979.

Piatelli-Palmarini, M. (ed.). *Language and Learning: The Debate Between Jean Piaget and Noam Chomsky*. Cambridge, Mass.: Harvard University Press, 1980.

Torrance, E. P. *Guiding Creative Talent*. Englewood Cliffs, N.J.: Prentice-Hall, 1962.

Vygotsky, L. S. *Thought and Language*. Cambridge, Mass.: MIT Press, 1962. (Originally published 1934).

Wallach, M. *The Creativity-Intelligence Distinction*. New York: General Learning Press, 1971.

Wallach, M. A. "Creativity Testing and Giftedness." In F. D. Horowitz and M. O'Brien (eds.), *The Gifted and Talented: Developmental Perspectives*. Washington, D.C.: American Psychological Association, 1985.

5

Creativity: Dreams, Insights, and Transformations

David Henry Feldman

In February of 1976 I had an experience that was a classic example of insight, with full, blazing impact and dazzling effect. I was even in the shower when it sent me out stark naked to tell the world, or at least a colleague with whom I was then sharing a hotel room. I can still remember that experience in detail, although no doubt it has become somewhat embellished with frequent retelling and reexperiencing. Nonetheless, I would like to use that experience as part of the basis for this essay. With recent emphasis in creativity research on breaking down the process into common elements (Perkins, 1981) or examining it through an information-processing lens (Hofstadter, 1985a, 1985b; Sternberg, 1986), or in terms of persistent lifelong struggles (Gruber, 1981), I think it well to remember that every now and then one of those blinding visions of a new reality actually does occur, and one occurred to me in 1976.

The support of the Jessie Smith Noyes Foundation, the Andrew W. Mellon Foundation, and the Spencer Foundation is gratefully acknowledged. Also, the members of our research team, the Developmental Science Group, made invaluable contributions: Thanks to Lynn T. Goldsmith, Margaret L. Adams, Ann C. Benjamin, Martha J. Morelock, and Ronald E. Walton for their help and support.

I shall begin by recounting what I saw in the shower, then describe some of the events that led to that moment when things came together so forcefully and dramatically as to nearly knock me off my feet. I shall also summarize what has happened with my insight since it first occurred more than 15 years ago, including a later insight episode. I shall use these personal experiences as a basis for describing certain aspects of creative processes. I make no claim that the way I have gone about it is the only way for creative work to be done, nor do I claim that these particular experiences of insight are of general substantive import. And yes, I am using introspective evidence— that most treacherous source of data. But on the other hand, these are the sources of information about creative processes that I know best, or at least firsthand. Based on my own experience, I am certain that moments of real insight are properly included within the realm of creativity research, even if they are not creativity itself.

I should distinguish at the outset between my own, more holistic work on insight and those efforts to strip insight processes down to their common elements (Perkins, 1981; Sternberg, 1986). At least one author, Maria Shrady, has put together a book describing major insight events, appropriately titled *Moments of Insight* (Shrady, 1972), and several others have produced significant works on the subject (e.g., Lonergan, 1957, cited in Shrady, 1972). My own personal favorite is Brewster Ghiselin's inspiring collection of first-person accounts of important aspects of such experiences, including some remarkable insights by notable contributors to the arts, humanities, and sciences (Ghiselin, 1952). Although these volumes may not represent a rigorous scientific literature, they certainly provide grist for the mill and kinship with others who have had moments of deep insight. I can compare my experience with the insights described by others and can look for some patterns that may speak more generally to creative processes; this is what I shall do in the second half of this essay.

AN AMUSEMENT PARK RIDE

For at least 3 years before my morning shower in February, I had been having a recurring dream—not every night, but perhaps as often as once a week. The dream consisted simply of an amusement park ride in motion. I was aware after several repetitions of the dream that this image was somehow related to my work, specifically to my efforts to understand development and creativity. I told almost no one about this dream, although I do remember once discussing it with the small group of research assistants I was working with at Yale. It was clear to me that this image was central and intimate and important, and I was embarrassed that I had no idea what it was. Let me try to describe what it looked like. The ride was one of those standard amusement park devices that had a kind of pod in the center, which housed the machinery driving the ride, and a number of struts or spokes emanating from the center to a set of small gondolas that held the riders. The gondolas moved in two planes, both around the central pod and up and down; indeed, the whole thing seemed to be moving and rotating in controlled but complex ways—and because it was a dream, the movements were not always strictly according to the ways in which the parts were connected. I have tried to sketch in Figure 4 what the ride looked like.

From time to time the image would change in subtle ways, but the basic parts were always there: central power source, rotating and rising peripheral containers with places for riders in them. Initially, I thought that perhaps the image was a neurophysiological image—something about how the neurons in the brain fire or interconnect—and that I was imaging my own central nervous system working. This left me somewhat dispirited, for I was familiar with enough neurophysiology to know that if this image was indeed neuropsychological, I would be unlikely ever to be able to make sense of it. So I had more or less resigned myself to the presence of this image in my dream life and more or less believed that it probably would be in someone else's lifetime, not mine, that the image would be interpreted.

There was something about this particular image, though, that was different from others in my dreams. I came to believe that this image was central to my work and was not about my emotional life, wishes, desires, or what have you—themes that filled many of my other dreams. These other dreams were quite different in how they "felt" to me and in the meaning that I derived from them. I have also had other dreams that were important for other aspects of my work, although none has had the persistent clarity of imagery or the persistent reappearance or has left me with the persistent feeling of importance that the amusement park ride did.

I should mention that my main preoccupation during this period was not with creativity per se. It was definitely on my mind; not long before, I had written a paper on the subject (Feldman, Marrinan, & Hartfeldt, 1972) and also a review (Feldman, 1975), but I did not see creativity research as my central activity. The closest I came to declaring my concern with creativity was shortly before I began having my amusement park dream. I gave a colloquium at Yale in 1973 in which I said that a model of developmental transitions that I was working on would yield some important new insights into creativity (Feldman, 1980). As a matter of fact, about 6 months after making the declaration in public that creativity and developmental transitions were somehow connected (Figure 5), I experienced a less dramatic insight than the amusement park ride, an insight that gave me the missing

Figure 4
The amusement park ride dream image.

Figure 5
Developmental regions from universal to unique.

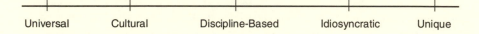

pieces for the "universal-to-unique" model of developmental domains. This model was made possible by my sudden realization (while sitting in a seminar on another topic altogether) that creativity was an extreme version of a stage development shift and could be linked to other such shifts through the conceptual framework for universal and nonuniversal developmental domains that was (I now know) partially completed at the time. By placing creative transformations at one extreme of a continuum and universal transformations at the other end, I was able to construct a pleasing representation of the range of developmental transitions that I wished to encompass in my theoretical work.[1] Creativity was thus "discovered" to be a special case of development in nonuniversal domains. Still, I had no idea that an image of an amusement park ride would provide me with additional information about creative processes. The truth of the matter is that 10 years later I was just beginning to appreciate that creativity is really what the image was about. But that gets ahead of the story.

A Friendly Catalyst

The meaning of the image of the amusement park ride was brought to light through the catalytic effects of Howard Gruber, who is coincidentally one of the foremost students of creativity, known particularly for his masterful study of the thinking of Charles Darwin (Gruber, 1981). Gruber was unaware of the role that he was to play; in fact, I am not sure to this day that he knows how critical a role he played in this particular episode of insight. Indeed, there is an irony in the fact that Gruber has spent much of his career trying to show the relative unimportance of moments of insight in major works of originality. His research of Darwin, for example, down plays Darwin's so-called Malthusian insight that led to the understanding that natural selection could play a positive as well as a negative role in evolution. Gruber has shown that this was only one among numerous other insights reported in Darwin's notebooks and that only in retrospect can it be claimed to be of major importance. Darwin himself gave no such indication in his notebooks (Gruber, 1981). In my own case, I know that the particular moment of insight was for me truly momentous and that it was helped into being by Howard Gruber, a scholar best known as a skeptic of such moments, an irony appropriate to the topic.

During the fall of 1975, I had been asked to review Gruber's book *Darwin on Man: A Psychological Study of Scientific Creativity* (Gruber, 1981), and I was so impressed with it that although I did not know him, I sent him a copy of my review. Gruber, being the kind of person that he is, called and thanked me for the review and mentioned that he would be in Boston shortly thereafter to give a lecture. He invited me to attend the lecture (I had since moved from New Haven to Tufts University in Medford). I went to his presentation (which was about the imagery Darwin used in his personal journals), and we met briefly afterward. Because there was little time to talk, we agreed that it would be worth trying to meet again. As it happened, Gruber was scheduled to come back to Boston soon.

In the meantime, another colleague and friend, Howard Gardner, was helping the Social Research Council in New York assemble a committee to review work in the area of giftedness in children. Gardner wanted both Gruber and me to join him on that committee. And because the first meeting of the committee was scheduled for the day after Gruber's next visit to Boston, we made plans to travel together to New York for the meeting. It was on the air shuttle between Boston and New York that the critical episode occurred that was to catalyze my insight. It was then that Gruber described to me his research on "images of wide scope," which had been stimulated by Charles Darwin's "branching tree" diagram—the only illustration in *The Origin of Species* (Gruber, 1981).

Gruber had begun to wonder if this kind of broad metaphorical image was common, particularly among those who had done original work. He was then engaged in an empirical effort to gather as many of these images as he could, and then to study them. He asked me if I was aware of any such images in my own work. For some reason, I felt comfortable enough to tell Gruber that I had been dreaming about the amusement park ride for better than 2 years. I told him also that I knew it somehow had to do with my work, but that I had no idea what its role might be. For the first time, I tried to draw a picture of what the image looked like. Unfortunately, that early drawing was lost. I had no idea that it would be of any particular importance, and I probably threw it away when we left the plane. It was the following morning that I went rushing into his hotel room across the hall and tried to explain what I had just learned in the shower.

The Concept of Co-incidence

I remember the flash of insight distinctly: What I actually said (out loud, I believe) was, "The ride is not inside, it's outside!" Remember that I had assumed that the carnival contraption was somehow connected with the brain, a neurophysical metaphor. Instead of a micro model, though, I realized in the shower that it was actually a macro model of the forces that contribute to developmental change. Perhaps I should have known from the outset that my model building would be done at the broadest level, because that is where I am most comfortable theorizing, as my critics well know. But the idea that the image that had preoccupied me for so long would turn out to represent an overarching organizing principle simply did not occur to me. Possibly this was because the ride resembled the way I imagined neuronal activity to occur. In fact, I came to see that there was no physical resemblance between the image and what it actually represents; it is an abstraction representing large-scale dynamic forces and their interrelationships. The image, in short, was one of "wide scope," rather than a reflection of the micro-level processes of the central nervous system.

I later came to label the image and what it represented as the processes of "coincidence" (Feldman, 1979, 1980, 1986a). I have developed this notion of coincidence from the original vivid image, and it has come to represent the idea that there are several dimensions of development that must be considered simultaneously if change is to be explained, particularly large-scale or extreme changes (see the chapters by Gardner and Csikszentmihalyi in this volume for complementary views). Development is not solely the result of changes within an individual, catalyzed by transactions with the environment, but is instead the result of a coinciding of a number of forces—some internal and some external—that set the stage, stimulate, and catalyze change. What I glimpsed in the amusement park ride was a system of great complexity, really a system of systems, that governs the development and expression of human potential. The center, or locus of intersection of the forces, I realized, is the whole individual person, and the surrounding pods represent various other forces contributing to the dynamic developmental calculus.

Co-incidence crystallized for me the idea that people do not master bodies of knowledge solely (or even primarily) because they themselves possess particular abilities, interests, or inclinations. Cognitive development within nonuniversal (and perhaps even universal) developmental domains of knowledge requires the coinciding and coordinating of a variety of forces and factors that prime, shape, and guide the individual's course of progress. These co-incidence forces include, for instance, the following: the evolving cultural context within the individual: the developmental trajectories of the significant other people who influence the child's development (parents, siblings, relatives, friends, teachers, institutional officials, etc.); the particular set of historical events that bear on that individual; the many disciplines and fields with which the child will come to interact and the developmental histories of these fields; and, finally, long-term evolutionary trends that provide the backdrop for the rest of the process. These trends do not refer simply to the sorting of the genes, but large-scale tendencies in human and other populations and the physical environment. In all, I sensed that there must be hundreds of possible vectors of influence on development, including the centrally important specific physical, emotional, and intellectual qualities of the individual whose development we are trying to comprehend.

When I stepped out of the shower in New York, I understood that the amusement park ride was an image capturing the multiplicity of dynamic forces that influence development and that do not at the same time compromise the integrity or importance of the individual's own contribution to the process. Development does not simply proceed inside the mind of the individual—stages are not inside anyone's head—but as a result of complex, dynamic processes of coordination, change, adjustment, and new coordinations among the individual, the physical environment, the crafted world, and the social milieu. Although this process is extremely complex and ever changing, it is also controlled and lawful.

As with many "new" ideas, there is much about the notion of co-incidence that is not all that new. I am far from the first to point out that development includes more than simply the expression of potential that is carried in the child's genome. A number of other theorists have called attention to the multifold character of the process of development, including most, if not all, of the forces that I discovered when I was able to "read" the image that had been rotating in my head for so long (Cavalli-Sforza, Feldman, Chen, Dornbusch, 1982). Perhaps the only thing really new was the connecting of the several dimensions of development with an image like a carnival ride, which may or may not actually add anything of importance. For my own part, I can say with certainty that this way of organizing developmental change processes has been greatly illuminating to me, particularly as I have tried to make sense of extreme cases, such as child prodigies. It is more difficult to say whether or not the notion of co-incidence has been of help to others. In fact, it is too soon to say one way or the other, even 15 years later. At this point I am able to say for sure only that the idea of co-incidence has been helpful to me, and also that it was a great relief to have discovered what I was trying to say to myself in my dream. I should also mention that I have not had a dream that included a carnival ride of any description since my rush from the shower. Not once. I take this as evidence that, for better or worse, what I was dreaming was well resolved in the concept of co-incidence that emerged into awareness so suddenly. In contrast to Piaget's idea of "seizing of consciousness" (by which he meant the process of making one's implicit understandings explicit), which became central in his epistemology later in life, I found that the rush to consciousness of this particular concept was not in the least seized. Rather, it seized my consciousness, but through no conscious effort on my part. At least not when it happened.

Co-incidence and Child Prodigies

When I claim that the insight I now call co-incidence was important to me, I can best illustrate that usefulness with respect to one particular problem I have been working on for more than a decade: how to explain the amazing phenomenon that we call the child prodigy. In fact, I see co-incidence as having been invented, at least partly, so that I might better deal with the matter of the prodigy. Even though I did not begin to study prodigies directly until 1975 (more than 2 years after I began dreaming about the ride with spokes and pods), it was not until I began to prepare to carry out the prodigy research that I made conscious sense of the dream.

That the idea of co-incidence came from a dream image that predated my research with prodigies is not in and of itself a problem for claiming that the concept was invented to explain prodigies. Even before I began a specific research effort, I had thought of the phenomenon of the prodigy as an extreme example of developmental processes that are shared with other individuals of less extreme ability. The amazing reciprocity between child and field that occurs in prodigies is very difficult to explain within traditional theories of development. I knew that I was looking for an alternative perspective to bring to bear on the matter of the prodigy that was part of an effort to bring an alternative perspective to developmental change in general.

It is therefore likely that I was assisted in discovering what my dream image was about by my work on prodigies. It may well have been my focus of attention on the particular and peculiar qualities of prodigies (their extreme precocity, domain specific abilities, single-mindedness of purpose, seeming wisdom, uncanny maturity, etc.) that moved me toward being able to interpret the carnival ride. It is even possible, I suppose, that co-incidence was one among several interpretations that I might have devised and that it prevailed because of the specific work I was doing on child prodigies. My own belief is that the prodigy work was catalytic, but did not predetermine the final outcome of the construction of the co-incidence idea.

What is it that I was able to say about prodigies after the co-incidence notion that I was unable to say before? With the co-incidence concept, I think I have been able to present a greater richness of interpretation, a fuller and more articulated explanation (rather than a radically different one) than I had before. I had selected the matter of the prodigy as an interesting topic for research because it seemed to shed light on other aspects of my theorizing (unrelated to the notion of co-incidence), and I had much to say about how prodigies might develop based on those efforts. That theoretical work is summarized elsewhere (Feldman, 1980, 1981, 1983, 1986b), but the basic idea was to try to fill in some of the gaps between universal developmental changes such as Piaget had tried to describe and the remarkable transformations that we associate with the truly unique human contributions. I saw the prodigy concept as a kind of map for some of the territory between these two poles: the universal and the unique (see Figure 5).

I did not think that prodigies would necessarily provide examples of the unique end of the spectrum, inasmuch as they do not necessarily transform the fields in which they perform, a critical attribute. Yet there is something about their uncanny mastery, both the speed and depth of it, that suggests a close proximity to creativity. And the frequently cited association between very early mastery and later creativity, although not well documented, seemed plausible to me, especially in music, in which prodigies seem the rule. I labeled the prodigy an example of "idiosyncratic development," along with esoteric specialists and scholars and those who engage in quirky, seemingly useless preoccupations such as collecting thimbles, comic books, or railroad schedules (Feldman, 1980, 1986b). The prodigy seemed to represent an exceptional pretuning to an already existing body of knowledge, one that countless others had spent time and energy developing and refining. It was this remarkable intersection of person and field that was so striking about the prodigy, almost as if the two had been made for each other. I remember wondering what would be the outcome if a child was preorganized to be a chess player but born at a time or in a place where chess was not known. Unhappiness? Frustration? Schizophrenia? Or possibly invention of a proto-chess game? These kinds of thoughts were certainly on my mind as I approached the plane ride with Howard Gruber that was to bring the concept of co-incidence from dream image to interpretive construct.

My assumption, following Piaget, was that developmental changes— major reorganizations of intellectual systems—are brought about by fundamentally similar processes at all places along the continuum of universal-to-unique developmental domains. I thought that because of their rapid movement through levels of mastery in their specific domains, prodigies present an exceptional opportunity to examine transition mechanisms while they are occurring. Instead of interpreting prodigies as anomalous, strange exceptions to the rules of development, I considered them to represent variations in speed and perhaps quality of processing that are not outside the laws of development. Unfortunately, the laws of developmental change still are not well understood; so the assumption that prodigies obey such laws was not a strong claim. It was more of a heuristic, a guiding notion that might allow for extreme examples of human variation in development to be encompassed within a single integrative framework. This has been, more or less, how I have interpreted the matter of the prodigy in my writing (Feldman, 1979, 1980, 1986a).

Once I saw the implications of the co-incidence insight, it seemed as if all development—not just that of the prodigy—could be interpreted as involving the same forces along the same dimensions, with variations in strength and quality of interaction in one or more of these accounting for the differences observed in behavior and abilities. In this account, when a prodigy appears, it is because of a highly improbable but still lawful set of forces that intersect and intertwine over a sufficient period of time. To specify what the forces of such a "co-incidence calculus" might be and how to weigh and analyze them seemed a good way to comprehend both the prodigy and other forms of development.

For the prodigy, a number of complementary sets of forces have to be sustained in nearly perfect coordination for early remarkable achievement to occur. In addition to the natural capabilities of the child, a set of responsive and interested parents must be there to recognize and support the early signs of extreme talent. A domain must be introduced early enough and in an appropriate manner to engage the energy, ability, and enthusiasm of the child. Domains themselves evolve and change with time, and the skills and abilities demanded by a domain during one period may not fully duplicate those demanded during another period. When and under what conditions a child comes into contact with a domain may also make a crucial difference. So, too, does the presence of other interests, friends, and practical constraints such as lack of money.

Teachers, schools, guilds, societies, and trades are also critical to the development of the prodigy. A tradition of pedagogy and sufficient structure to move into and through a field must be present for the child and child's parents to chart their way. When dealing with a child 5 or 6 years of age, decisions about who will teach, and how long and in what manner, are vital parts of a co-incidence equation. Cultures and geographic locations vary in their receptiveness to various kinds of talent, to various domains of knowledge and skill. When a climate of receptivity exists for certain fields, such as for the visual arts in fifteenth-century Florence, for scientific fields in Vienna in the 1920s, or for high technology in Silicon Valley in the 1980s, it is because a set of cultural rewards and practices and values crystallizes uniquely in a given place at a given time (Csikszentmihalyi & Robinson, 1986; Feldman, 1986b; Simonton, 1984). Although relatively little is known about just what kinds of things must be present for such an outpouring of creative energy, clearly these aspects of talent expression must be reckoned into any explanation.

Finally, there are longer-term influences that can play vital though sometimes less obvious roles in the appearance and development of extremely early talent. The traditions that run in families are sometimes very explicit and clear, sometimes implicit or even unknown at a conscious level. When known, these traditions can have profound channeling effects, such as in the case of a family of musicians or doctors or artists. For a child born into such a family, the environment is filled with the signs of commitment made by a family and its members, and it seems as natural as any other environment. This is one reason why music prodigies have such an advantage when they come from musical families. Music is all around them from their earliest days, even before birth, and it is played and enjoyed and lived as if it is the most important and central thing that a person can do, and for such families it often is. It should also be noted that strong family traditions can be troublesome for children who have no talent or inclination for the family's preoccupation. This only serves to underline the point that it is the combining and coordinating of all the co-incidence forces that give rise to exceptional early achievement. Remove or mistime any one of these, and the changes are substantially reduced that something really extraordinary will happen with the child.

In families in which there has been a strong tradition, but in which for one reason or another it has been lost or repressed, the effect can still be powerful, but more indirect. In the case of the Menuhin family, for example, a long-standing tradition of producing religious prodigies seems to have been transformed and redirected into preparation of a secular talent: violinist Yehudi Menuhin (Feldman & Goldsmith, 1986). It seems that a centuries-old tradition of producing religious prodigies in this family was suppressed by Menuhin's parents, and the children were unaware of it. Yet, in looking at the pattern of the parents' child-rearing decisions and their organization of resources to bring Yehudi's talent to full flower, the Menuhins repeated many of the same techniques used by their ancestors, even as they re-directed their emphasis into a secular realm.

Another aspect of the prodigy phenomenon that became clearer within the framework of co-incidence is the importance of coordination of resources, a task that often falls to families of prodigies. If it is true of development in general that it requires that child, parents, environment, society, and culture be working in harmony, then the prodigy requires a much more precise and carefully timed sequence of appropriate events and experiences. Because the prodigy is unlikely to be capable of making many of the decisions about how to negotiate the early phases of preparation (if for no other reason than extreme youth), others must take on this task. This means that an essential part of prodigy preparation is a finely tuned coordinating function that marshals and deploys just the right kinds of resources and secures optimal early experiences.

Of course, some co-incidence forces simply are not controllable: The child must possess talent, and it must be very powerful; the domain must exist in a form that engages and challenges the child; chance or environmental circumstances that arise must not disrupt the process in any significant way. Only so much of the co-incidence process can be controlled or coordinated by even the most masterful manager. But the things that can be brought into synergistic relationship must be if the co-incidence process is to yield extreme expression of potential.

I am not suggesting that those who have taken responsibility for managing the coordination of co-incidence forces for talented young children are always fully aware of what they are doing. From my experience with several families of prodigies, it is clear that these parents see their role as simply facilitating and furthering the largely autonomous development of their child's talent. Were they to fully appreciate the magnitude of the problem and the complexity of the task they face, many would no doubt be discouraged from taking it on. The planning, coordination, and execution of a prodigy's preparation is a prodigious task in itself, and only with the full attention and energy of someone very determined is it likely to be successful (Feldman, 1986b).

It is an enormous challenge to raise any child, but at least the target for development is not such a narrow one for most children. Parents of most 6-year-olds want to help their children learn to write and sing, for example, but the children are not specifically driven to write novels or symphonies. Although parents often have aspirations for what they would like their offspring to become, usually it is not obvious what their talents will lead to, so that decisions about how to respond to interests, enrich, and guide have wide margins of error. Parents of prodigies seem to know how crucial their decisions could be for the successful development of their child's talent, particularly in a society like this one, in which the burden for responding to extreme talent falls heavily on the shoulders of parents.

In my research with prodigies, I noticed that most of the families showed signs of stress and were in a continuing (yet, on the whole, successful) struggle against disintegration. The co-incidence notion helped me to see why this would tend to occur in such families. Preparing a prodigy requires vast adjustments in childrearing, family life, and aspirations, as well as the willingness of at least one parent to devote virtually total attention to the prodigy's development. That these conditions should create stress seems more than reasonable; I began to wonder how the families I observed did as well as they did under the circumstances.

Seeing the development of the prodigy as a process involving several sets of factors that have to be coordinated has helped me to understand why it is important for prodigies also to be blessed with at least a modicum of general organizational/analytic ability, a healthy dose of pragmatism, and a strong sense of inner confidence (Feldman, 1986b). Because so little is explicitly understood about how the various forces of co-incidence intertwine, and even less about how to keep them in effective reciprocal relation to one another, a good deal of the burden for maintaining the trajectory of development falls directly on the prodigy.

Was the Insight Creative?

I have been trying to describe the episode of insight that was the most dramatic one in my experience. There have been many others, some of which had similar qualities of suddenness and flashing power, most of which did not. I have also elaborated on the meaning of the co-incidence insight itself. Much of what I have said about co-incidence is based on subsequent reflection and analysis of that sudden moment of comprehension. The process of interpretation continued after the insight as it had before, but it was more tightly focused. My insight in the shower transformed a dream image into a tool to work with. Through the process that I have just described, I was able to focus and further my conscious efforts to make better sense of prodigies in particular and the nature of developmental change more generally.

That the co-incidence insight was important for me is, of course, clear. Not only was its arrival marked by fireworks and fanfare, but it has remained an important part of my mental landscape ever since, to be explored over a period of more than 15 years. There is no question, then, that the carnival ride insight was significant for me and, in a real sense, personally creative. I mean that it had the effect of helping transform and reorganize my way of thinking about matters that were and are of vital importance to me. I have found the distillation of the amusement park image into a model of certain aspects of development to be a source of stimulation and satisfaction, and I believe that my thinking is clearer and better organized than it was before. In short, I believe that the experience contributed to my own knowledge and understanding of developmental processes. Of course, it remains to be seen just how much this new knowledge will add to the more formal, distilled body of knowledge we call the field of creativity research or, more broadly, the field of developmental psychology.

How did my personally powerful insight fare in the larger arena of creativity research? I can report one instance in which it seems to have made a difference. My colleague Howard Gardner also studies creativity. He has had a particular interest in co-incidence. His initial reaction to the idea was not enthusiastic. It sounded like overlearning to him, or overdetermined behavior. If the co-incidence concept posits that a large number of forces must conspire to produce prodigious behavior, Gardner reasoned, the outcome is inevitable. Since this first exposure to co-incidence, he has warmed to the idea considerably, as should be evident in his recent writing, including his chapters in this volume. Gardner came to realize, and helped me to realize as well, that it is not enough to invoke a framework that points to the complexity of factors that impinge on and control development, nor even to intone the critical function of qualities like coordination and balance, as I have done. Few would argue that development is not complex, and most would acknowledge that the main vectors of influence identified by the co-incidence model are well chosen. But the manner in which the various forces interact is of critical importance, and this is rarely, if ever, explicitly considered in the co-incidence model.

Asserting that natural talents and personal qualities are not sufficient to account for development, prodigious or not, is of value only if something new about these forces and their manner of interacting is discovered. What patterns of capability, family forces, teachers, peers, institutions, cultural features, and so forth, would lead to one outcome versus another? Is it possible to predict later instances of remarkable behavior from a thorough analysis of the forces that were present during the early years? Given the limited success of psychometric instruments to predict later creativity, might co-incidence offer a way to improve prediction? And what, if anything, does the co-incidence idea have to say about the actual process involved in doing creative work—of carrying out an effort to transform or reorganize a domain?

These well-intentioned challenges led to further reflections about and extensions of the notion of co-incidence. Howard Gardner proposed a possible distinction between a child prodigy and a creative worker. Gardner suggested that co-incidence forces for prodigies tend to work in amazing harmony and coordination, posing few major obstacles or impediments to the fulfillment of their potential, as, for example, was the case with Yehudi Menuhin (Feldman & Goldsmith, 1986). For creativity of a major sort to occur, in contrast, perhaps it is necessary that there be well-timed discordances, failures in coordination, or other instances of less than optimal timing, sequencing, and calibrating of experience. Creativity, then, would depend in part on adversity, on less than optimal circumstances, whereas prodigious achievement would thrive on sustained, amazing coordination among the critical co-incidence forces (see chapter 2).

It is true that most child prodigies do not go on to make truly creative contributions, in the sense that they do not bring about significant changes in the structure and organization of a domain. Most prodigies are able to do something very difficult in a very short time, but what they do is not unlike what others do, except that others take more time and perhaps have less talent (Feldman, 1986b).

The challenging question, of course, is what combination of qualities and forces, coordinated in what ways, over what period of time, will result in a truly creative contribution to a field of knowledge. At what point will a given combination move in a new direction if it encounters obstacles? Is it true that the old idea of creativity as a response to difficult and frustrating life circumstances has merit after all? Are prodigies an indication of well-being in their own developmental courses and in the domains in which they perform, whereas creative reorganizations and revolutions betoken a malady, plateau, or effort to forestall a dead end in a given field? These seem to be the right sorts of issues to consider when sorting out distinctions between and among different forms of giftedness and talent, and between precociousness and creative accomplishment.

When a domain is stable, it offers a valued place for the canonical performer. It is not likely in such circumstances that a person would find it necessary to transform the field. A case of this sort is provided by the violinist Yehudi Menuhin, whose experience seems to have been one long, happy, highly rewarding road from prodigy to world-class performer.

Menuhin's autobiography, written when he was about 60 years old, has an almost smug tone. In the Preface, Steiner (1977) writes:

> Luck was there from the beginning: in a brilliantly gifted family, in a childhood guarded but also stretched to fulfillment, in a series of true teachers—Persinger, Enesco, Busch—in an accord between mind and sinew which enabled the very young virtuoso to pass almost unknowing from mechanical display to the inward meaning of a score. International acclaim followed as of itself, in an era, now lost, of transatlantic liners, firelit hotel suites, and a freemasonry of musical culture that admitted no frontiers.

Contrast this with the agonizing of one who has not found that wonderful meshing of talent and domain, who has a need to express himself, but no medium through which to do so. Here are the words of the young Van Gogh, sometime preacher, not yet a painter, who felt himself to be a person with a mission:

> Prisoners in an I-don't-know-what-for horrible, horrible utterly horrible cage. . . . Such a man often doesn't know himself what he might do, but he feels instinctively; yet am I good for something, yet am I aware for some reason for existing! I know that I might be a totally different man! How then can I be useful, how can I be of service! Something is alive in me: what can it be! (Ghiselin, 1952, p. 13).

The foregoing examples credibly support Gardner's idea that a major difference between creativity and prodigiousness is the extent to which the forces of co-incidence are in positive alignment. The prodigy takes full advantage of the existing composition of a domain and, through a rapidly accelerated process, masters its expressive potential. Creative work also requires mastery of a domain, but it does not have mastery as an end point; rather, significant extension and transformation of the domain are its goals. Whereas the prodigy experiences an amazing harmony, the creative worker may deliberately attend to misalignments, gaps, and anomalies. In doing so, the creative worker may construct a different perspective on the domain, one that affords perception of its limits and provides glimpses of a fundamental reorganization. For a prodigy, forces must be in a nearly optimal and sustained coordination, whereas for significant works of creativity, some misalignments must occur. Precisely which elements must be coordinated or misaligned, for how long, and in what ways, is just the kind of question that I have been exploring (Feldman, 1986b).

The concept of co-incidence, then, may prove useful for thinking about the broad contextual factors that facilitate prodigious behavior or creativity or both. Although this seems to be true, it is also true that creativity will not be adequately explained by a broad framework alone, no matter how appropriate such a framework might be. What we need in order to explain creativity more adequately are models, theories, and frameworks at several levels of specificity. The co-incidence concept provides a general framework, and its usefulness is limited by virtue of this (as is its particular utility defined by it). The more specific qualities and characteristics of each of the major co-incidence forces (individual, society, culture, historical trends, evolutionary patterns, etc.) form more specific processes involved in solving problems and making associations, and they, too, need attention.

Juxtaposing my own experience of a blockbuster insight, for example, and the concept of co-incidence (what that insight turned out to be), it is clear that the latter only loosely and indirectly "explains" the former. That is, the framework of co-incidence is at best a rough guide to the experiences and qualities that may have led me to the moment when reorganization yielded insight. The concept of co-incidence sheds little light on why or how I might have produced such an idea, specifically, or where it might have come from. As a particular component of an overall explanation for creative work and how it is done, co-incidence is of value, but many other components are needed to complement it. In the remaining parts of this chapter I shall briefly discuss some additional possible components, and one in particular that lies at a more fine-grained level of detail.

As it happens, I also came upon this component by way of an insight process, although it was a much more recent one and was more subtle and quiet in announcing itself. I do not believe that the addition of this new component in any sense "completes" the picture of creativity, but it does represent an effort to work at another level and illustrates how efforts at one level of explanation can lead to efforts at another level.

THE TRANSFORMATIONAL IMPERATIVE

Once again there was a series of dreams, and once again there was an insight, but the experience was very different from the co-incidence experience. For the past 2 years or so I have been dreaming in a very particular way, a way different from anything I can remember from earlier dreams. Not a recurring dream, but rather a recurring tendency, it was as if each dream was intended to go a step farther into detail than the last. I do not remember the content of these dreams at all, but I know what my impression was when I would wake and think about them. What was striking about these dreams was the incredible detail that they had generated. The details in these dreams were lovingly displayed, as if my mind were telling me to pay attention and it would show me what it was able to do. Normally I have little interest in details; this certainly tends to be true of my work (as a number of critics have pointed out). I enjoy thinking at broad levels, my theoretical work tends to be about very general phenomena, and I have little memory for specific events. These detail dreams, then, were totally anomalous with respect to both my previous dreams and my normal way of thinking, so far as I am able to determine.

The other thing that was true of these dreams was that the details they produced were of things, people, and places that I had never seen. It was as if each dream was intended to be more amazing than the last in terms of the extent to which the images could not plausibly have come from my direct experience, nor even from my vicarious experience via books, television, hearsay from others, and so forth. The point these dreams seemed to be making was that they could not have come directly from my experience alone. For several months there was a tendency in these dreams to escalate in vividness, specificity, and fineness of detail. It reminded me of the technique of "zooming in" that is used in cinema and video for highlighting the importance of a particular feature of a scene, what is called "lavish" in cinema criticism; indeed, my colleague and friend Gavriel Salomon has used a contrived version of zooming in as a research tool for teaching thinking skills about attention to detail (Salomon, 1979). It felt as though I was teaching myself in my dreams to pay more attention to details—but not just particular details, for almost all details seemed equally important. I also remember something in Stephen Jay Gould's book about intelligence testing to the effect that both God and the devil lie in the details (Gould, 1981). My dreams were telling me that I had been ignoring details for too long, but why were they important?

A clue to why they were important led to the insight that has directed my work on creativity since the fall of 1985. In contrast to the amusement park insight, this one arrived quite without fanfare. It is more than 10 years newer than the co-incidence idea, and already I have all but forgotten when it happened. I simply woke up one morning or sometime during the night and knew what the point of all the details was. As with the previous experience of dreaming described here, I knew for some time that this series of dreams was important for my work, and also that it was of a different character than my usual dream experience. I had been telling my wife Lynn about the detail dreams, but otherwise was not attending to their meaning during consciousness.

For some reason, when I finally realized why the dreams were important, I did not immediately tell Lynn. I sort of let the insight sit for a while, not feeling compelled to run out and tell the world, or even Lynn. Perhaps a week or so later I told her that I knew what the detail dreams were about, but that it would take a while to explain, and so the description in words of the meaning of the detail dreaming process was again delayed. Finally, I began to feel that I might get hit by a truck and not have anyone know about my new perspective on creativity and development; so I managed to find a time to tell her what I thought the dreams were about. As was the case with co-incidence, the effort at explanation did not match the clarity of the feeling of understanding. This lack of ability to articulate what I "knew" did not surprise me this time, and I expect that it will take another 10 years before it becomes clear what the meaning of that set of experiences really is. As best I could articulate it, the important point is that the mind naturally and effortlessly is taking liberties with reality, transforming it.

An additional piece of the puzzle is an extension of something I have been thinking about and saying for several years. I have been involved with efforts to try to demonstrate that major new developmental changes not only occur but also are central features of what it means to be human. This may not sound like much of an issue, because people by and large assume that development of this sort does occur. There are powerful voices, however, that claim otherwise, and these voices have of late been more and more influential in the scholarly field. I am referring to the neonativist views of Noam Chomsky, Jerry Fodor, and others who claim that qualitative changes in thinking not only do not occur but also are in principle impossible (Chomsky, 1980; Fodor, 1983). Their view traces back to Aristotle, who claimed that everything must come from something else and that therefore there is fundamentally nothing new. It also assumes an encoding of reality as its basic process (Campbell & Bickhard, 1986). The argument would apply to creativity, of course, as it does to development in general.

If nothing really new is possible, then development itself is impossible, and it follows that creativity is impossible as well. These sorts of arguments, along with some ideas about genetic determinism, have led to an increasing move in the field in the direction of innatism, even predeterminism, that places the potential for everything that a person will ever do as existing at the beginning of life. The argument is clear, it is parsimonious, it is compelling, and it helped Chomsky and his followers shine in the only direct encounter to occur between them and Piaget (Piattelli-Palmarini, 1980).

I have been disturbed by the position taken by neonativists for a number of years and have even written a bit about what form an alternative view might take (Feldman, 1983, 1986a). I also have been encouraged to find that I am not the only one who believes that a radically nativist explanation for change based on encodingism is unacceptable (Bickhard, 1979, 1980; Campbell & Bickhard, 1986). Long before I began dreaming my detail dreams, then, I was consciously working on a solution to the paradox of development, the claim that something new can indeed be constructed even though all the elements of that new thing are not present in the potentials of the physical stuff of the human organism. I even went so far as to assert that there should be a field of inquiry called "developmental science" to balance and contrast with the "cognitive science" that has become such a prominent force in the academic field (Feldman, 1983, 1986a; see Pea & Kurland, 1984, for a complementary view).

As was the case with the co-incidence insight, a series of parallel efforts toward solution of a problem was going on, one set consciously directed toward a solution through direct application, the other set through less conscious, indirectly applied processes that manifested themselves in certain kinds of dreams, of whose purpose I became increasingly aware. At a certain point it seems that the two lines of attack were brought into contact with each other through reflection on a dream or set of dreams, and by my efforts at interpretation of these dreams that I have described as examples of insight.

This experience about how insight works does seem to run counter to David Perkin's recent observations of "loud thinking" by artists, poets, and other workers who reported their thoughts "on line," as it were (Perkins, 1981, 1986). In Perkin's work, insight is seen as relatively mundane and undifferentiated from more typical processing and thinking. For better or worse, however, it is an inescapable conclusion that, in my own case at least, sustained semiconscious and perhaps unconscious processes were applied to problems in parallel with, and eventually in concert with, conscious processes. And the process was not at all mundane or typical. This dual sort of effort took place over a period of years, because in both cases reported here at least a 2-year period elapsed between the earliest dream of a particular type and the insight that, in each case, ended that series. The detail dreams, too, ceased immediately on my realization of what they were trying to "teach" me. And what was that? What was I trying to teach myself?

Essentially, the dreams were showing me that my mind was producing things that I had never seen or heard or been exposed to in any direct way. My mind was quite spontaneously *making new things*. That these new things may have been produced in part out of already existing things does not diminish the fact that by the hundreds and thousands, my mind was showing me that it had the ability to produce a virtual torrent of small transformations and to produce them in coherent, organized ways. I was at times transforming things so rapidly and fluidly that it seemed as if my mind were designed to do nothing else.

I know as well as anyone that in the waking state my mind is not up to these antics. Even daydreaming and preconscious activity touch reality quite actively. But when I thought about the dreams, the unbelievable dreams of detail, I knew that their meaning must be to prove that the mind (or at least my mind) works in at least two complementary ways, one trying to sort, categorize, and otherwise keep things the same, the other taking the most extravagant liberties with things, sometimes seemingly just for the hell of it.

CREATIVITY: A THREE-PHASE MODEL

There is, of course, nothing really new in the fact that the mind does fantastic things. Dreams have been subjects of intense investigation for decades and are known to play a large role in psychological functioning. It is even known that dreams have sometimes been important for creativity, as in the case of Kekulé's snake turning on itself as the image for the benzene ring, or Picasso's description of painting as "successive crystallizations of the dream" (Ghiselin, 1952; Hartmann, 1984). What seems new is to link this large body of evidence to a more general point of view about mind—that it is capable of producing astoundingly new images, thoughts, and ideas based only most remotely on anything that came in from outside, and that these transformations are purposeful and productive. Indeed, they are part of a larger process of overall coordination and direction in the use of mind.

It seems then that there are at least three essential aspects to creativity. The first I have just described as a natural tendency of the mind to take liberties with what is real, mostly in nonconscious ways. These transformations, nonetheless, have the possibility of being or becoming conscious. Indeed, the manners and kinds of transformations produced may be directed in some way by the conscious purposes of the individual, as I had discovered myself through my two series of dream episodes. The second aspect is the conscious desire to make a positive change in something real, to, in effect, change the external world to make it conform more fully to one's wishes. I mean this not necessarily in any lofty or cosmic sense. The part of the real world that one wishes to change can be modest and mundane; there is always room for a better mousetrap. The claim here is that it is a natural part of being human to want to change the world, to experience this wish consciously, and to set about using whatever resources are available to do so. These resources include the capability to guide internal transformation and harness its productions to a conscious goal of change. To do so may not be easy or straightforward (as was the case with my sets of "harnessed" dreams), but it can be done. This conclusion was not reached through an insight process, but seemed to follow from the other parts of the system.

Finally, the third aspect of the process concerns the results of previous efforts by other individuals labeled at changing the world or their environments. I have labeled this aspect "the crafted world." The artifacts of creative work are available to the person who desires to make further changes in the world. These previous efforts, as represented in a culture's products, models, technologies, and so forth, are of enormous value to the aspiring creator for at least two reasons: They illustrate that it is possible to make a difference and have that difference incorporated into the environment, and they make it possible to reduce the "mental distance" one has to go to be able to make a meaningful change. This is at least partially what Newton meant when he exclaimed that he stood on the shoulders of giants.

I shall now try to show how what I have just discussed makes Aristotle's dictum that everything must come from something else true but irrelevant to my point. The Aristotelian tradition, which has seen its fullest expression in Western rationalism, has to do with the part of mind that tries to keep things the same, that gives us something to hang on to, that provides for continuity of experience and a stable sense of reality. The other side of mind aims to continuously change and transform, to show that constructing a stable reality is a device for not going insane, a way to keep the forces of transformation from holding sway. Indeed, conscious versus unconscious thought may have been an evolutionary adaptation for keeping these two functions—transformation and categorization—from destroying each other. This interplay becomes productive and central in the process of making something both new and useful.

Why New Ideas Really Do Occur

I have called the presumably universal tendency to produce new things "the transformational imperative." I call it this because I want to stress the deep and uniquely human quality that I believe operates when a conscious effort is made to change the world. I think that this tendency is as fundamental a quality of cognition as any. It has even led me to propose that Piaget's two most important change processes are not sufficient to account for new ideas. Piaget proposed that there are two complementary processes, assimilation and accommodation, that account for all change in thought structures. Assimilation refers to the tendency to keep reality just as it is, to take in information and put it into existing ways of organizing experience, even if that information must be distorted in the process. On the other hand, accommodation represents the tendency to make adjustments in how reality is interpreted when it becomes impossible to live with the distortions that assimilation demands. The interplay of these two modes of responding to experience accounts for all developmental change, according to Piaget (1971, 1972/1981).

One well-known problem with Piaget's account is that it does not deal well with novelty, with producing really new restructurings of experience. Piaget was well aware of this problem and tried mightily to overcome it (Piaget, 1971, 1972/1981, 1975). Piaget's final attempt to solve the novelty problem was both formal and rational. He claimed that a process called "reflective abstraction" (also sometimes called reflexive abstraction) might be able to explain how genuinely novel ideas could be formed. He was aware that his argument with the nativists hangs on being able to produce a plausible account of novelty (i.e., of changes that represent true advances in thought and that are constructed by the individual mind). Rather than consider the possibility of a nonrational, nonreflective ingredient of the process of novelty production, Piaget persisted in trying to find a conscious, rational, and directed solution to the problem. Of course, there is a conscious, directed aspect to the process, but there is also more. As usual, Piaget was on the right track and laid the groundwork for further progress.

This was not the only difficulty Piaget faced as he worked on the novelty problem (some of the other problems are discussed in Feldman, 1980), but it may have been the most devastating. In order to solve the novelty problem, Piaget would have had to look to an aspect of mind he had self-consciously excluded from his framework for more than 50 years. Little wonder that he was unable to entertain the idea of coordinated efforts between two polar casts of mind in explaining the construction of novelties.

The fact of the matter is that the fruits of the dream or any other transformation process are of little use unless they eventually become connected with the rational, conscious work of the mind aiming to solve a problem or render something more pleasing. As easily as the less conscious mind is able to transform, it seems to have little idea of why it is doing so or how to use its fantastic possibilities. This job is directed by the aspects of mind that are in contact with the world of real things, real people, and real problems. It seems that only when the whole of mind is somehow harnessed to complementary purposes is it likely that something both new and useful will be constructed. And part of what is available is outside the mind altogether. Interestingly, this is more or less what Brewster Ghiselin, a student of creativity, wrote more than 30 years ago:

New life comes always from outside our world, as we commonly conceive our world. This is the reason why, in order to invent, one must yield to the indeterminate within him, or, more precisely to certain ill-defined impulses which seem to be of the very texture of the ungoverned fullness which John Livingston Lowes calls "the surging chaos of the unexpressed." Chaos and disorder are perhaps the wrong terms for that indeterminate fullness and activity of the inner life. For it is organic, dynamic, full of tension and tendency. What is absent from it, except in the decisive act of creation, is determination, fixity, and commitment to one resolution or another of the whole complex of its tensions. (Ghiselin, 1952, p. 13)

Ghiselin had his finger on part of the transformational imperative, but did not extend his description to include use of the external world as a critical source of inspiration for creativity. Ironically, some of Piaget's most interesting experiments were with external physical reality of just the sort that I am referring to. He asked children to imagine what a piece of wire would look like when it was bent in various positions, or he asked how a set of two blocks, one on top of the other, would change in appearance if one block was moved a bit off center. What Piaget found was that the ability to mentally represent movement (i.e., physical transformation) was one of the last to be achieved in children. As late as 8 or 9 years, children were unable to carry out even simple mental transformations and make accurate predictions based on an understanding of physical properties in transformation. It was as if the children were locked into the appearance of the object and unable to make it change in state through mental manipulation (Piaget, 1969).

Piaget's ingenious experiments show, I believe, that the conscious rational mind does not deal easily with transformation, but is nonetheless able to learn about it through experience with changed and changing reality. It is as if the conscious mind has been constructed to create a constant world, to behave as if things are not changing, but static, and to go about its business with this purpose as a central goal. Only reluctantly does the conscious mind entertain transformation.

When Piaget's experimental results with physical transformation are compared with dream states, which are suffused with transformations, movements, extrapolations, extrusions, and all manner of wild imaginings, it is a wonder that the conclusion that there are really two quite distinct simultaneously active functions did not occur to Piaget as the key to the novelty problem. As extreme as one way of organizing experience is, the other tends toward the opposite extreme. When both are put in the service of a goal that calls on the best efforts of the full range of waking and dream states, conscious and unconscious processes, conserving and transformational capabilities, a genuinely new idea or work or solution may be constructed. This is a long way from Piaget's idea of reflective abstraction. It is more like reciprocal exchange: on the one hand, an effort to abstract and categorize and organize, to put things in their place; on the other hand, to stir up and change and expand.

Piaget was close to the mark, but he stopped a bit short. He was right to insist that internal novel thoughts are constructed by individuals and that they are achieved through a process of abstraction. Reflection of the sort Piaget described is part of the process, but is limited to conscious effort and directed analysis, necessary but not sufficient for something new to be made. When something new occurs, it is because the fruits of the transformational imperative are made available to the reflective rational mind, and also, in some ways, vice versa. Assimilation and accommodation are useful only if they have the right material to work on, and the transformational imperative helps take care of that. Rather than two invariant functions, assimilation and accommodation, we must propose that there are three: assimilation, accommodation, and transformation. Because the latter, transformation, seems so alien to the rational conscious mind, as Piaget's own experiments showed, Piaget did not see that it is as involved in changes in thinking as the other two functions, but in a different way. The transformational imperative may also be mediated by Vygotsky's "inner speech" (Vygotsky, 1934/1962), as it seems to have qualities of both rational and irrational thought. In any case, the coordinated interplay of the powerful operations that Piaget studied and the fluid productions that I dreamed seems central to the construction of novelty.

Creativity: The Construction and Appreciation of Crafted Transformations

Having just proposed to add a third invariant function, transformation, to the broad process of developmental change that Piaget proposed, we may be in range of specifying a mechanism that can account for qualitative change, for novelty. Because the mind is clearly able to construct ideas and images that are not directly part of its experience, it need not be limited to what is represented, copied, perceived, or taught of the world as it exists. In fact, as I have just tried to illustrate, part of the mind seems to do almost nothing but transform. Were it not for the rational, orderly, logical, largely conscious function to balance it, experience would have no stability at all. Yet the transformational imperative is not itself enough to explain development and creativity, to refute the antidevelopmental position of Chomsky and Fodor. It still could be possible that all that is happening in the mind when it "transforms" is to make modifications and combinations based on previous experience, on representation, not really constructing anything new. This would be particularly true if, as the neonativists assert, the basic rules of thought are present, and all that happens is to build even more complex and varied combinations of those rules. This is essentially the argument made by Chomsky for the "creative" feature of language. No two sentences need be quite the same; yet all sentences follow the same deep rules of grammar.

What is needed to complete the mechanism of creativity (or at least to have a sketch of what it might be like) is the additional component I have called the crafted world. It was expressed in nascent form in my work *Beyond Universals in Cognitive Development* (Feldman, 1980) in a chapter with Lynn T. Goldsmith on novelties, where we likened the existence of humanly crafted parts of the environment to Darwin's observations of the unbelievable diversity of living things:

> Although we have taken no voyage comparable to Darwin's it occurred to us that the variety of human inventions seems in its own way as overwhelming and inexplicable as the infinite variety of life forms that Darwin saw. (Feldman, 1980, p. 36).

At that time I was not able to say what kind of process might produce human inventions, only to marvel at their variety and pervasiveness. This was true as well of Darwin when he was unable to propose a plausible mechanism for producing variation, a mechanism later identified as genetic recombination (Gruber, 1981).

The full impact of my insight about transformation as an inherent part of human thought—a functional invariant in Piaget's terms—was to come when I combined the two ideas that I have just summarized—the transformational imperative and the existence of innumerable *products* of human invention, perceived and attributed to the efforts of other human beings. I was able at last to glimpse a plausible process that could account for the construction of genuinely new ideas and at the same time refute the antidevelopmental claims of neonativists and other radical, biological determinist types.

The essential point is that thinkers since at least Plato's time have either put the source of creativity outside the individual altogether (coming from the gods or some other unknown place) or put it entirely inside the individual, having no other source of inspiration than the individual's own experience in the use of a developed craft. Piaget went a long way toward breaking this logjam when he claimed that development is not a matter of one source or the other, outside or inside, but must consist of both sorts of forces. Piaget's central epistemological assumption was that knowledge is constructed through the individual's inherent tendencies to know, in confrontation with the inherent properties of the physical world to be known. With this formulation, he had the components needed to show how novelty occurs, except for two: the most internal and the most external aspects of the process. He had the right idea, that it took individuals reflecting on their own experience from transactions with the world of objects and people in order to gain new knowledge (Campbell & Bickhard, 1986). What he missed were the amazing possibilities of the non-conscious, nonrational, expressive side of mind and also the myriad examples of such tendencies expressed in ideas, artifacts, symbol systems, technologies, artforms, and the like, creating an environment that is itself constantly changed through the efforts of purposeful human beings (Gruber, 1981).

To put the matter another way, consider the insight of Aristotle that everything comes from something else. The conclusion that we have incorrectly tended to make from that insight is that nothing new is ever constructed. Aristotle said:

> And so, as . . . a thing is not said to be that from which it comes, here the statue is not said to be wood but is said by a verbal change to be wooden, not brass but brazen, not gold but golden, and the house is said to be not bricks but bricken (though we should not say without qualification, if we looked at the matter carefully, even that a statue is produced from wood or a house from bricks, because coming to be implies change in that from which a thing comes to be, and not permanence). (Rothenberg & Hausman, 1976, p. 35)

Aristotle recognized change, but did not seem to notice that the particular *kinds* of changes described, as in this passage, are a consequence of human effort. Or, to be more accurate, he noticed but did not give special status to changes brought about by "thought" or "art." In fact, however, it is a crucial distinction to make between changes that are "natural" and changes that are the result of human effort.

Plato and Aristotle both placed the source of change outside the individual, and in doing so they set the course of Western thought on creativity for more than 2,000 years. Kant put the source of change inside the individual, and only there. It was Piaget who revolutionized thought by placing the source of change in the process itself, a crucial and irreversible change in the history of ideas. Piaget, the quintessential rationalist, ironically opened the door for a dynamic, process-oriented explanation of development that begins to capture the fluid, changing, transformational tendencies of the human mind; in doing so, he made possible an explanation of novelty, the key to creativity.

How, then, is it possible for truly new things to be constructed? It is possible because everything need not come from outside, nor from inside. Things are available in the man-made or crafted environment to provide examples of novel ideas brought to fruition, expressed in real form, by other human beings. They show that it is possible to change the world and make things that are there to be further modified by others. It must, of course, be assumed that something like the transformational imperative exists, that individuals acted on it in the past, and that they externalized their ideas into products. Otherwise, the availability of products of human effort would not necessarily be critical to further change.

The extent to which one might act on a tendency to transform further the crafted world can range from idle "tinkering around" to focused, sustained, systematic, organized, long-term, sophisticated efforts to transform entire fields or bodies of knowledge or cultures. Perhaps the first human to take a stick and make marks in the dirt was exhibiting a playful tendency to bring transformational possibilities to concrete external expression, with eventual profound consequences for all civilization. Examples of the latter, more deliberate sort include all the great works of Darwin, Freud, Einstein, and Piaget. Transformational tendencies that have taken concrete expression and irreversibly changed the human environment include spiritual, cultural, political, and economic revolutions. And, yes, even the invention of nuclear weapons must be included, for few transformations have had such a profound set of consequences; the context within which every individual uses the transformational imperative has been irreversibly altered by the nuclear threat.

To account for human creativity, then, it is not necessary to assume that something comes from nothing. Something can come in part from the outcomes of innumerable previous efforts at transformation—available, waiting, and also visibly changing the environment. Each one of these products is for a time a survivor of cultural selection pressures somewhat like those of Darwin's "survival of the fittest" (Feldman, 1980). Furthermore, the products of transformational tendencies need not just lie there, waiting for an interested individual to be intrigued with them. Human beings can actively transmit the most important transformations to others, and in doing so they introduce members of the group to the most powerful resources available in their culture. Clearly, such capabilities as speech, writing, reading, counting, and calculating are highly distilled products of many centuries of efforts at expressive transformational possibilities by countless individuals, some of whom were no doubt just tinkering around. These resources provide some of the tools for achieving new products and examples of new products to build on.

Real development, significant internal reorganization that is not preordained, can thus be helped to occur through transactions among individuals who are trying to express their thoughts and ideas and who have done so by changing their cultural world. By being given or taught or confronted with the work of others, the actual material that a person is working with can be added to and enhanced. Therefore, not only is there something new under the sun, there are countless new things being made all the time, each bringing with it the possibility of adding features to the manmade, crafted environment and possibly becoming part of the perceived environment of others.

Development is real even if it is not altogether internally generated. Creativity is therefore also real, a special form of development that yields a product that is new and valuable not only to an individual but also to a field. Spontaneous and directed transformations are the processes that make possible both development and creativity. Plato, Aristotle, Kant, Piaget, and even Chomsky have all contributed to this conclusion, as have countless others. Creativity, therefore, is at once the most individual and the most social developmental process of all, because it depends directly on the efforts of others to provide the material that makes possible a new idea.

CONCLUSION

In this chapter I have described two insight experiences, one that occurred more than 15 years ago, another much more recent. Each of these experiences has turned out to reflect an aspect of the creative process as well as to provide a source of information about how to form a plausible account of significant acts of creativity. The earlier insight was a blockbuster type, arriving with dazzling suddenness and intensity. The second was the opposite, appearing quietly and with no fanfare. They have been equally important. Each insight was also built over several years, with hints about its meaning in a series of recurring dreams. It was clear long before the meaning of the dreams was discovered that they would shed important light on my work. In the first instance, it was not creativity per se that was the focus of the insight; in the second it was. In both cases, however, the consequences have been profound and continue to be influential.

I have tried to make two points. The first is to show how large-scale insight is a valuable process for studying creativity and for helping to unravel its mysteries. The second is that insight, or, more broadly, illumination, occurs through the loosely directed reciprocal interplay of conscious and less efforts to understand or solve a problem and to produce a work that changes the world, however slightly. The impetus to express a new idea in a form that can be understood and used by others leads to the directed use of both rational and nonrational mental processes for construction of cultural artifacts, which in turn are a unique human environment that may stimulate, nurture, and catalyze efforts at transforming a part of the culture. These new artifacts make the environment different from what it was, an awareness of which is a critical and unique quality of human experience.

Taking the two points together, I have come to the conclusion that genuine, qualitative novel thoughts and ideas do occur. It is possible to make something new under the sun that is not directly a function of the biological potential of the individual. In fact, when one looks around at the results of humanity's efforts to transform the world, it is stunning to reflect on how much of our reality consists of a continuously emerging set of humanly crafted new things. Anyone who argues against development in the sense of true constructed novelty must ignore these manifest fruits of human labor and expression to an amazing degree.

Although I must caution that most of what I have learned is based on my own experience, and is also highly speculative, I know that I did not contrive the typewriter I am using, the chair I am sitting on, or the light that I use to illuminate my office, nor, for that matter, the numerous other things that are being changed in my culture even as I write. To doubt creativity under such circumstances is simply beyond my comprehension.

NOTE

1. It was somewhat later that I changed the name of creative developmental transitions to "unique" (Figure 5).

REFERENCES

Bickhard, M. H. (1979). On necessary and specific capabilities in evolution and development. *Human Development*, 22, 217–224.

Bickhard, M. H. (1980). A model of developmental and psychological processes. *Genetic Psychology Monographs*, 102, 61–116.

Brandt, R. S. (1986, May). On creativity and thinking skills: A conversation with David Perkins. *Educational Leadership*, pp. 12–18.

Campbell, R. L., & Bickhard, M. H. (1986). *Knowing levels and developmental stages*. Basel: Karger.

Cavalli-Sforza, L. L., Feldman, M. W., Chen, K. H., & Dornbusch, S. M. (1982). Theory and observation in cultural transmission. *Science*, 218, 19–27.

Chomsky, N. (1980). On cognitive structures and their development. In M. Piattelli-Palmarini (Ed.), *Language and learning: The debate between Jean Piaget and Noam Chomsky* (pp. 35–54). Cambridge, MA: Harvard University Press.

Csikszentmihalyi, M., & Robinson, R. E. (1986). Culture, time, and the development of talent. In R. Sternberg & J. E. Davidson (Eds.), *Conceptions of
giftedness* (pp. 264–284). Cambridge University Press.

Feldman, D. H. (1974). Universal to unique: A developmental view of creativity
and education. In S. Rosner & L. Abt (Eds.), *Essays in creativity* (pp. 45–
85). Croton-on-Hudson, NY: North River Press.

Feldman, D. H. (1975). Doing for creativity research what evolution did for
biology: A review of Gruber and Barnett's *Darwin on man. Phi Delta
Kappan*, 57, 56–57.

Feldman, D. H. (1979). The mysterious case of extreme giftedness. In H. Passow
(Ed.), *The gifted and the talented. Yearbook of the National Society for
the Study of Education* (pp. 335–351). University of Chicago Press.

Feldman, D. H. (1980). *Beyond universals in cognitive development.* Norwood,
NJ: Ablex.

Feldman, D. H. (1981). Beyond universals: Toward a developmental psychology
of education. *Educational Researcher*, 10, 21–31.

Feldman, D. H. (1983). Developmental psychology and art education. *Art Education*, 36, 19–21.

Feldman, D. H. (1986a). How development works. In I. Levin (Ed.), *Stage and
structure: Reopening the debate* (pp. 284–306). Norwood, NJ: Ablex.

Feldman, D. H. (1986b). *Nature's gambit: Child prodigies and the development of
human potential.* New York: Basic Books.

Feldman, D. H., & Goldsmith, L. T. (1986). Transgenerational influences on the
development of early prodigious behavior: A case study approach. In W.
Fowler (Ed.), *Early experience and competence development* (pp. 67–
85). San Francisco: Jossey-Bass.

Feldman, D. H., Marrinan, B. M., & Hartfeldt, S. D. (1972). Transformational
power as a possible index of creativity. *Psychological Reports*, 30, 335–
338.

Fodor, J. (1983). *The modularity of mind.* Cambridge, MA: MIT Press.

Ghiselen, B. (1952). *The creative process.* New York: Mentor.

Gould, S. J. (1981). *Mismeasure of man.* New York: Norton.

Gruber, H. (1981). *Darwin on man: A psychological study of scientific creativity*
(2nd ed.). University of Chicago Press.

Hartmann, E. (1984). *The nightmare: The psychology and biology of terrifying
dreams.* New York: Basic Books.

Hofstadter, D. R. (1985a). On the seeming paradox of mechanizing creativity. In
D. R. Hofstadter (Ed.), *Metamagical themas* (pp. 526–546). New York:
Basic Books.

Hofstadter, D. R. (1985b). Variations on a theme as the crux of creativity. In D. R.
Hofstadter (Ed.), *Metamagical themas* (pp. 232–259). New York: Basic
Books.

Menuhin, Y. (1967). *Unfinished journey.* New York: Knopf.

Pea, R., & Kurland, D. M. (1984). On the cognitive effects of learning computer programming. *New Ideas in Psychology*, 2, 137–168.

Perkins, D. (1981). *The mind's best work*. Cambridge, MA: Harvard University Press.

Perkins, D. (1986, May). Thinking frames. *Educational Leadership*, pp. 4–10.

Piaget, J. (1969). *The mechanisms of perception*. New York: Basic Books.

Piaget, J. (1971). The theory of stages in cognitive development. In D. R. Green, M. P. Ford, & G. B. Flamer (Eds.), *Measurement and Piaget* (pp. 1–11). New York: McGraw-Hill.

Piaget, J. (1975). *The development of thought: Equilibration of cognitive structures*. New York: Viking Press.

Piaget, J. (1981). Creativity. In J. M. Gallagher & D. K. Reid (Eds.), *The learning theory of Piaget and Inhelder*. Monterey, CA: Brooks-Cole. (Original work published 1972).

Piattelli-Palmarini, M. (Ed.), (1980). *Language and learning: The debate between Jean Piaget and Noam Chomsky*. Cambridge, MA: Harvard University Press.

Rothenberg, A., & Hausman, C. R. (Eds.). (1976). *The creativity question*. Durham, NC: Duke University Press.

Salomon, G. (1979). *Interaction of media, cognition, and learning*. San Francisco: Jossey-Bass.

Shrady, M. (1972). *Moments of insight*. New York: Harper & Row.

Simonton, D. K. (1984). *Genius, creativity and leadership: Historiometric inquiries*. Cambridge, MA: Harvard University Press.

Steiner, G. (1977). Foreword. In Y. Menuhin, *Unfinished journey*. New York: Knopf.

Sternberg, R. J. (1986). A triarchic theory of intellectual giftedness. In R. J. Sternberg & J. Davidson (Eds.), *Conceptions of giftedness*. Cambridge University Press.

Vygotsky, L. (1962). *Thought and language*. Cambridge, MA: MIT Press. (Original work published 1934).

6

The Domain of Creativity

Mihaly Csikszentmihalyi

In this chapter I will take stock of what I have learned about creativity in the past quarter century. I will describe how I started with an interest in the personality traits and cognitive processes of creative people, and how as time went on I became convinced that the epistemological grounds of such a quest were largely unsound. The more I tried to say that "creative people are such and such" or "creative people do this and that," the less sure I became about what creativity itself consisted of and how we could even begin to figure out what it was.

Finally, I came to the conclusion that in order to understand creativity one must enlarge the conception of what the process is, moving from an exclusive focus on the individual to a systemic perspective that includes the social and cultural context in which the "creative" person operates. Being trained as a psychologist, I came to this conclusion reluctantly; but now I am convinced that it is not possible to even think about creativity, let alone measure it, without taking into account the parameters of the cultural symbol system (or domain) in which the creative activity takes place, and the social roles and norms (or field) that regulate the given creative activity. But before exploring this expansion of the notion of creativity, I shall briefly describe the chain of studies that led up to it.

PERSONALITY, MOTIVATION, AND THE DISCOVERY OF NEW PROBLEMS

My involvement in the domain of creativity research started in 1963, as a graduate student working with Professor J. W. Getzels at the University of Chicago. We had just begun what was to be a longitudinal study of several hundred artists in their early twenties, hoping to understand why some of them produced work that in the course of time would be judged creative while others did not. My doctoral thesis focused on a subset of fine art students, describing in detail the cognitive and behavioral patterns used by art students whose work was rated as original and contrasting them with the patterns employed by students whose work artists and critics rated as lacking originality (Csikszentmihalyi, 1965).

The results of these studies, especially those concerning personality traits and cognitive processes, were widely reported at the time Csikszentmihalyi & Getzels, 1970, 1973; Getzels & Csikszentmihalyi, 1966, 1967, 1968a, 1969, 1975). A volume titled *The Creative Vision* provided an integrative summary of these findings and presented some of the results of the first follow-up of the students a few years after they had graduated from art school (Getzels & Csikszentmihalyi, 1976). The second follow-up was conducted 18 years after the initial study. At this point, some of the former art students were being hailed as creative artists and their work was being exhibited in first-rate museums, while others had settled in routine jobs and entirely given up creative ambitions. Some of the results of this phase were reported in Csikszentmihalyi, Getzels, and Kahn (1984), Kahn, Zimmerman, Csikszentmihalyi, and Getzels (1986), and Csikszentmihalyi and Getzels (1988).

It is difficult to summarize the wealth of data collected in these investigations. Here I will focus on three main issues that have stood the test of time and that I think are important in explaining the phenomenon of creativity. They concern three aspects of the person, corresponding to the three classical dimensions of psychological functioning described by Hilgard (1980): emotion, cognition, and conation. They are the personality and value system, the ability to discover and formulate new problems, and the intensity of interest and motivation in the chosen domain.

Personality and Values

Giorgio Vasari in the sixteenth century and Cesare Lombroso in the nineteenth century were fascinated with the relationship between genius and personality. One of the first empirical studies of creative people, conducted by Anne Roe (1946, 1952) over forty years ago, investigated the personality traits of creative scientists and creative artists. Our studies very clearly substantiated previous findings to the effect that strong personality and value differences characterize young people who embark on a creative career, and further differentiate those who succeed in it (Csikszentmihalyi & Getzels, 1973; Getzels & Csikszentmihalyi, 1968a, 1968b, 1976).

For example, in terms of values, young art students held social and economic values in much lower esteem and endorsed aesthetic values much more than average college students; the more original art students' values were even more extreme, in the same direction, than the less original art students', and the successful artists' early values were still more extreme. In other words, each successive step toward becoming a creative artist coincides with further reductions in the regard in which money and status are held and an increasing regard for the value of the domain, for the activity itself, which in our case was art.

In terms of personality, the cluster familiar to other investigators in the field was confirmed (e.g., Albert & Runco, 1986; Cross, Cattell, & Butcher, 1967; MacKinnon, 1964). Original art students tended to be sensitive, open to experiences and impulses, self-sufficient, uninterested in social norms and social acceptance (Csikszentmihalyi & Getzels, 1973; Getzels & Csik-szentmihalyi, 1968a, 1968b, 1976). Over the years, the trait that most consistently differentiated the successful artist from those who gave up a creative career has been the trait of cyclothymia, or a cold and aloof disposition (Csikszentmihalyi, Getzels, & Kahn, 1984).

Of course, our studies did not address creativity in the abstract, so to speak, but looked at creativity embedded in a specific domain—namely, the domain of art. Thus it is difficult to know whether what we found out about values and personality tells us something about creative *artists*, or about *creative* artists. Perhaps being cold and aloof, for example, would not be an important trait for a creative scientist but only for a creative artist. To a certain extent we were reassured that several of our findings replicated those of researchers who had been studying creativity in other domains, such as the physical and biological sciences, engineering, or architecture (e.g., Cattell & Drevdahl, 1955; MacKinnon, 1964).

On the other hand I was getting less and less sure that it made sense to talk about creativity as a process independent of domains. There were indications in our studies that different personality traits were more salient in being judged a creative art student than in being judged a creative artist. In art school, a student whose personality resembled that of the introverted, tortured, intrinsically motivated stereotype of the artist was viewed as very original and creative by teachers. But when students left school, if they lacked the extroversion and street smarts that attracted the attention of critics, gallery owners, and media, they tended to disappear from the art scene, never to be heard of again. If personality traits played such a different role in the recognition of creativity within the same domain, in a time span of only a few years, how different an effect must they have in the same point in time? We shall see later how these questions may eventually be resolved. Now let us return to what our results suggested about the cognitive processes involved in artistic creativity.

Discovery and Problem Finding

Just as previous researchers, we also failed to find any relationship between traditional measures of intelligence and criteria of creative accomplishment, either in art school or afterward. However, the discovered problem-finding approach, developed theoretically by Getzels (1964) and operationalized by Csikszentmihalyi (1965), showed strong empirical relationships with original performance in art school (Csikszentmihalyi & Getzels, 1970, 1971; Getzels & Csikszentmihalyi, 1976) and afterward with success as a fine artist (Csikszentmihalyi & Getzels, 1988; Csikszentmihalyi, Getzels, & Kahn, 1984; Getzels & Csikszentmihalyi, 1976).

Many creative individuals have pointed out that in their work the formulation of a problem is more important than its solution and that real advances in science and in art tend to come when new questions are asked or old problems are viewed from a new angle (e.g., Einstein & Infeld, 1938, p. 92). Yet when measuring creative thinking processes, psychologists usually rely on problem solution, rather than problem formulation, as an index of creativity. Even "divergent" thinking tests ask subjects to solve a task defined by the experimenter. They thus fail to deal with one of the most interesting characteristics of the creative process—namely, the person's ability to define the nature of the problem.

It was in part to fill this conceptual and methodological gap that Getzels (1964) developed his model of problem finding. The model describes intellectual activity as taking place on a continuum between two poles: presented problems at one end and discovered problems at the other. A presented problem is one that is clearly formulated, has an accepted method of solution, and has a generally agreed-upon solution. A puzzle, for example, presents the problem of assembling the pieces so as to form a picture; how to do it and when the task is completed are clear to everyone. A person confronted by a presented problem needs only to apply the accepted methods until the desired solution is achieved.

At the other end of the continuum is a discovered problem. Here instead of a clearly formulated task there is only vague unease and dimly felt emotional or intellectual tension. Because the problem itself has yet to be defined, there cannot be an agreed-upon method for resolving the tension. For the same reason, one cannot even imagine in advance what a "solution" might be. Great creative breakthroughs, the achievements of a Newton, a Freud, a Darwin, or an Einstein, involve this kind of cognitive approach. Similarly, great works of art, such as da Vinci's Mona Lisa or Beethoven's Seventh Symphony are creative because they could not have been predicted from knowledge of previous works in their respective domains—they were solutions to "discovered" problems.

In our studies, we designed a naturalistic experiment to measure the discovery orientation of artists. It consisted in leading each of a group of 31 male art students, one at a time, into a studio where there were two tables. A few dozen visually interesting objects were arranged on one table; on the other, drawing papers and dry media (pencils, charcoals, and pastels) were provided. After he entered the studio, the student was asked to look at the display of objects, select the ones he wanted to draw, and then start drawing at the other table. The instructions stressed the fact that once the drawing started the student could do what he wanted—he could ignore the objects and do an entirely different or abstract drawing. The task was finished when the student felt that he had produced a drawing he liked. In practice the length of the drawing session lasted from 15 minutes to almost five hours. Photographs of the evolving drawing were taken at three minute intervals. After the task was completed, each student was asked in an interview to reconstruct the thoughts he had been aware of during the drawing process.

Even this naturalistic experiment had some of the characteristics of a "presented" problem. The students were confronted with a task structured by us, and we provided them with the elements of the problem. But the essential characteristics of a "discovered" problem were also present. First of all, the students were asked to draw something, but they were free to choose *what* to draw. Therefore, either they could formulate the problem in a presented way, by resorting to a tried-and-true still-life arrangement, or they could try to formulate a discovered problem, by finding a uniquely meaningful reason for drawing what they wanted to draw. Second, they had to decide *how to go about* doing the drawing. Here again, they could follow a presented solution procedure by applying an accepted rendering technique to the task they had defined, or they could experiment with various media, or with different techniques, until they found the best fit between ends and means. And, finally, they had to decide *when to call the problem solved*. For those who went about the drawing in a presented way this was easy: As soon as the drawing resembled the picture they had intended to represent at the very beginning, they could quit because the task was finished. In contrast, the students who approached the situation as a problem to be discovered had a harder time knowing when the picture was finished and the problem solved. Their formulation of the problem evolved slowly all through the drawing process, and even at the end the stopping point was somewhat arbitrary because they thought the drawing could evolve still further.

These possible distinctions between a presented and a discovered way of approaching the experimental situation yielded ten behavioral variables and three interview variables for measuring a person's *discovery orientation*. For example, the number of objects a person touched before starting to draw was used as an indication of the number of possibilities he considered before starting to formulate the problem. The higher the number, the more likely that the problem was approached in the mode of discovery. Another behavioral variable concerned the number of changes a person introduced in the drawing process: how often he changed the arrangement of objects, their perspective, the paper he used, the media, or the technique of representation. Again, the greater the number of changes, the more likely it was held that a process of discovery was in effect.

When these variables were analyzed, we found that established artists and art teachers rated drawings produced by students who had used discovery orientation much higher on originality and aesthetic value than the drawings of students who had adopted a presented problem-solving orientation. At the same time, they rated the two sets of drawings equal on craftsmanship.

The correlation between discovery orientation and success as a creative artist was still significant 7 years later (Getzels & Csikszentmihalyi, 1976) and 18 years later (Csikszentmihalyi & Getzels, 1988): Those artists who as students approached the experimental drawing task as offering an opportunity to formulate a new problem were exhibiting their work, and attracting the attention of critics and collectors, much more than artists who as students took the experiment to be a presented problem.

These findings gave a strong indication that at least some of the cognitive parameters of artistic creativity were open to investigation and prediction. Moreover, because problem finding is so often mentioned in the context of scientific creativity, there is good reason to believe that the same process may account for creative accomplishments in other domains as well. Certainly, discovery orientation seems to be a very strong candidate for explaining the thought process peculiar to creativity.

At the same time, even this conceptually sound and empirically promising attempt to capture the essence of creativity suffers from an epistemological weakness. How do we know that discovery orientation is a necessary condition for creative achievement? After all, it is possible that the relationships we found depend on time-bound conceptions of what is creative—a product of particular cultural and social conditions. The rejection of old problems, the restless search for new solutions, and the emphasis on discovery and novelty may be just a passing phase in humankind's attempt to recognize and describe creativity. Does discovery orientation explain how Michelangelo, Bach, or Newton actually thought? Or how future geniuses will think?

Intrinsic Motivation

A certain type of personality and values and a cognitive orientation toward discovery, may be necessary for an individual who aspires to be creative, but they are not sufficient. I have become convinced that an essential ingredient for sustaining creative effort is intrinsic motivation, or the ability to derive rewards from the activity itself rather than from external incentives like power, money, or fame. Of course, motivation is intimately related to values and personality. A would-be artist who values economic success, for instance, is less likely to be intrinsically motivated to make art than one whose aesthetic values are stronger.

There are two ways in which intrinsic motivation affects creativity. The first is in terms of immediate information processing, as suggested by Amabile (Amabile, 1983; Amabile, Hennessey, & Grossman, 1986); the second is in terms of the sustained involvement with a set of problems that is necessary for achieving a creative outcome, described by Gruber (Gruber, 1974/1981; Gruber & Davis, 1988).

A person who is too involved with achieving goals external to the activity itself, and whose main concern is winning, cannot pay undivided attention to what he or she is doing. Creative achievements depend on single-minded immersion in the domain. Painters must want to paint above all else, and scientists who hope to advance science must love their labs more than fame. Concern for extrinsic rewards dilutes this unflinching concentration and tends to interfere with the fragile process of discovery (Csikszentmihalyi, 1985, 1988c). If the artist in front of the canvas begins to wonder who will like the painting, and how much he or she will sell it for, it is likely that he or she will approach the task as a presented problem—trying to produce a picture that will fit the tastes of the relevant public. Several of our former art students found themselves trapped in this situation, unable to paint original works any longer because they were always worrying whether the canvas would meet the gallery owner's approval or some critic's praise.

After a while, an artist in this situation may develop a "painter's block," often giving up painting altogether.

Thus intrinsic motivation affects not only the momentary focus of attention but also the long-term dedication to creative endeavors. In the summary of our early investigations with art students we wrote:

> The unanimity with which extrinsic motivations were disregarded was strik-ing. If the students really expected their rewards to come from the activity itself rather than from its results, then one can understand why they are able to persevere in their hazardous vocation—a vocation that is both without financial security or immediate social recognition. (Getzels & Csikszentmi-halyi, 1976, p. 19).

The importance of intrinsic motivation in providing the perseverance necessary for the pursuit of a creative career is well illustrated in a recent doctoral thesis by Jean Carney (1986). She and an associate coded TAT stories told by the art students in 1963 for extrinsic versus intrinsic motiva-tion, and correlated these scores with their artistic success in 1981. What she found is that students who told stories filled with extrinsic success imagery—stories of artists making it big, getting money and glory for their work—tended to drop out of art unless they were successful immediately after leaving school. Students whose stories focused more on the joy of making art, on self-discovery, on the process rather than on the product, tended to keep on painting or sculpting even if they were not immediately recognized, and it is from their ranks that most of the successful artists eventually emerged.

But if we look at the issues from a broader historical perspective, it again seems that intrinsic motivation may not be essential component of creativity. At different times, in different cultural settings, a concern for fame and money does not seem to have detracted from creative accomplishment. A notorious example is in the autobiography of Benvenuto Cellini, considered one of the foremost mannerist artists of the Renaissance, and certainly its most original goldsmith. If we go by Cellini's account, he rarely made a sculpture without incessantly wondering how much gold the French king, or Cardinal X, would pay for it; and he always compared his work with that of other artists, bragging all the time how much better he was than anyone else. Even the great Leonardo da Vinci calculated who would be the most generous patron for his work and kept moving from court to court according to market conditions.

THE LIMITS OF A PERSON-CENTERED VIEW OF CREATIVITY

Personality, values, intrinsic motivation, and discovery orientation give valuable clues as to who may turn out to make a creative contribution in art—and perhaps other domains as well—in the last decades of the twentieth century. But in the course of our investigations it became very clear that a prediction based on these factors left much of the variance in creative achievement unexplained.

For instance, although women art students scored just as high as men—or higher—in measures of creative potential, 18 years out of school very few women worked full-time as artists, and none had succeeded in reaching first-rank recognition (Csikszentmihalyi, Getzels, & Kahn, 1984). The student with the highest score on discovery orientation was a Black man; but like almost all Black art students, he stopped painting in the late 1960s in order to do something more relevant politically and financially—such as educating Black children in African culture or becoming a set designer. Whether these women and Blacks continued to be creative is a moot point: The fact is that, by stopping producing art, it will be impossible for them to be recognized as creative artists.

Conversely, some of the least promising students in terms of creative potential became respected creative artists, often because of seeming fluke accidents. All of these facts suggest that personal characteristics such as personality, values, or discovery orientation are at best only correlates of creativity, conditions that facilitate its occurrence. They do not tell anything directly about what creativity *is*. This state of affairs has convinced me that the empirical problem of measuring creativity will not be resolved until the conceptual issues surrounding the nature of creativity are clarified.

If one turns to the literature of creativity research and asks the simple questions: What is being measured? What is creativity? One soon realizes that the entire research enterprise moves on very thin ice. One finds out that it is impossible to define *creativity* independently of a judgment based on criteria that change from domain to domain and across time (Csikszentmihalyi, 1988a; Csikszentmihalyi & Robinson, 1986). In most research about the creativity of children, the dependent variable consists in teachers' or experimenters' ratings of childish behaviors or products. And the raters' notions of the signs of creativity in children are often based on very parochial values. But even in the best of cases, when real-life adult accomplishments are evaluated by experts, judgments are based on criteria that cannot be separated from current values and norms. Hence one must conclude that *creativity is not an attribute of individuals but of social systems making judgments about individuals.*

For instance, at this moment there is a general consensus that Rembrandt was a very great and original painter. But if we showed his work to persons who are not versed in the history of art, they would be unable to know whether his work was creative or not. They might like it and think it was great painting, but they couldn't tell whether it was creative or not because they lacked a comparative context in which creativity can be assessed. Rembrandt's contemporaries did not believe he was that creative and preferred the works of several painters less well known to us, such as Jan Lievens or Adrien van der Werff (e.g., Alpers, 1988). Rembrandt's "creativity" was constructed after his death by art historians who placed his work in the full context of the development of European painting, and who pointed out novelties and differences between his work and that of his predecessors. This highlighted Rembrandt's originality.

The point is that without the comparative evaluation of art historians, Rembrandt's creativity would not exist. And if different criteria of evaluation had to be used, or if art historians had developed a different taste, it is very likely that Rembrandt would have stayed in relative obscurity and a different artist would have emerged as the most creative painter of the seventeenth century. Thus we could never understand Rembrandt's creativity just by studying his personality, his thoughts, or his behaviors. Even if we had his complete genetic blueprint, or if we had a moment-to-moment account of all he did or all that went through his mind, we could not get a full understanding of what made him creative. To do this we would also have to know what other relevant people around him did, thought, and valued.

It could be argued that this view applies only to the arts, where judgments are subjective and fallible. But the same social constitution of creativity appears to hold in the more exact sciences, even though in those domains revisions are less likely to occur. Brannigan (1981) has argued, for instance, that Mendel's experiments with peas were considered by everyone—including himself—as elegant demonstrations of how to hybridize plants but that they were without great theoretical implications. The implications were appreciated only half a century later, when evolutionary theory had progressed far enough for William Bateson and other British biologists to realize that the segregation of traits Mendel had observed could fit the genetic model of evolution that they were interested in proving. So Mendel's creativity was defined posthumously, in interaction with theoretical advances and evaluations that originally played no part in Mendel's own thought. If this is true, it is very difficult to see how Mendel could have been creative independent of the theoretical context that others developed only later and within which his work acquired a significance it would have lacked by itself.

What was true in Mendel's case is true of creativity in general: It only exists within a framework of attributions based on the criteria of domains, and these change with time. The evaluations of relevant experts also vary. So creativity is not a "natural kind," a trait that can be measured objectively such as height, strength, perfect pitch, reaction time, or knowledge of languages or mathematics. Rather it is an attribution based on the current conditions of the social system—more like judgments of taste, beauty, or goodness.

To say that creativity is relative to the conditions of the social system does not mean that it is any less important, or less real, than if it had an independent, objective existence. But it does mean that if we wish to understand creativity we must search for it outside the boundaries of the individual person. The usual question of creativity research—What is creativity?—may have to be replaced by a different question—Where is creativity?

THE SYSTEMS VIEW

The best way to conceptualize the systems view proposed here is in terms of a dynamic model, with creativity the result of the interaction between three subsystems: a domain, a person, and a field. Each subsystem performs a specific function. The domain transmits information to the person, the person produced a variation, which may or may not be selected by the field, and the field in turn will pass the selected variation to the domain. The subsystems influence each other, and no act or product with claims to creativity can exist without an input from each of these subsystems.

I will try to illustrate with a recent example how these subsystems conjointly constitute a phenomenon that might be called creativity. During the 24th modern Olympic games that took place in Seoul, a television sportscaster covering the final synchronized swimming events kept referring to the performance of the Canadian duet as being outstandingly "creative." At first I found this use of the term inappropriate, partly because I felt synchronized swimming to be aesthetically abhorrent, and partly because it seemed to me that such a recently invented and trifling activity should not be dignified with the attribution of creativity. On further thought, however, I had to admit that whether I liked it or not, synchronized swimming met the criteria of the dynamic model and thus it fit the definition of creativity. Let use see in more detail how this works out.

What is the *domain* of synchronized swimming? Although I am no expert, I gather that swimmers in this activity are judged on the basis of four-minute performances that consist in a series of compulsory and voluntary moves, based on more than 100 variations of the "jackknife." These moves constitute a set of rules, a vocabulary with a grammar and a syntax, out of which many different four-minute performances can be put together. They constitute the symbolic system, or domain, of synchronized swimming. Until the 1930s, when various athletes, coaches, and promoters got together and agreed upon what the parameters of the emerging domain would be, it would have been impossible to be a "creative" synchronized swimmer, simply because there were no benchmarks in terms of which performance could be evaluated as creative.

But performance is never evaluated automatically in terms of the domain. The judgment of creativity is made by a different subsystem, what in this model we call the *field*. The field is composed of individuals who know the domain's grammar of rules and are more or less loosely organized to act as gatekeepers to it. The field decides whether an individual's performance meets the criteria of the domain. It also decides whether an individual performance that departs from the standard rules of the domain is "creative" and thus should be added to the domain, or whether it is simply "deviant" and thus should be ignored or censored. In the case of synchronized swimming, the field is composed of swimmers, former swimmers, coaches, producers of water ballets, judges at various competitions like the Olympics and world championships, and media critics such as the television commentator who originally started this whole trend of thought. These interested parties became officially recognized as members of an organized amateur sport in 1954 by the international swimming federation (FINA), and the event was first admitted to the Olympics in 1984. Now it does not matter much whether you or I think that Betty is a creative synchronized swimmer, because we have no standing in the field, and presumably we do not know the domain well enough to make an informed judgment. But if enough people who are recognized in the field think Betty's moves are creative, she may go down in history. To be more precise, because her performance stood out sufficiently from previous achievements, she may be remembered and her performance recorded in the evolving domain of synchronized swimming.

This leaves us to consider the third element of the systems model: the *individual*. In the last analysis, who is a creative swimmer? It is a person who has assimilated so well the various moves of the domain that she can convince the field that her variations are an original extension on previous performances. Thus a swimmer who can use the vocabulary of the domain to express possibilities inherent in it, but never expressed before by others, and whose performance is recognized by the field, is likely to be remembered as creative. Such a person will probably have the characteristics that distinguish creative people—the appropriate personality traits, values, problem-finding orientations, intrinsic motivation, and so on. But these characteristics only affect one of the subsystems that constitute creativity: the person. They have no direct influence on the other two, and, therefore, they can never determine creativity by themselves.

I chose to dwell on the rather trivial example of synchronized swimming for two reasons: First, because the domain involved is simple to understand, and, second, because the field is of recent constitution. Simplicity and recency make it easier to see how a type of individual performance that could not have been creative 50 years ago can now be talked about in terms of creativity, because the existence of a domain and a field makes it possible.

But the same argument applies to domains that are far richer and more ancient. The fact that we know of so few European artists prior to the Renaissance is not because there was a lack of potentially creative artists in the Middle Ages—in fact, the contrary is true. An enormous number of works were produced in that period that we would not call creative. But before the Renaissance the domain of art had no independent existence; painters and sculptors were essentially part of architectural teams whose job was to decorate and illustrate buildings or furniture. Their work was not evaluated separately from the functional context in which it was embedded, and there were no widely shared standards by which novel performances could be judged.

And before the princely patrons began to exercise their taste, there was no field to give voice and legitimacy to aesthetic value judgments. To be socially recognized, artists had to belong to marginally related craft associations, like the guilds of dye makers, pharmacists, or goldsmiths. Under such conditions an exceptionally gifted artist could only gain a local reputation, and for lack of a common standard of judgment, his or her work could not be meaningfully compared with that of others. This made an attribution of creativity next to impossible. The same argument applies to any other area of human endeavor. A person could be the most brilliant scientist but could never be a creative chemist or physicist unless these domains existed and the relevant fields had been constituted.

To study creativity by focusing on the individual alone is like trying to understand how an apple tree produces fruit by looking only at the tree and ignoring the sun and the soil that support its life. It is a step forward, but not nearly enough, to recognize that one must consider the entire individual as an evolving system rather than just his or her thought processes in isolation

(Gruber & Davis, 1988), or that one must consider environmental influences (Hennessey & Amabile, 1988), social and cultural conditions (Simonton, 1975, 1984), the variation in the universality of domains (Feldman, 1980), or the influence of families on the creative person (Albert, 1983).

Nor is it possible, in my opinion, to preserve the primacy of the individual by separating creativity into a "process" that takes place within the individual mind and into "persuasion," which refers to whether the person is accepted by a field (Simonton, 1988, p. 417). The problem with this dichotomy is that there is no way to get evidence for a "creative" process taking place in a person's mind independent of social validation. Because these two components cannot be separated, the rule of parsimony in scientific explanations suggests that we postulate a single process rather than two.

The person-centered approaches cited above give due credit to variables external to the individual, but they still see the individual as the crucible inside which external influences are transmuted into the gold of creativity. In my model the creative process takes place outside the person, in the *interaction* between the three subsystems. In such a scheme, the individual does not have a privileged epistemological position. In other words, if one wants to understand creativity, it does not make any more sense to turn to a study of the individual than it would to a study of the field or of the domain. Real understanding may, however, come from investigating the interaction among all three.

To see how the dynamics within the system operate, we may turn to another historical example drawn from the arts. There is no question that some of the greatest original works of art in Europe were produced in Florence in the early fifteenth century. For a few decades that city had an unprecedented density of creative architects, sculptors, painters, and decorative craftsmen. How do we explain such a sudden flourishing of creativity? A person-centered approach would say that the social and cultural conditions at that time favored the development, or the expression, of individual creativity. The systems approach would come to a very similar conclusion, but with a crucial difference: It would claim that the social and cultural conditions, interacting with individual potentialities, brought about the objects and behaviors we call "creative."

The artistic creativity of Renaissance Florence cannot be understood without the sudden transformation of the domain of art brought about by the discovery of ancient buildings and statues and the analysis of their aesthetic characteristics by humanist scholars. These interpretations established a new vocabulary, or original idiom, that artists then used in novel ways. For instance, the dome that Brunelleschi designed for the Florentine cathedral in 1420, which is generally considered one of the most brilliant achievements of the Renaissance, was made possible by the recently completed studies of how the Romans had built the dome of the Pantheon. It does not make sense to say that these developments in the domain of art "facilitated" or "influenced" the creativity of a Donatello or a Brunelleschi. They were just as essential to it as anything these individuals brought to the process.

During the same years, the financial and political leaders of Florence were developing what turned out to be a uniquely creative field for the generation of art. In a life-and-death struggle with neighboring city-states, the Florentines set as their goal remaking their city into a new Athens (Hauser, 1951, p. 23). The prestige and the economic support made available to artists attracted many outstanding young men, who in earlier times would have become lawyers or clergymen, to careers as architects, sculptors, and painters. "In this environment," writes Heydenreich (1974, p. 13), "the patron begins to assume a very important role: in practice, artistic production arises in large measure from his collaboration." And Hauser (1951, p. 41) is even more definitive: "In the art of the early Renaissance . . . the starting point of production is to be found mostly not in the creative urge, the subjective self-expression and spontaneous inspiration of the artist, but in the task set by the customer." In other words, the social environment not only facilitates the expression of individual creativity, it often takes the initiative in, and it is always an essential component of, the creative process.

The specific functions of the three elements in the creative process are analogous to the three aspects of all evolutionary processes: variation, selection, and transmission (Campbell, 1960, 1974). Individuals produce variations in domain; the field selects one variation among many, and adds it to the domain; and finally the domain transmits the selected variant to a new generation of individuals. In this sense, creativity is a special case of cultural evolution (Csikszentmihalyi, 1988b; Csikszentmihalyi & Massimini, 1985). Just as it makes no sense to talk about evolution only in terms of changes in the structure of chromosomes without taking into account how well adapted these are to the environment, and how they will influence future heredity, so it makes no sense to talk about creativity only with reference to what happens inside the individual without reference to the field and the domain.

As I have already suggested, the causal chain is not a simple linear progression from individual variation to social selection to cultural retention and transmission. The system is more intimately connected than that; and, depending on one's perspective, one may be able to see causation running from cultural transmission to individual variation to social selection, or in any number of other permutations. Moreover, occasionally, new fields and domains emerge (Gardner, 1988), making new kinds of creative behavior possible.

IMPLICATIONS OF THE SYSTEMS PERSPECTIVE

The difference between a person-centered and a systemic view of creativity is not simply a matter of semantics or metaphysics. The two views suggest quite different testable predictions. If the person-centered perspective is closer to the truth, and creativity is an individual trait, then it should be possible to identify a set of individual characteristics associated with creative performance across different domains, social contexts, and historical periods, and these characteristics *should be both necessary and sufficient for an attribution of creativity to be made.*

The systems perspective admits that individual traits may be necessary for a person to be recognized as creative, but it postulates that these cannot be predicted a priori. It holds, instead, that one must also consider the characteristics of domains and fields before one can predict what a creative person will be like. *The specific individual traits associated with creativity will depend on characteristics of the other two subsystems.* For example, the systemic perspective suggests that, in the domain of fine arts, a young person who becomes a painter in a period when abstract expressionism is the reigning style will be more likely to be recognized as creative if he or she is emotional, imaginative, and antisocial. In a period when the favorite idiom of art is photorealism, however, a cool, precise, and relatively conformist young person may be more likely to make a contribution judged to be creative.

I will now turn to each of the three subsystems in turn, in order to illustrate the kind of research questions suggested by the model. These, in turn, might define the domain of creativity research according to the perspective advanced here.

The Person

In the systemic model, the person's function is to provide variations in a domain. Hence the kind of questions we need to address are these: What personal traits facilitate the production of viable variations? Are these traits innate and relatively impervious to change or can they be affected by the environment? Are these traits the same in widely divergent domains, such as physics and synchronized swimming? Does a person who will produce a viable variation approach the domain differently from a person who will not? How are variations produced in different domains? What is the relationship between the production of variation and the kinds of encouragement or discouragement the person receives from the field?

In practice, the characteristics of creative persons I discussed at the beginning of this chapter are likely to be important sources of variation across most situations. For instance, at least since the late Renaissance, artists have tended to feel deeply ambivalent toward their field. They want its recognition, but they often fear that if they are too responsive to money and fame they will compromise their vision. As a result, artists tend to develop certain traits to protect themselves from what they see as potentially destructive external influences. Low economic and low social values will help ensure that artists stay independent of the field, so that they can play around with variations regardless of external rewards. High aesthetic values, on the other hand, keep their attention focused on the domain. The same results are accomplished by low-extrinsic and high-intrinsic motivation.

This tension between innovators and their public may be universal, and hence these individual traits may be prerequisites of the creative process regardless of the domain and the social context. But one may imagine that in a culture like Bali, where the arts are respected and widely practiced yet no great financial or status gains accrue to artists, a person would feel free to make variations in the domain even if he or she had high economic and social values. In any case, from the point of view of our model such values would not be characteristics of *creative persons* but of persons who are part of a *creative system*.

Personality traits and cognitive skills, such as discovery orientation, play a similar role in the genesis of creative performances. In other words, they enable a person to produce variations that, if the other elements of the system are conducive to it, will be selected, preserved, and transmitted to future generations as valued contributions to the domain.

However, the model also suggests that certain individuals who have achieved creative accomplishments may have been entirely unique in their psychological makeup. If creativity were a strictly individual trait, then one would expect every creative person to exhibit more or less the same characteristics. But if it is a systemic trait, then the personal contribution will vary according to the states of the other subsystems. Hence it is possible to imagine that at some peculiar conjunction of social and cultural conditions creative variations will be produced by persons who are unlike any other "creative"person who lived earlier or later.

The Field

The field is that part of the social system that has the power to determine the structure of the domain. Its major function is to preserve the domain as it is, and its secondary function is to help it evolve by a judicious selection of new content. Taking the domain of psychology as an example, certain committees of the American Psychological Association, together with state legislators, are currently developing the power to decide what the domain of psychology shall be. They decide what kind of training, what type of knowledge, and what sequence of examinations and tasks define a psychologist. The selective function of the field is more informal; it is performed by editors and referees of major journals, the authors of textbooks, the review committees of major funding agencies, and the faculties of prestigious universities. Of the thousands of new ideas and research findings they come across each year, the field selects a few for inclusion in journals and texts. The *Citation Index* is a rough and preliminary record of this selection process. Which theories and methods the next generation of students will encounter when they begin to study psychology depends on what the field decides to include in this selection. And it is against this background of ideas and methods that new variations introduced by young psychologists will be evaluated.

Some of the questions that will help us understand the impact of fields on creativity are as follows: Is the main concern of the field to preserve or to change the domain? How many new variations is the field equipped to recognize? What are its resources for controlling the rate of individual variations? What are its selection criteria concerning new variations? What is the status of the field relative to other fields in the social system? Is the field autonomous, made up of practitioners in the domain, or is it controlled by external institutions? Each of these questions opens up a rich agenda for creativity research.

In contemporary American art, for example, there are two major fields with very different characteristics that operate in complete isolation from each other. The first one is the New York art establishment with subsidiaries in the major urban centers. It is made up of a few thousand leading artists, collectors, art critics, historians, professors, gallery owners, and museum curators. They trace their genealogy to earlier artistic fields in London, Paris, and Berlin and thus own a certain ideological legitimacy. They take pains to verbalize, defend, and explain their choices in terms of accepted historical and conceptual claims. And because of their control of large sums of money and the media, they are in a position to decide what is good art and which new works of art are worth attention.

The second major context in which art is produced in this country is western and Native American art. The number of people involved in making, collecting, and appreciating it may be greater than that for mainstream art, and the financial value of its exchange equivalent, but the field of western art is much more loosely organized. It consists of a professional association, many minor but few major collectors, publications that emphasize description but not the critical analysis of works of art, a network of galleries—but it lacks the academic and intellectual components necessary to legitimize its choices and values. The major concern of this field is not to encourage creativity but to preserve and develop a narrowly defined aesthetic idiom. Yet some artists who work in this idiom produce variations recognized as creative by the field. However, western artists who are thought to be creative are little known outside the circle of collectors because the domain is not well articulated with the rest of the culture. Of course, eventually such a domain may evolve, and if it can demonstrate its superiority in terms of existing cultural values, it may overshadow current establishment art.

The Domain

Any symbolic system that has a set of rules for representing thought and action is a domain. For example, mathematics, music, the Mormon religion, the game of bridge, and now synchronized swimming all have clear conventions that specify mental or physical performances and, therefore, qualify as domains. The function of a domain is to preserve desirable performances selected by the field and transmit them to a new generation of people in a form that will be easy to learn.

Usually domains are nested inside larger domains, and where one wishes to draw their boundaries is often a matter of convenience. For instance, experimental social psychology could be treated either as a separate domain or as a subset of social psychology, which in turn could be assimilated into psychology. A good rule of thumb is that, when a symbol system develops its own field, composed of people who take on the task of preserving it, then we have a full-fledged domain.

Domains vary in terms of what type of behavior they are concerned with—motor performance, the manipulation of numbers, beliefs, or political action are only a few examples. They also vary in terms of complexity; some are fairly easy to learn, others can never be entirely mastered. Some, like religion, medicine, or the law, are fairly central to the values of the culture; others are peripheral or held to be trivial.

The issues that concern research on the domains of creativity are of the following type: How clear are the rules of the domain? How easy is it for a person to learn to operate in it? How difficult is it to produce a variation? Are there particular ways of ordering a domain that are more conducive to creative variations? What kinds of controls does the field have over the domain?

THE DOMAIN OF CREATIVITY RESEARCH

At this point it is difficult to carry out research in creativity according to the systemic approach because each investigator typically looks at the issues only from the perspective of his or her discipline. In a study now being completed, we find that problems that logically should belong under the heading of "creativity" are investigated under different names depending on the domain in which the researcher is working. In economics and business, creative processes are referred to as *entrepreneurship*, in sociology as *innovation*, and, in history or literature, a variety of terms are used. Only in psychology and education is *creativity* the term of choice.

But when psychologists study creativity, they almost invariably look at it as an individual trait or as an individual process. They ignore the role that the field and domain play in the process. Sociologists are more aware of institutional effects on creativity, and anthropologists have paid attention to the cultural dimensions, but then they have little to say about the person.

This fragmentation of effort will continue until research in creativity itself becomes a domain instead of being, as it is now, an extension of several other domains. If this were to come about, what could it encompass? A useful matrix for organizing the kind of problems that creativity research might address has been drawn up by the Hungarian "creatologist" Istvan Magyari-Beck (1976). In his scheme, there are four levels on which creativity could be studied: that of the culture, the institution, the working group, and the person. And there are three main forms in which the creative process manifests itself: as a trait, as a process, and as a product.

This 4 x 3 matrix generates 12 cells that provide a general map of what creativity research entails. For example, at the level of the group, which might include such instances as the Bloomsbury circle or the Cavendish laboratory at Cambridge University in the 1920s, one would investigate characteristic traits of working groups that produce creative results, group processes that result in creativity, and how group interactions result in creative products.

In addition, Magyari-Beck's model takes into consideration four methodological options in each of the 12 cells: whether the investigation is quantitative or qualitative and whether it is empirical or normative. Thus his matrix specifies 48 possible directions for creativity research. And because there are already thousands of psychological studies concentrated in just one of these cells—the quantitative, empirical approach to individual traits—it is clear that the domain is potentially very rich.

It is unlikely that creativity research will ever become an entirely independent symbol system, with its own special theoretical constructs, methods, and procedures. Instead, it is more likely to become an interdisciplinary domain in which humanists and social and biological scientists retain their own conceptual tools and approaches but find a way of integrating them to study processes that do not admit one-dimensional explanations.

Whether this is the direction creativity research will take is at this point a moot question. Whichever way it goes, however, it will not go very far unless we who work in it recognize that creativity is not something that takes place inside the head of a person but is the product of a far larger and more mysterious process.

REFERENCES

Albert, R. S. (Ed.). (1983). *Genius and eminence: The social psychology of creativity*. New York: Oxford University Press.

Albert, R. S., & Runco, M. A. (1986). The achievement of eminence: A model based on a longitudinal study of exceptionally gifted boys and their families. In R. J. Sternberg & J. E. Davidson (Eds.), *Conceptions of giftedness* (pp. 332–360). New York: Cambridge University Press.

Alpers, S. (1988). *Rembrandt's enterprise: The studio and the market*. Chicago: University of Chicago Press.

Amabile, T. M. (1983). *The social psychology of creativity*. New York: Springer-Verlag.

Amabile, T. M., Hennessey, B. A., & Grossman, B. S. (1986). Social influences on creativity: The effects of contracted-for reward. *Journal of Personality and Social Psychology*, 50, 14–23.

Brannigan, A. (1981). *The social basis of scientific discoveries*. New York: Cambridge University Press.

Campbell, D. T. (1960). Blind variation and selective retention in creative thought as in other knowledge processes. *Psychological Review*, 67, 380–400.

Campbell, D. T. (1974). Unjustified variation and selective retention in scientific discovery. In F. J. Ayala & T. Dobzhansky (Eds.), *Studies in the philosophy of biology* (pp. 139–161). London: Macmillan

Carney, J. (1986). *Intrinsic motivation in successful artists from early adulthood to middle age*. Unpublished doctoral dissertation, University of Chicago.

Cattell, R. B., & Drevdahl, J. E. (1955). A comparison of the personality profile (16PF) of eminent researchers with that of eminent teachers and administrators. *British Journal of Psychology*, 46, 248–261.

Cross, P. G., Cattell, R. B., & Butcher, H. J. (1967). The personality pattern of creative artists. *British Journal of Educational Psychology*, 37, 292–299.

Csikszentmihalyi, M. (1965). *Artistic problems and their solution*. Unpublished doctoral dissertation, University of Chicago.

Csikszentmihalyi, M. (1985). Emergent motivation and the evolution of the self. In D. Kleiber & M. H. Maehr (Eds.), *Motivation in adulthood* (Vol. 4, pp. 93–119). Greenwich, CT: JAI.

Csikszentmihalyi, M. (1988a). Society, culture, and person: A systems view of creativity. In R. J. Sternberg (Ed.), *The nature of creativity: Contemporary psychological perspectives* (pp. 325–339). New York: Cambridge University Press.

Csikszentmihalyi, M. (1988b). Genes vs. memes: Notes from the culture wars. *Reality Club Review*, I(1), 107–127 (see also chapter 7).

Csikszentmihalyi, M. (1988c). Motivation and creativity: Toward a synthesis of structural and energistic approaches to cognition. *New Ideas in Psychology*, 6, 159–176.

Csikszentmihalyi, M., & Getzels, J. W. (1970). Concern for discovery: An attitudinal component of creative production. *Journal of Personality*, 38(1), 91–105.

Csikszentmihalyi, M., & Getzels, J. W. (1971). Discovery-oriented behavior and the originality of artistic products: A study with artists. *Journal of Personality and Social Psychology*, 19(1), 47–52.

Csikszentmihalyi, M., & Getzels, J. W. (1973). The personality of young artists: A theoretical and empirical exploration. *British Journal of Psychology*, 64(1), 91–104.

Csikszentmihalyi, M., & Getzels, J. W. (1988). Creativity and problem finding. In F. H. Farley & R. W. Neperud (Eds.), *The Foundations of aesthetics, art, and art education*, (pp. 91–106). New York: Praeger.

Csikszentmihalyi, M., Getzels, J. W., & Kahn, S. P. (1984). *Talent and achievement: A longitudinal study of artists* (Unpublished report to the Spencer and MacArthur Foundations). Chicago: University of Chicago Press.

Csikszentmihalyi, M., & Massimini, F. (1985). On the psychological selection of bio-cultural information. *New Ideas in Psychology*, 3(2), 115–138.

Csikszentmihalyi, M., & Robinson, R. (1986). Culture, time, and the development of talent. In R. J. Sternberg & J. E. Davidson (Eds.). *Conceptions of giftedness* (pp. 264–284). New York: Cambridge University Press.

Einstein, A., & Infeld, L. (1938). *The evolution of physics*. New York: Simon & Schuster.

Feldman, D. (1980). *Beyond universals in cognitive development*. Norwood, NJ: Ablex.

Gardner, H. (1988). Creative lives and creative works: A synthetic scientific approach. In R. J. Sternberg (Ed.), *The nature of creativity: Contemporary psychological perspectives* (pp. 298–321). New York: Cambridge University Press.

Getzels, J. W. (1964). Creative thinking, problem-solving, and instruction. In E. R. Hilgard (Ed.), *Theories of learning and instruction* (63rd Yearbook of the National Society for the Study of Education, pp. 240–267). Chicago: University of Chicago Press.

Getzels, J. W., & Csikszentmihalyi, M. (1966). The study of creativity in future artists: The criterion problem. In O. J. Harvey (Ed.), *Experience, structure, and adaptability* (pp. 349–368). New York: Springer.

Getzels, J. W., & Csikszentmihalyi, M. (1967, September). Scientific creativity. *Science Journal*, pp. 80–84.

Getzels, J. W., & Csikszentmihalyi, M. (1968a). The value-orientation of art students as determinants of artistic specialization and creative performance. *Studies in Art Education, 10*, 5–16.

Getzels,J. W., & Csikszentmihalyi, M. (1968b). On the roles, values, and performance of future artists: A conceptual and empirical exploration. *Sociological Quarterly*, 9, 516–530.

Getzels, J. W., & Csikszentmihalyi, M. (1969). Aesthetic opinion: An empirical study. *Public Opinion Quarterly*, 33, 34–35.

Getzels, J. W., & Csikszentmihalyi, M. (1975). From problem-solving to problem-finding. In I. A. Taylor & J. W. Getzels (Eds.), *Perspectives in creativity* (pp. 90–116). Chicago: Aldine.

Getzels, J. W., & Csikszentmihalyi, M. (1976). *The creative vision: A longitudinal study of problem-finding in art*. New York: John Wiley.

Gruber, H. (1981). *Darwin on man: A study of scientific creativity*. Chicago: University of Chicago Press. (Original work published 1974).

Gruber, H., & Davis, S. N. (1988). Inching our way up Mount Olympus: The evolving-systems approach to creative thinking. In R. J. Sternberg (Ed.), *The nature of creativity: Contemporary psychological perspectives* (pp. 243–270). New York: Cambridge University Press.

Hauser, A. (1951). *A social history of art*. New York: Vintage.

Hennessey, B. A., & Amabile, T. M. (1988). The conditions of creativity. In R. J. Sternberg (Ed.), *The nature of creativity: Contemporary psychological perspectives* (pp. 11–42). New York: Cambridge University Press.

Heydenreich, L. H. (1974). *Il Primo Rinascimento*, Milano: Rizzoli.

Hilgard, E. (1980). The trilogy of mind: Cognition, affect, and conation. *Journal of the History of the Behavioral Sciences*, 16, 107–117.

Kahn, S. P., Zimmerman, G., Csikszentmihalyi, M., & Getzels, J. W. (1986). The relationship between identity and intimacy: A longitudinal study with artists. *Journal of Personality and Social Psychology*, 49(5), 1316–1322.

MacKinnon, D. W. (1964). The creativity of architects. In C. W. Taylor (Ed.), *Widening horizons in creativity*. New York: John Wiley.

Magyari-Beck, I. (1976). *Kiserlet a Tudomanyos Alkotas Produktumanak Interdiszciplinaris Maghatarozasara*. Budapest: Akademiai Kiado.

Roe, A. (1946). The personality of artists, *Educational and Psychological Measurement*, 6, 401–408.

Roe, A. (1952). *The making of a scientist*. New York: Dodd, Mead.

Simonton, D. K. (1975). Sociocultural context of individual creativity: A transhistorical time-series analysis. *Journal of Personality and Social Psychology*, 32, 1119–1133.

Simonton, D. K. (1984). *Genius, creativity, and leadership*. Cambridge, MA: Harvard University Press.

Simonton, D. K. (1988). Creativity, leadership, and chance. In R. J. Sternberg (Ed.), *The nature of creativity: Contemporary psychological perspective* (pp. 386–426). New York: Cambridge University Press.

7

Memes versus Genes: Notes from the Culture Wars

Mihaly Csikszentmihalyi

Humanity discovered evolution just a little more than a century ago. For the span of a few generations we thought this meant that the future belonged to mankind. During the Victorian era and up to World War I, it seemed that we were slated to be benevolent rulers of the entire planet. This brief period of optimism had barely time to blossom before it already seemed part of a nostalgic past. As we approach the end of the century it is getting more and more difficult to believe that we are making progress toward the rational control of evolutionary processes. Indeed, the very concept of evolution is coming under attack.

Despite these setbacks, evolution still seems the best way to explain what has happened in the past, what is happening now, and, to a certain extent, what will happen in the future. But in order to understand events in human history from the evolutionary perspective, which so far has taken into account changes in the biological structure and function of living organisms, must be expanded to include events of a different kind, following different laws from those that hold for the transmission of genes—changes that take place in the realm of society and culture.

Scholars have debated the relative contributions of biology and culture to human evolution, especially after Edward O. Wilson formulated the theses of sociobiological determinism. The question is whether changes in art, science, religion, economics, politics, and other cultural systems obey their own rules, or whether they are shaped by the same forces that account for the selection and transmission of genes.

It makes sense to assume that evolution consists of the interaction of two parallel but related processes, one biological and the other cultural. They have separate mechanisms for producing new information, for selecting certain variants, and for transmitting them over time.

For example, art historians trace the evolution of dome like structures in Western Europe from the Roman Pantheon rebuilt by Hadrian in the second century, through the baptistery of Florence in the twelfth century, through Brunelleschi's dome of the Cathedral of Florence in the fifteenth century, and ending with Michelangelo's dome over St. Peter's in Rome about a hundred years later. The changing shapes of the dome were not due to genetic mutations in the architects' chromosomes, but to attempts to improve on culturally mediated instructions—plans, theories, calculations, and information passed on from masters to apprentices. Each dome may not have been "better" than the previous one, but it is clear that one "evolved" from the other in the sense that the latter included the technical and aesthetic knowledge of earlier forms, plus changes that had not been possible before.

This means that cultural forms can evolve and grow without necessarily enhancing the biological fitness of the individuals who produced them. The monks who developed European culture in the Middle Ages transmitted art and learning instead of genes. That these two ways of transmitting information across time are often in conflict was recognized long ago by the Latin saying *libri aut liberi*—books or children. It is indeed difficult to spawn biological and cultural progeny at the same time.

Occasionally people try to eliminate information they fear. The Romans systematically destroyed everything written in Etruscan so that they could impose their cultural hegemony over Italy. When the great library of Alexandria was put to the torch, much of our Greek heritage perished with it. During the Great Cultural Revolution the Chinese lost so much of their culture that very few people are left now who know how to read the ancient texts that were saved from the flames. But the opposite also happens: Ideas, beliefs, and wrong information kill people perhaps more often than the other way around. Sometimes a small difference in religious interpretation leads to the death of tens of thousands of people, as during the Albigensian wars of the thirteenth century.

Cultural forms depend on the environment of human consciousness. Ideas and artifacts reproduce and grow in the mind, responding to selective pressures that are in principle independent of those that constrain genetic evolution. Because of this independence, it is perfectly possible to start up trains of thought that in the long run will be injurious to our survival. We tend to select new cultural forms that promise to give more power, comfort, or pleasure. But like selective mechanisms that operate in biological evolution, this one, too, has potential dangers as well as obvious advantages.

Cultural evolution can be defined as the differential transmission of information contained in artifacts—in objects, concepts, beliefs, symbols, and behavior patterns that exist only because people took the trouble to make them. While artifacts are human products, they in turn shape human consciousness. A person with a gun, for instance, is different from an unarmed man. It makes no sense to say, as the National Rifle Association does, that "guns don't kill people, people do." People in the abstract don't exist. They are made by the culture in which they live, by the objects they use, the words they hear, the ideas they come across. We have biologically programmed propensities for aggression as well as for compassion and for cooperation. Which of these potentials we realize depends on the cultural environment. When everyone carries a gun, it becomes "natural" to act out the aggressive script instead of the cooperative one.

Artifacts contain implicit instructions for how to behave because they define the reality within which we operate. Children born in a fishing village automatically adapt to a technology of boats and nets, just as spontaneously as they adopt the local language. Some artifacts also contain *explicit* directions for actions; they are the norms, regulations, and laws. They parallel even more clearly the function of genetic instructions that direct behavior. But while genetic instructions are coded chemically in the chromosomes, the information contained in artifacts is coded and stored outside the body—in the action potential inherent in objects, drawings, texts, and the behavior patterns of other individuals with whom one interacts. We might use the term "meme," coined by Richard Dawkins for the replicating unit of cultural information.

We like to believe that cultural evolution serves the goal of human adaptation. According to this view, memes survive only if they enhance the inclusive fitness of the individuals who use them. Artifacts evolve because they help to make our lives better. Cultural forms become destructive and dangerous only when they are misused. For instance, the reason armaments have evolved from stone axes to space lasers is that we have not been able to resolve competition for resources without resorting to aggressiveness. If men only learned to curb their belligerence, weapons would cease to multiply. This perspective on the evolution of culture is basically reassuring because it holds that the growth of artifacts is held in check by human control.

But thinking this way might blind us to the real state of affairs. It is possible that weapons and other artifacts evolve regardless of our intentions.

In effect, the multiplication and diffusion of artifacts follows its own logic to a large extent independently of the welfare of its carriers. The relationship of memes to humans is sometimes symbiotic, sometimes parasitic. Although they need consciousness as their growth environment, this dependence is not different, in principle, from our dependence on plants or on a breathable atmosphere. And just as we might kill the environment that made and supported us, the artifacts we created could well destroy us in the end.

Memes often spread in human cultures despite people's initial opposition. Some of the most important steps of civilization, such as the transition from the free life of the hunters to the more regimented life of the nomadic shepherds, and then to the even more restricted life of the farmers, were at first bitterly resisted. The diffusion of coins and currency across the globe initially caused an enormous amount of unhappiness. People just didn't take easily to a money economy, which seemed so much more impersonal and arbitrary, and so much less fun, than bartering had been.

Whenever there is a change in the culture, we assume that it was something we meant to happen, even though on reflection it seems that we are rather helpless in the matter. For instance, most people believe that new car models are introduced because manufacturers are greedy. But in reality they can't help doing what they do. As long as customers automatically prefer novelty, each new advance in technology makes it mandatory to add the latest gimmicks to existing models. In a free market this means that even if all the manufacturers declined to change, new capital would be attracted to produce a car that included the up-to-date features. We are in the habit of thinking that businessmen use technology to achieve competitive advantages. From a less anthropocentric viewpoint, the same scenario could be described as technology using producers and consumers as a medium in which to prosper. Unless actively restrained, memes continue to grow and multiply on their own.

Cultural evolution has its own propaganda apparatus, complete with ideology and slogans that people repeat over and over mechanically. One of my favorites is the phrase "It's here to stay," applied to new products and processes. It serves as a handy Trojan horse to lull our sense of judgment. This innocuous-sounding phrase heralds the territorial ambitions of the meme: Ready or not, here I come.

Weapons provide a clear example of how memes change and propagate. The information in a weapon, when decoded by our mind, says that the amount of threat must be countered with a weapon that contains at least as much threat as the first, and possibly more. Thus, the threat of the knife begets the sword, the sword begets the spear, the spear begets the arrow, the arrow begets the bolt, the bolt begets the bullet . . . and so on to Star Wars.

This progress may or may not benefit the biological survival of the human host. There is no evidence, for example, that the people of the Tuscan city of Pistoia, who first manufactured the pistol more than five centuries ago, have received any particular benefits in terms of inclusive fitness over their neighbors. On the other hand, the relative decline of the American Indians is due in large part to the fact that the Caucasian invaders had more and better firearms.

Like other patterns of organization, whether physical, chemical, biological, or informational in their composition, memes will propagate as long as the environment is conducive to growth. There is no reason to expect, for instance, that weapons will stop taking over more and more resources unless their growth environment in human consciousness is made less hospitable. The problem is, of course, that many people find the information contained in weaponry congenial. For some, paradoxically, weapons provide a relief from existential anxiety. Others find in the manufacture of weapons a source of profit. A few are intellectually challenged by the technology—Robert Oppenheimer used to refer to his work on the nuclear bomb as "that sweet problem."

Weapons are an obviously problematic species of memes, but the same argument holds for cultural forms that on the surface appear to be more benign. The control over the transformations of matter that modern physics and chemistry have brought about, when translated into uncontrolled technology, has reached a point of diminishing returns. Physical energy gets compressed in ever more explosive concentrations, without a clear idea of whether we shall be able to control its release. New substances are being created regardless of how useful they are, simply because it is possible to produce them. As a result the planetary environment, polluted by noxious substances, is getting to be increasingly unfit for human existence. And when genetic engineering becomes a going concern, it is doubtful that the new forms of life that gene splicing makes possible will be designed with the ultimate welfare of human life in mind—partly because it is impossible to know at this point what that is. Rather, the proliferation of new life forms will be dictated by whatever the technology can accomplish, regardless of consequences. Unless, of course, mankind realizes that its physical survival might be threatened by the evolution of culture, and it is willing to take this threat seriously.

Because artifacts are born and develop in the medium of the human mind, in order to understand the dynamics of cultural evolution it is necessary to consider how consciousness selects and transmits information.

While the *content* of socio-cultural evolution exists outside the body, the *process* that makes it possible takes place within consciousness. The three phases common to all evolutionary processes—variation, selection, and transmission—are mediated by the mind. Cultural variation begins when new memes arise as ideas, actions, or perceptions of outside events. Selection among variant memes, and retention of the selected ones, also involves a more or less conscious evaluation and investment of attention. And so does the transmission of the retained meme. Unless people invested time and attention—psychic energy—in the new variant, it would not survive long enough for the next generation to be aware of its existence. New products, political ideas, and path-breaking works of art will disappear without a trace unless they find a receptive medium in the minds of a large enough audience.

This difference between biological and cultural evolution has some important consequences. Perhaps the most important is that in genetic evolution, selection is to a very large degree accomplished by impersonal environmental conditions. Whether a given mutation will be retained or not generally depends on the climate, the nature of the food supply, the mix of predators and parasites, plus a myriad of other factors that interact with the mutation and determine its contribution to the fitness of the organism. In socio-cultural evolution, selection is mediated by consciousness. Whether a new idea or practice is viable does not depend directly on external conditions, but on our choices.

This does not mean, of course, that such things as climate or predators have no effect on cultural evolution. To the contrary, external conditions often dictate which innovations are selected. Two of the most fundamental early cultural inventions, fire and stone weapons, are obvious examples: They were selected because they helped us cope with the climate and compete for the food supply. Our current fascination with nuclear physics is basically not that different: The energy of the atom is sought both to warm our homes and to destroy our enemies. But in cultural evolution the constraints of temperature and competitive pressure do not affect the survival of information through the differential reproductive rates of the organisms that carry it. The constraints are represented in human consciousness, and it is there that the decision is made whether to replicate the meme. It is clearly not the case that atomic reactors have multipled because those who developed them have had more children—if anything, the contrary is probably true.

Because the variation, selection, and retention of memes occur in consciousness, we must consider their dynamics in order to understand socio-cultural evolution. Perhaps the most fundamental issue is the limitation of the mind as an information-processing apparatus. There is so much we will never know, simply because our brain is not equipped to handle the information. The limitation is both qualitative, referring to the kind of things we are able to recognize, and quantitative, referring to how many things we can be aware of at a given time. Although the qualitative limitations of consciousness are probably the most interesting in the long run, in this context only the consequences of quantitative limitations will be explored.

Information matters only if we attend to it. It is impossible to learn a language or a skill unless we invest a sizable amount of attention in the task. This means that each person is an informational bottleneck; there are only so many memes that he or she can process at any given time. According to the best estimates, the human organism is limited to discriminating a maximum of about seven bits—or chunks—of information per unit of time. It is estimated that the duration of each "attentional unit" is of the order of 1/18 per second; in other words, we can become aware of about 18 times seven bits of information, or 126 bits, in the space of a second. Thus a person can process at most in the neighborhood of 7,560 bits of information each minute. In a lifetime of 70 years, and assuming a waking day of 16 hours, it amounts to about 185,000,000,000 bits of information. This number defines the upper limit of individual experience. Out of it must come every perception, thought, feeling, memory, or action that a person will ever have. It seems like a large number, but in actuality none of us finds it nearly large enough.

To get a sense for how little can be accomplished with the amount of attention at our disposal, consider how much it takes just to follow an ordinary conversation. It is claimed that extracting meaning from speech signals would take 40,000 bits of information per second if each bit had to be attended to separately, or 317 times as much as we can actually handle. Fortunately, our species-specific genetic programming allows us to chunk speech into phonemes automatically, thereby reducing the load to 40 bits per second—or approximately 1/3 of the total processing capacity of attention. This is why we cannot follow a conversation and at the same time do any other demanding mental task. Just to decode what other people are saying, even though it is to a large extent an effortless and automated process, preempts any other task that requires a full commitment of attention.

As the above example suggests, "chunking" information greatly extends the limits for processing it. Some people conclude from this fact that consciousness is a boundless "open" system, and that the information we can attend to can be indefinitely multiplied. This optimistic reading of the situation, however, flies in the face of the facts. Despite our spectacular success in chunking phonemes, it is still impossible to listen to more than three conversations at the same time. It is unlikely that we will ever be able to pull up two socks simultaneously, and it is difficult to imagine a person being able to talk to a child and write a sonnet at the same time.

Because attention is the medium that makes events occur in consciousness, it is useful to think of it as "psychic energy." Any nonreflex action takes up a certain fraction of this energy. Just listening to an ordinary conversation closely enough to understand what is being said takes up one-third of it at any given time. Stirring a cup of coffee, reaching for a newspaper, and trying to remember a telephone number all require information-processing space out of that limited total. Of course, individuals vary widely in terms of how much of their psychic energy they use (how many bits they process), and in terms of what they invest their energy in.

The limitations on the information-processing capacities of consciousness have clear implications for the evolution of culture. Only a few new memes out of the variations constantly being produced are noticed, few are retained, and even fewer are transmitted to a new generation.

The rate at which new variations are produced depends to a large extent on how much attention free from survival demands is available. In addition, it depends on what cultural instructions there are regarding new memes. Some cultures, like the ancient Egyptian civilization, actively discouraged variants. Others, like current Western societies, are ideologically primed to encourage their overproduction. Thus, how frequently new memes appear is a function both of the basic scarcity of attention and of the social organization of attention that may either facilitate or inhibit the emergence of new artifacts.

After a new meme is produced, its retention is also constrained by the amount of attention available in the given human environment. According to the census there are at present about 200,000 Americans who classify themselves as artists. It is probably safe to assume that no more than 1 in 10,000 from among their works will be preserved even one generation from now as part of the information that constitutes the symbolic system of the visual arts. Every year about 50,000 new books are published in the United States. This number already constitutes a selection from probably 1,000,000 manuscripts submitted, most of which do not get published. But how many of these volumes will be remembered in ten years, now many in a hundred? The same argument holds for scholarly articles, inventions, popular songs, or new products. The environment of consciousness that allows artifacts to exist is restricted and provides a severe selective pressure on their survival.

The rate of selection and retention of new memes is again a function of both the scarcity of attention and the social organization thereof. Each person must have a theoretical upper limit on how many paintings he or she can admire, how many scientific formulas he can remember, or how many products of each kind he can consume. Thus, societies must also have limits on how many works of art, scientific facts, or commercial products they can recognize and assimilate. It is naïve to assume that progress can be enhanced by encouraging more people to be creative: If there is not enough psychic energy available to recognize creative changes, they will simply be wasted. At certain historical periods, some communities have disposed of unusual amounts of free attention. Greece twenty-five centuries ago, Florence five hundred years ago, and Paris in the nineteenth century were able to stimulate and to retain cultural variations at unusually high rates. Occasionally communities become specialized niches for certain kinds of memes; music flowered in eighteenth-and nineteenth-century Vienna; Göttingen in the late nineteenth century and Budapest in the early twentieth century provided fertile soil for mathematics; Goethe's Weimar was receptive to poetry, and so forth. But eventually no human community has enough attention to keep more than a few of the many new artifacts that are constantly produced. At the point of saturation, a selective process begins to operate.

Of the few innovations that eventually end up in the symbolic system of society, even fewer will be transmitted to the next generation. It is not enough for a meme to be preserved in a book or an object. To survive, it has to affect the consciousness of at least some people. A language that is no longer spoken or at least read becomes a "dead" language. When people forget the key to its meaning, as has happened with Etruscan, the language loses its informational structure and stops growing and reproducing. The transmission of cultural information through time requires expensive investments of attention. Several institutions exist primarily to carry out this function. For instance, schools specialize in the transmission of memes, although anyone familiar with them knows what a small fraction of the cultural heritage is actually passed on within their walls. Another example are the public behavioral instructions codified in political constitutions. All of the nations of the world have constitutions that specify appropriate behaviors concerning the same dozen or so units of information (such as work, property, income, education, decision-making, and so on), although the hierarchical relations between these units vary. The continuity of constitutional texts can be traced back to Roman law and the British Magna Charta. But they don't survive naturally. Great social resources must be invested for their preservation. Without courts, judges, lawyers, police, schools, and a host of other institutions, the instructions contained in constitutions would be disregarded and eventually forgotten.

Human environments favorable to cultural evolution are characterized by surplus attention, by a social organization that encourages novelty, by social arrangements that facilitate the retention and transmission of new variants, and by informational skills that are far enough developed to recognize and integrate the variation within their symbol systems. When a society has these characteristics, it becomes a favorable medium for the spread of artifacts. But whether this will benefit the people who become hosts to cultural evolution is another issue entirely.

The survival of new memes does not depend only on environmental factors, such as the amount and the social organization of attention in the human milieu. It also depends on how the information itself is patterned. In other words, some memes are fitter than others in the sense that the information contained in them is going to spread to more minds, and to be remembered longer. It is impossible to give a general description of what makes a new artifact successful, any more than it is possible to describe a successful genetic mutation, and for identical reasons. Just as the fitness of a new mutation depends on the environment to which the phenotype is adapted, so is the viability of a new cultural form dependent on the prior state of the culture and the human environment in which it appears.

Nevertheless, it is possible to point out some characteristics of memes that help their diffusion in a wide range of contexts. The first requirement of a new cultural form is that it be identifiable as such. Every symbolic domain has formal or informal criteria for establishing whether a meme is a genuine new variant. The Patent Office and the copyright laws use formal definitions, while in other fields like science and art a consensus of experts decides whether an artifact is really new. To be so identified a variant must depart from previous artifacts to a substantial extent, yet not so much as to be unrecognizable. The range of optimal variation is one characteristic that defines the viability of new memes.

In social contexts where new memes are seen to be dangerous, elaborate institutions might be established to test new ideas and other artifacts to determine whether they constitute variations from the accepted orthodoxy. In some historical periods the Christian Church spent great efforts to identify "heresy," which referred to cultural variants that had to be eliminated from the consciousness of the population. Even now the function of the Vatican's Sacred Congregation for the Doctrine of the Faith, a successor to the Inquisition and to the Holy Office, is to eliminate books and teachings that introduce unacceptable variations into the religious meme pool. Similar institutions existed in the Soviet Union, and in all societies built on the assumption that the structure of information they already have is superior to any possible new form. Such mechanisms of social control try to separate new artifacts that are beneficial to the commonwealth from those that are not. In principle this could be a useful function once it is admitted that cultural evolution need not coincide with human welfare. Historically, though, the censorship of new ideas has been informed more often by the desire to maintain a particular power structure than by the desire to maximize the well-being of the population.

Once it is established that an artifact is genuinely new, the next question becomes: Should it be preserved? A great variety of reasons determines why one meme will be selected for retention while thousands of others are eliminated and forgotten. Economy is one general criterion. Any artifact that saves scarce human resources has a better chance of surviving. And, attention being one of the most precious resources, artifacts that save time and concentration generally have an edge in fitness. Thus, the evolution of symbol systems representing language, quantities, and other forms of representation always tends toward memes that will accomplish equal or better effects with a saving of attention. The ascendancy of the metric system over competing systems of measurement or the general adoption of the North Semitic alphabet are good examples of how savings in attention will positively select a more efficient set of symbols. The same is true of the evolution of tools, appliances, and social customs. A cheaper price is just a corollary of the same principle, since the advantage of saving money is simply a special case of saving attention—money being what is exchanged for psychic energy invested into productive tasks. If a book or a car is less expensive than an equivalent brand, buying the cheaper one saves psychic energy that would have gone into earning the difference in price; the attention saved can then be invested either into making more money or into pleasurable experiences.

While economy of attention is a very important criterion for the selection of artifacts, it is certainly not the only one. Perhaps the most universal qualification of positively selected artifacts is that they improve the quality of experience. Whenever a new cultural form promises pleasure or enjoyment, it will find a receptive niche in consciousness. This reason for the adoption of a new artifact is well expressed by the Greek poet who welcomed the invention of the water mill two thousand years ago, as quoted by the historian Marc Bloch: "Spare your hands, which have been long familiar with the millstone, you maidens who used to crush the grain. Henceforth you shall sleep long, oblivious to the crowing cocks who greet the dawn." Compared to the millstone, the water mill offered women smoother hands, less physical effort, and more disposable time—presumably adding up to an overall improvement on the quality of life.

Clearly enjoyment is the main reason why we select and retain most works of art. Painting, music, drama, architecture, and writing are symbolic skills adopted because they produce positive states of consciousness. So do mystery novels and television programs, which appear to "waste" psychic energy but do so while providing pleasurable information in return for the investment of attention.

But some of the most utilitarian artifacts also survive because they provide enjoyment to those who use them. In discussing the introduction of the first metal objects at the end of the Stone ages, Colin Renfrew writes:

> In several areas of the world it has been noted, in the case of metallurgical innovations in particular, that the development of bronze and other metals as *useful* commodities was a much later phenomenon than their first utilization as new and attractive materials, employed in contexts of display. . . . In most cases early metallurgy appears to have been practiced primarily because the products had novel properties that made them attractive to use as symbols and as personal adornments and ornaments, in a manner that, by focusing attention, could attract or enhance prestige.

Products with novel properties continue to attract attention regardless of utilitarian considerations. Interest in automobiles started not because of their usefulness, but because stunts and races captured people's imagination. A recent promotional brochure from Alfa Romeo states: "In 1910, a car company was created that was destined to distinguish itself from all others. A company built on the simple philosophy that a car shouldn't be merely a means of transportation, but a *source of exhilaration* . . ." This is wrong only in claiming that such a "philosophy" was unique to this particular manufacturer; in fact, most early cars were built with that goal in mind (a point recognized six pages later in the same brochure: "The Triumph TR3. The Austin Healey 3000. The Jaguar XKE . . . They were sleek, sensual, agile . . . Designed and built for the sheer joy of driving, *they made no pretense whatsoever of practicality*"). The same trend can be recognized at the inception of many cultural innovations, from the airplane to the personal computer.

According to the great Dutch cultural historian Johan Huizinga, human institutions originally arise as games that provide enjoyment to the players and the spectators; only later do they become serious elements of social structure. At first, the thoughts and actions these institutions require are freely accepted; later they become the taken-for-granted elements of social reality. Thus, science starts as riddling contests, religion as joyful collective celebrations, military institutions start as ceremonial combat, the legal system has its origins in ritualized debates, and economic systems often begin as festive reciprocal exchanges. Those forms that provide the most enjoyment are selected and transmitted down the generations.

But once a set of memes, for whatever reason, finds a niche in consciousness, it can go on reproducing without reference to the enjoyment of its hosts. Coins were first minted to enhance the prestige and the economic power of kings and to facilitate trade. When the exchange of necessary products becomes dependent on a monetary system, however, people become helpless to resist its spread and will have to adapt to it whether they like it or not. As Max Weber noted, capitalism began as an adventurous game of entrepreneurs but eventually became an "iron cage," an economic system with peculiar shortcomings from which it is very difficult to escape.

If it is true that artifacts exploit enjoyment as their medium for survival, any account of cultural evolution must give consideration to what people enjoy doing. People enjoy experiences in which they are faced with opportunities for action—or challenges—that are high and that are matched with an equivalent level of personal skills. Worry and anxiety result when there are more challenges than skills, apathy and boredom when the situation is reversed. When challenges and skills are out of balance, people seek to restore the optimal condition in which their experience is most positive. The simple formula for enjoyment, Challenges/Skills $=1$, was originally developed in the context of empirical studies with urban American adults. Since then it has been confirmed by studies in a variety of European and Asian contexts.

Because of this relationship, people tend to overreproduce memes that raise the level of existing challenges, provided that at the same time they can raise the level of their own skills. Anything we do for a long time eventually becomes boring. At that point we look for new opportunities for action, which in turn forces us to develop greater skills; this dialectic leads to a process of *complexification*. This principle accounts for both the generation of new artifacts and, to a lesser extent, for their subsequent acceptance and transmission.

The relationship between complexification and enjoyment does not mean that people are constantly motivated to seek higher challenges. In fact, the opposite is true. When free to use time at their discretion, most people most of the time prefer to relax. They engage in low-intensity activities such as sitting with a bottle of beer in front of a television set. "Pleasure" is a homeostatic principle that drives people to save energy whenever possible, and to derive rewards from genetically programmed actions that are necessary for the survival of the species, such as eating and sexuality.

Enjoyment that requires developing new skills to meet increasing levels of challenge is relatively rare. Yet this is the experience that people all around the world mention as the high point of their lives. Thus, while pleasure is generally conservative, selecting and transmitting already exist-

ing artifacts, enjoyment that leads to complexification is more often responsible for generating and selecting new cultural forms.

At the most general level, then, it can be said that the process of
complexification, which is experienced as enjoyable, defines the symbiotic
relationship between the evolution of human beings and the evolution of
culture. Cultural forms that offer the possibility of increasing enjoyment
will survive by attracting attention. Similarly, people who invest attention
in such forms acquire a more complex consciousness. In each generation,
individuals who develop and learn to use new artifacts form a new breed.

Up to a point, this coevolution is beneficial both to us and to the world
of things. However, there is always the possibility that memes will move
from a symbiotic to a parasitic relationship. To prevent this from happening,
we must entertain the possibility that culture does not exist to serve our
needs. As organized matter and information, artifacts compete for energy
with other forms of organization, including ourselves. When this possibility
is faced, it becomes easier to evaluate cultural forms more objectively, and
to make decisions on a sounder basis concerning which ones to encourage
and which ones to restrain.

The joint complexification of consciousness and culture, brought about
by the evolved trait of finding joy in complexity, has given the human race
a great advantage in its competition with other forms of organized matter.
Because the mind enjoys a challenge, people have lustily explored the
hidden potential in all forms of information, thereby acting as midwives to
artifacts of every kind. In so doing they have learned how to survive at the
expense of other animals and plants they found useless. But just because
enjoying the challenge of complexity has served us in the past does not
guarantee that it will do so in the future. There is increasing evidence that
this Faustian restlessness is making us vulnerable to the mindless replication
of artifacts. If we are to take charge of the direction of evolution, a first step
might be to recognize the fact that unless we find ways of controlling the
evolution of culture, our own survival might be in serious jeopardy.

8

Conclusion: Creativity Research on the Verge

Having presented our joint general perspective on the topic of creativity, and having placed before the reader some of our own most recent work, we now pause to reflect for a moment on what the prospects for the future of work on creativity look like at the moment. If it is "on the verge" of something, as the title of this conclusion suggests, what might that something be? Is the field positioned to take (or retake) its place among the major lines of thinking and research to occupy the social science community over the next several decades? Or will the traditional intractability and inscrutability of creativity (an imperviousness to explanation that has persisted for more than two millennia), render it likely that once again its central meaning will elude us, in spite of the confident claims of the artificial intelligence community that creativity is nothing more than a set of common mechanisms carrying out an uncommon set of activities.

Our view is that the cognitive science community is probably overly optimistic in its claims that creativity is in principle no more difficult to understand than any other process of the human nervous system, and that it will be only a matter of time before convincing simulations of creative processes are available, if indeed they are not available already.

There is, we believe, good reason to think that the still mysterious and baffling aura that surrounds creativity will be with us for the foreseeable future, especially if contributions of the first rank are the focus of interest, as they are for us. There is little danger that the wonder and awe we feel when confronted with truly amazing works will be replaced with algorithms or neural network diagrams that "explain" the process.

On the other hand, if we are right, and the field has taken a decisive turn toward rejuvenation, if new vistas have been sighted, we may well be able to look forward to a period of new discovery and deepened understanding of creative processes. Using some of the recently developed techniques of the social, cognitive, computer, physical, and neural sciences, it should be possible to mount a coordinated research effort that could yield extraordinary new knowledge. It is not yet clear if the kind of collaborative enterprise that is needed will come to exist. It does not exist at this time, but many of the critical elements seem to be at hand. Perhaps most encouraging is that, in the past ten years or so, there has been a resurgence into the field of high-quality new talent, willing to stake their careers on their success at studying creativity. The talent pool is also widening, including scholars from a variety of disciplines not typically seen in the field of creativity research.

The degree to which these able new scholars, along with their more seasoned colleagues, are able to coordinate and maintain joint efforts will determine how far the work will go toward major new understandings of creativity. Our joint purpose in preparing this book has been to try to offer to the field, and to anyone else who is interested, a framework for organizing the effort to penetrate more deeply into the nature of creativity. To the degree that an overall approach guides the field, to that degree will we feel that our labors have been worthwhile, even if the framework that guides the field does not turn out to be quite the one we have been proposing in this book.

While it is true that each of us will continue to pursue creativity-related research topics that interest us, and these are certainly rewarding in and of themselves, in the present work we wanted to show how the work we have been doing is actually part of a broader, collaborative enterprise that grew out of our years together on the Social Science Research Council's Committee on Giftedness, Development, and the Learning Process. As a number of other groups have done under the sponsorship of the SSRC, we set out to try to help an ailing field of research get back on its feet.

As we have said more than once, this collaboration has influenced each of us to the extent that it is not clear anymore where our ideas on creativity have come from. This is probably true as well of the other long-term committee members, Jeanne Bamberger and Howard Gruber, whose influence on us has been profound. We also argue a lot, lest the reader think that the work has proceeded in tranquility and order. Yet, to have been able, through the process, to make our shared approach to the study of creativity more explicit, to have hammered out areas of agreement and disagreement, has been a richly rewarding experience in our careers. We believe that the support of collaborative efforts such as ours, but on a much larger scale, is key to the future of creativity research.

We are of course hoping that the field will rally behind our banner of a tripartite, developmentally oriented, interdisciplinary team approach to creativity. Were a better framework to appear, we would be happy to shift our allegiances to it, but the way of organizing the field we have offered seems to us sufficiently broad, yet clear, to guide work on creativity for some time into the future.

To change the world, as we have argued, is the unique province of human beings. As we have seen, we are the only residents of the universe likely to possess self-consciousness of purpose and the ability to reflect on our own and others' efforts to accomplish their purposes. These qualities bring with them a unique opportunity but also a unique responsibility to use them well. Our little group sees the study of creativity—the process of change perhaps most uniquely human—as a worthy human purpose and one most likely to produce knowledge that will provide leverage over the ever more challenging problems we most surely will confront as our species moves, however haltingly and poorly prepared, into a new millennium.

Bibliography

Abra, J. (1988). *Assaulting Parnassus: Theoretical views of creativity*. Lanham, MD: University Press of America.

Amabile, T. (1983). *The social psychology of creativity*. New York: Springer-Verlag.

Bamberger, J. (1991). *The mind behind the musical ear*. Cambridge, MA: Harvard University Press.

Boden, M. (1990). *The creative mind*. New York: Basic Books.

Brannigan, A. (1981). *The social basis of scientific discoveries*. New York: Cambridge University Press.

Briggs, J. (1989). *Fire in the crucible*. New York: St. Martin's Press.

Csikszentmihalyi, M. (1990). *Flow: The psychology of optimal experience*. New York: Harper.

Feldman, D. H., with L. T. Goldsmith. (1986, 1991). *Nature's gambit*. New York: Teachers College Press.

Feldman, D. H. (1994). *Beyond universals in cognitive development* (2d ed.). Norwood, NJ: Ablex.

Gardner, H. (1983, 1993). *Frames of mind*. New York: Basic Books.

_____ . (1993). *Creating minds*. New York: Basic Books.

Getzels, J., and M. Csikszentmihalyi. (1976). *The creative vision: a longitudinal study of problem finding in art*. New York: John Wiley.

Ghiselin, B. (ed.) (1952). *The creative process: A symposium*. New York: Mentor.

Gordon, W.J.J. (1961). *Synectics*. New York: Harper & Row.

Gould, S. J. (1981). *Mismeasure of man*. New York: Norton.

Gruber, H. (1974, 1981). *Darwin on man*. Chicago: University of Chicago Press.

Horowitz, F., and M. O'Brien (eds.) (1985). *The gifted and the talented: Developmental perspectives*. Washington, DC: American Psychological Association.

Howe, M.J.A. (ed.) (1990). *Encouraging the development of exceptional skills and talents*. Letchworth, UK: The British Psychological Society.

John-Steiner, V. (1985, 1987). *Notebooks of the mind*. New York: Harper.

———. (1992). Creative lives, creative tensions. *Creativity Research Journal*, 5, 99–108.

Langley, P., H. Simon, G. L. Bradshaw, and J. Zytow. (1986). *Scientific discovery: Computational explorations of the creative process*. Cambridge, MA: MIT Press.

Ochse, K. (1991). *Before the gates of excellence*. New York: Cambridge University Press.

Perkins, D. (1981). *The mind's best work*. Cambridge, MA: Harvard University Press.

Piaget, J. (1982). Creativity. In J. M. Gallagher and D. K. Reid (eds.), *The learning theory of Piaget and Inhelder*. (pp. 221–229). Monterrey, CA: Brooks/Cole.

Piirto, J. (1992). *Understanding those who create*. Dayton, OH: Ohio Psychology Press.

Runco, M., and R. S. Albert (eds.), (1990). *Theories of creativity*. Newbury Park, CA: Sage Publishers.

Simonton, D. K. (1984). *Genius, creativity, and leadership: Historiometric inquiries*. Cambridge, MA: Harvard University Press.

Sternberg, R. (ed.) (1988). *The nature of creativity*. New York: Cambridge University Press.

Wallace, D., and H. Gruber (eds.) (1989). *Creative people at work*. New York: Oxford University Press.

Watson, J. D. (1968). *The double helix: A personal account of the discovery of the structure of DNA*. New York: Signet Books.

Weisberg, R. W. (1993). *Creativity: Beyond the myth of genius*. San Francisco: Freeman.

Index